Sarah McKimm is a solicitor who, after a first career in commercial litigation, has been specialising in education law for the last 20 years. In 2008 she became Principal Solicitor and later Deputy General Secretary for the Independent Schools Council. She was also until recently Head of Legal & Policy at the Independent Schools Inspectorate (ISI).

'This detailed, practical guide provides authoritative guidance for senior leaders in independent schools seeking to remain up to date with the requirements of the Independent School Standards Regulations.'

– Julie Robinson, Chief Executive Officer, Independent Schools Council

'A clearly written, fully comprehensive reference book which is a must-have for all senior leaders and governing bodies in both independent schools and academies.'

– Kate Richards, former Chief Inspector Independent Schools Inspectorate, Chair of Governors and educational consultant.

'A really handy resource for schools which provides a route map through a blizzard of guidance, old and new. Great to see it updated for September 2022.'

– Rudolf Eliott Lockhart, CEO Independent Schools Association

'Highly detailed and most useful.'

– Clive Rickart, Chief Executive Officer, The Society of Heads.

'This book is the definitive work for those involved in the detail and setting policy for safeguarding in schools. The information is accessible logical and entirely up-to-date.'

– John Murphie, Chief Operating Officer, the Independent Schools' Bursars Association

'For several years I had the privilege to work alongside Sarah McKimm whose unparalleled knowledge of and authoritative insight into the Independent School Standards Regulations were crucial to the success of the inspectorate on many fronts; now anyone with an interest in understanding the standards can have access to her knowledge and insight, expressed succinctly and practically.'

– Durell Barnes, Head of Governance and Compliance at RSAcademics, former Chair of the Independent Schools Examinations Board.

A Practical Guide to the Independent School Standards

September 2022 Edition

A Practical Guide to the Independent School Standards

September 2022 Edition

Sarah McKimm

Solicitor, MA (Oxon), MA (KCL)

Law Brief Publishing

Published 2022 by Law Brief Publishing, an imprint of Law Brief Publishing Ltd
30 The Parks
Minehead
Somerset
TA24 8BT

www.lawbriefpublishing.com

Paperback: 978-1-914608-59-9

To Daniel, Connie, Hector and Alice.

FOREWORD TO THE
FIRST EDITION

Sarah McKimm has been giving advice to Independent Schools Council schools for many years – as a senior official and lawyer working for ISC and then for the Independent Schools Inspectorate. She has also been closely engaged with the Department for Education in the construction and updating of the Independent School Standards – the requirements the government places on all independent schools. There is, therefore, arguably no one better placed to write an informed and up-to-date commentary on these Standards.

The text is written for lawyers but schools will be interested to read it. She covers the implementation of the Standards but with extra materials about human rights and issues like SEND and mental health.

As a user of the Independent School Standards I must say that I found them hard to read and hard to understand fully. Sarah unpacks the true intent of the standards and in so doing illuminates them for us. We should be grateful to her for this work.

Professor Barnaby Lenon CBE
Chair – Independent Schools Council

PREFACE

Some years ago, when I was new to education law, I heard an experienced education lawyer refer to the independent schools sector as 'The Wild West! The place where anything goes'. That comment roused my curiosity. Could the sector really be unregulated, as is often its reputation? I knew of local schools which were either Ofsted 'outstanding' or ISI 'excellent'. As a lawyer and parent, I wanted to understand the real difference. Was it just about history, resources and class sizes or was there something else? Did children and parents have the same rights and protections in both sectors? If so, were they enforceable in the same way? The independent school leaders I knew often felt they were over regulated. These conundrums led eventually to my working at the interface between the independent school sector and the Department for Education. This book sets out to answer some of those questions and to provide an introduction and overview for others new to the sector.

Independent schools in England are subject to laws applicable to other organisations such as charity, contract, tax and employment law, all of which are well served by other legal textbooks. The focus of this text is on the independent school standards only. It aims to bring the guidance they incorporate, other official advice and the limited body of case law which informs interpretation, into a single coherent narrative for ease of reference while also signposting additional material which will help the reader further develop their understanding. Where the independent school standards incorporate other regulations, statutory frameworks and standards, such as the National Minimum Standards for Boarding Schools and the statutory framework for the Early Years Foundation Stage, it has not been possible to cover these comprehensively. Some obvious connections are highlighted but they are largely flagged for the reader's own exploration. This is a textbook primarily for legal advisors but it is hoped that it may also be of assistance to parents and schools.

Structure

Part one sets the scene, explaining why the independent school standards exist from a human rights perspective and outlining concepts from key pieces of legislation which form important building blocks of what follows.

Part two introduces the standards.

Part three applies the standards to some common issues, starting to show readers how to work with them. It closes by looking forward to future changes.

Date at which the law is stated

Education law is constantly changing and developing. Key guidance to which schools must 'have regard' is updated frequently in response to emerging issues. Case law continues to develop our understanding although many legal points have not yet been settled by the courts. However, it is hoped that nearly 20 years on from publication of the first standards, there is now a sufficiently stable core of regulation and guidance to warrant a source book.

In the first edition, I committed to addressing major changes through updated editions. In the few months since that was written, IICSA has reported on safeguarding in schools, the NMS for boarding have been comprehensively overhauled, KCSIE has been updated, the Covid regulations have been withdrawn and various other key pieces of guidance have been updated or introduced. Forensic readers of the underlying documents will notice that while some issues have been addressed, a few new fissures have opened up, such as in the cross-referencing between the independent school standards and NMS for boarding. I have chosen not to highlight these in this introductory text but to focus on the bigger picture.

This second edition seeks to offer practical guidance to the independent school standards as I understand them as at **31 July 2022**, in readiness for the start of the 22/23 academic year. It is not provided and should not be relied on as legal advice.

What follows applies to England only

This book addresses the law applicable to independent schools in England only.[1]

Acknowledgements

I take this opportunity to thank again my dear friends and former colleagues Liza Gilhooly and Clare Wigzell for all their wisdom, support and humour over the years. I am also immensely grateful to the numerous ISI inspectors and other colleagues at ISI, ISC, the associations and the DfE from whom I have learned so much. I pay tribute to their dedication to the best interests of children in independent schools.

Sarah McKimm
July 2022

ERRATA

The text of the statutory guidance, *Keeping Children Safe in Education* (KCSIE) 2022, was published by the DfE in June 2022 for September implementation. However, the addition of a new paragraph 94 and new footnotes 38, 45 and 147 to KCSIE on 1 September 2022 mean that some of the references to KCSIE cited in this text are mis-numbered.

To find the correct references, readers should:

- add one to KCSIE paragraph numbers over 94

- add one to KCSIE footnote numbers 38 – 43, add two to footnotes 44 – 147 and add three to footnotes 144 and over.

---

[1] Government of Wales Act 1998 – Government of Wales Act 2006, Schedule 7. Responsibility for education in Wales has been gradually devolved to the National Assembly for Wales by a series of measures between 1998 and 2011.

CONTENTS

PART TWO – THE STANDARDS 85

LIST OF TERMS AND ABBREVIATIONS

DfE – Department for Education

DSL – Designated safeguarding lead

ECHR – European Convention for the Protection of Human Rights and Fundamental Freedoms

EHC plan – Education Health and Care plan made under the Children and Families Act 2014

EHRC – Equality and Human Rights Commission

EqA 2010 – Equality Act 2010

EYFS – Early Years Foundation Stage

GIAS – Get Information About Schools

HMCI – Her Majesty's Chief Inspector of Education, Children's Services and Skills (Ofsted)

HRA – Human Rights Act 1998

IICSA – The Independent Inquiry into Child Sexual Abuse

ISI – The Independent Schools Inspectorate

ISS 16 (example) – Paragraph 16 of the independent school standards, in the schedule to The Education (Independent School Standards) Regulations 2014, as amended

KCSIE – The statutory guidance: *Keeping children safe in education*

LA – Local authority

LSP or LSCP – Local safeguarding partners or Local safeguarding children partnership

NMS for boarding schools 2022 – National Minimum Standards for boarding schools

NMS for residential special schools – National Minimum Standards for residential special schools

PCP – Provision, criterion or practice

Proprietorial schools – Colloquial term for independent schools owned and run by a private individual, who may also be the head, or by a single family, as a business

PSHE – Personal, social, health and economic education

PSED – Public Sector Equality Duty

RSE – Relationships and sex education

Secretary of State – Secretary of State for Education

SEN – Special educational needs

SENCO – Special educational needs co-ordinator

SEND – Special educational needs and disabilities

School – Independent school unless the context indicates otherwise

SLT – Senior leadership team

SMSC – Spiritual, moral, social, and cultural development of pupils

SVGA 2006 – Safeguarding Vulnerable Groups Act 2006

WT – The statutory guidance: *Working together to safeguard children*

UNCRC – The United Nations Convention on the Rights of the Child

PART ONE

INTRODUCTION

CHAPTER ONE

STATE AND INDEPENDENT EDUCATION – HOW THEY DIFFER AND WHY

Introduction and overview

Education in state schools is controlled and funded by the state operating through the Secretary of State for Education who works through the Department of Education (DfE) and agencies such as local authorities (LAs).[1]

Parents are required to ensure their children receive efficient full-time suitable education but do not have to take up the education offered by the state.[2] They have the right to educate their children independently of the state[3] and in accordance with their own religious and philosophical convictions,[4] whether at an independent school or otherwise.[5]

At the same time, children have rights to effective education,[6] to be safe and in due course to make their own choices as they mature.[7]

In recognition of the freedoms and rights of parents, the Secretary of State does not exercise the same degree of control over independent

---

[1] See for example, the Education Act 1996, sections 10,11 and 13.

[2] 'Suitable' means: *'suitable to the child's age, ability and aptitude and to any special educational needs he may have'*, section 7 Education Act 1996.

[3] Art. 8 ECHR

[4] Art. 2. Protocol 1 ECHR and also Art.s 8, 9 and 14 ECHR and Education Act 1996, section 9.

[5] Education Act 1996, section 7 and 9.

[6] Art. 2. Protocol 1 ECHR and Belgian Linguistics Case (No.2)(1968)1 EHRR 252 at 280-3.

[7] Art.s 8, 9 ECHR and Gillick etc.

education as s/he does over state education. There remains a role for the state, however, in setting standards firstly to provide assurance to parents that any independent school they may choose will keep children safe and provide a good education and secondly to balance parental rights against those of their children, ensuring that parental choices do not lead to the rights of their children being compromised.

This is achieved through a system of compulsory registration of independent schools and a set of registration standards known as the independent school standards ('the standards' or sometimes 'ISS') which are prescribed in regulations.[8] Failure to meet the standards can lead to regulatory action against a school, including de-registration, by the Secretary of State through a process defined in legislation.[9]

The standards create a safe space in the education system where parents and schools can exercise their independence, continue their own distinctive heritage and traditions, where children are safe and education can develop in ground-breaking creative ways. The approach preserves the huge variety of schools within the independent sector in England, from schools providing an all-round education to those with a strong academic or sporting focus, to world renowned schools of dance or music, to the small schools serving faith communities, to specialist schools catering for pupils with particular needs, and within each type, co-educational and single sex, day and boarding, prep, senior and all-through schools. The standards are the same whether the proprietor is a charity, a small family business, a large international enterprise, a religious community, a college, profit-making, not-for-profit, or a one-person operation.

The standards do not confer direct, actionable rights although they may have evidential value in litigation, but they do seek to ensure protections for children and provide certainty and assurance to parents about what they are buying into. Their implementation is monitored through regular inspections, as discussed in Chapter Three.

---

[8] The Education (Independent School Standards) Regulations 2014.

[9] Education and Skills Act 2008, sections 114 – 116.

The most common requests for legal advice are likely to be from schools who are keen to understand and implement the standards in contexts such as seeking registration, policy drafting, handling regulated matters (such as safeguarding and other welfare issues), inspection preparation, post-inspection action plans, or from parents, schools, current or former pupils in the context of a private law dispute.

Children's rights to education

Article 2, Protocol 1 (A2P1) of the European Convention for the Protection of Human Rights and Fundamental Freedoms (ECHR) provides:

> ### Right to education
> *No person shall be denied the right to education.*
>
> *In the exercise of any functions which it assumes in relation to education and to teaching, the State shall respect the right of parents to ensure such education and teaching in conformity with their own religious and philosophical convictions.*

This is incorporated into domestic law by the Human Rights Act 1998 (HRA). Despite the negative formulation, A2P1 has been held to guarantee a right of access to an 'effective' form of education.[10]

The first sentence protects the rights of a child; the second, the rights of parents. [11]

---

[10] Belgian Linguistics Case (No.2)(1968)1 EHRR 252 at 280-3.

[11] The right of respect does not oblige the state to provide a particular type of education. It is largely a right of non-interference – Belgian Linguistics case. It also does not prevent the state from providing factual information in a context that is objective, critical and pluralistic – Kjeldsen, Busk, Madsen and Pedersen v Denmark (1976) 1 EHRR 711.

The purpose of education

The <u>UN Convention on the Rights of the Child</u> (UNCRC) provides further context.[12] In Article 28, State parties *'recognise the right of the child to education ...'.* Article 29(1) is instructive in formulating a purpose for education:

> *States Parties agree that the education of the child shall be directed to:*
>
> a) *The development of the child's personality, talents and mental and physical abilities to their fullest potential*
>
> b) *The development of respect for human rights and fundamental freedoms ...*
>
> c) *The development of respect for the child's parents, his or her own cultural identity, language and values, the national values of the country in which the child is living, the country from which he or she may originate, and for civilisations different from his or her own*
>
> d) *Preparation of the child for responsible life in a free society, in the spirit of understanding, peace, tolerance, equality of sexes, and friendship among all peoples, ethnic, national and religious groups and persons of indigenous origin*
>
> e) *The development of respect for the natural environment.*

The vision is for an education which prepares children for adult life in a modern pluralist society in which they are able to play their part and fulfil their potential.

Perhaps oddly in a convention about the rights of children, there is a second part to Article 29 UNCRC which concerns the rights of adults to run schools. It provides that no part of that article:

> *... shall be construed so as to interfere with the liberty of individuals and bodies to establish and direct educational institutions, subject always to the observance of the principle set forth in paragraph 1 of*

---

[12] The UNCRC was adopted by the UN in 1989 and ratified by the UK in December 1991 with effect from January 1992 but is not part of domestic law.

the present article [above] *and to the requirements that the education given in such institutions shall conform to such minimum standards as may be laid down by the State.*

The best interests of the child

UNCRC Article 3 introduces the notion of the *'the best interests of the child'* as *'a primary consideration'*, of the state taking steps to ensure the protection and care of children while taking into account the rights of adults (parents and others)[13] and again of conformity to institutional standards:

> *3(3) States Parties shall ensure that the institutions, services and facilities responsible for the care or protection of children shall conform with the standards established by competent authorities, particularly in the areas of safety, health, in the number and suitability of their staff, as well as competent supervision.[14]*

In the contexts of both education and welfare, the UNCRC recognises the rights of adults and envisages a role for the state in setting minimum standards to protect and balance the rights of children.

Freedom from interference

Article 8 of the ECHR also provides for a right of respect for private and family life. This is as relevant to children as it is to their parents. The state is restricted from interfering

> *… except such as is in accordance with the law and is necessary in a democratic society in the interests of national security, public safety or the economic well-being of the country, for the prevention of disorder or crime, for the protection of health or morals, or for the protection of the rights and freedoms of others.[15]*

When it comes to parental choice, 'others' includes their own children. In <u>R v Secretary of State for Education and Employment and others ex</u>

---

13   UNCRC Art. 3(1) and 3(2).

14   See also UNCRC Art. 19(1) requiring states to take action to prevent abuse, neglect and maltreatment.

15   ECHR Art. 8(2).

parte Williamson [2005] UKHL 15, the House of Lords discussed the limits on parental rights. A group of Christian parents challenged the outright legal ban on all corporal punishment in independent schools on the basis that it infringed their religious freedom.[16] Baroness Hale saw '*the essential question*' as

> ... *whether the legislation achieves a fair balance between the rights and freedoms of the parents and teachers and the rights, freedoms and interests, not only of their children, but also of any other children who might be affected by the persistence of corporal punishment in some schools.[17]*

The House of Lords agreed that the parents' rights had been infringed but held that this was justified in the interests of the legitimate aim of protecting the rights and freedoms of children.[18] The legislative prohibition had achieved a fair balance between the religious rights and freedoms of the parents and those of their children to be free from physical punishment. [19]

Domestic law

We see some of these principles filtering into domestic law in places such as the welfare principle in section one of the Children Act 1989; sections 7 and 9 of the Education Act 1996; and the Education and Skills Act 2008 which permits individuals and bodies to set up schools and requires the Secretary of State to set standards to regulate them.

---

[16] Art. 9 (Freedom of thought, conscience and religion) and 9(2) for a similar qualification on the right, ECHR.

[17] R v Secretary of State for Education and Employment and others ex parte Williamson [2005] UKHL 15 at para. 74.

[18] See for example, Baroness Hale at para. 72 and 80. Art 9(2) in that case provided the 'mechanism for achieving balance'.

[19] See also Beis Aharon Trust v Secretary of State for Education [2016] UKFTT 270 (HESC) at para. 93, the state does not have to respect the right of parents to provide their children an education which did not meet the standards.

Freedoms of independent schools

What does independence translate to in practice? An independent school is, by definition, independent of the state. Much of the legislation, regulations and guidance which apply to state-funded schools are, therefore, not compulsory for independent schools. It is not always understood by parents, however, that in choosing independent education they are opting out of some of the statutory rights, systems and certainty afforded to pupils and parents in the context of state education.

Does it apply? Key differences between state and independent schools

Does it apply?	State-funded schools	Independent schools
National curriculum	Yes	No
Teacher qualifications are prescribed	Yes	No – with rare exceptions[20]
SEND Code of Practice: 0-25 years	Yes	No in practice, except for publicly funded provision[21]
Requirement to have a SENCO	Yes	No[22]

---

[20] In the EYFS, managers' qualifications are prescribed and the adult:child ratios vary according to the level of qualification of the staff. See the statutory framework for the EYFS para. 3.28 et seq.

[21] Independent schools are included among those to whom the Code applies in relation to functions under Part 3 of the Children and Families Act 2014 – section 77(1)(b), (f) and (g). But usually there are no such functions for the duty to bite on in practice, unless schools have pupils with EHC plans, are approved under section 41 of the Children and Families Act 2014 or are early years providers receiving public funding to provide free childcare. So, yes in theory, but with limited effect in practice.

[22] Special educational needs and disability regulations 2014, regulations 2 and 49 (interpretation) and Children and Families Act 2014, section 83(2) for meaning of 'mainstream school'.

Statutory guidance: *Supporting pupils with medical conditions at school*	Yes	No[23]
Statutory Admissions Code	Yes	No
Statutory guidance on exclusions	Yes	No
Statutory codes for recording registration	Yes	No
Statutory number of sessions (380) and term-time dates fixed by local authority[24]	Yes	No
Constitution for governing bodies	Yes	No
Safer recruitment training	Yes[25]	Yes[26]
School teacher pay and conditions document	Yes	No
Public sector equality duty (PSED)	Yes	No
Teachers' Standards (statutory)	Yes	Part one – No Part two – Yes
Statutory guidance for safeguarding: • *Keeping children safe in education* • *Working together to safeguard children*	Yes	Yes
Statutory framework for the Early Years Foundation Stage (EYFS)	Yes	Yes – partial exemptions available

---

23 Children and Families Act 2014, section 100.

24 Education Act 2002, s32 and The Education (School Day and School Year) (England) Regulations 1999 .

25 Reg. 9 of the School Staffing (England) Regulations 2009.

26 A 'should' duty under para. 207 of KCSIE 2022.

National Minimum Standards for Boarding Schools	Yes	Yes
Statutory guidance: *Relationships Education, Relationships and Sex Education (RSE) and Health Education (HE)*	Yes	Yes – RSE No – HE
Statutory guidance: *Careers guidance and access for education and training providers*	Yes	No
Daily act of worship	Yes	No
Equality Act (other than PSED) e.g. duty to make reasonable adjustments	Yes	Yes
Freedom of Information Act	Yes	No
Data protection law	Yes	Yes
The Regulatory Reform (Fire Safety) Order 2005	Yes	Yes
Inspections under section 5 or 8 Education Act 2005	Yes	No
Inspections under section 109 Education and Skills Act 2008	No	Yes – except for academies

Registration and the role of the independent school standards

The relative lack of prescription for independent schools does not leave them to operate in a vacuum. All independent schools are required to register with the Secretary of State, operating through the DfE. It is an offence to run an unregistered school. Anyone who does so is liable on summary conviction to imprisonment and/or a fine.[27] The Secretary of State sets standards which must be met as a condition of registration. A

---

27 Education and Skills Act 2008 section 96.

pre-registration inspection and regular inspections thereafter monitor whether the standards are met.

Essentially, while state schools are provided with a curriculum and told how to handle key issues through various statutory codes, independent schools are largely able to design their own approaches:

> The school … is entrusted by the legislation to run a school according to its own values and standards so long as it can guarantee compliance with those demanded by Parliament in the Act and Regulations.[28]

Each school's practices must be recorded in policies and made available to parents.[29] The policies must be implemented rigorously. 'Independence' is therefore better understood to mean freedom for schools to design their own systems rather than permission for unstructured anarchy. The benefit of the approach from the perspective of independent schools is freedom; the downside is the greater attention given by the regulatory system to school policies compared to the state sector.

Market forces

Market forces have a part to play in informally regulating the quality of independent education. Parents wishing to invest in their children's education take great care over their choice of school but it can be difficult to know what really goes on at a school and a school's reputation may be a lagging indicator of quality. Market forces, though important, cannot therefore be relied on alone to secure children's rights to effective education. One of the functions of the standards and inspection is to assist the market to function properly by ensuring parents have access to certain information when making their decisions. Provision of further information is covered in Chapter Fifteen.

---

28 Beis Aharon Trust v Secretary of State for Education [2016] UKFTT 270 (HESC) at para. 88.

29 See Chapter Fifteen on the Provision of Information standard for the detail.

The parent/school contract

The relationship between parents and independent schools is one of contract. Parent/school contracts tend not to cover the matters regulated by the standards, which are the focus of this book, although there may be overlap particularly in relation to behavioural expectations for pupils. Parent/school contracts typically focus on financial arrangements, co-operation between the parties and the circumstances in which the relationship can be terminated. It is always important for advisors to check the particular contract in case it has any bearing on the issue on which they are advising.

Parents and schools cannot contract out of the requirement for the school to meet each of the independent school standards. [30]

The curious position of academies

Academies are registered as independent schools and funded directly by central government, rather than by parents or LAs as in the case of traditional independent or maintained schools.

In their earliest conception, academies were not subject to all the statutory codes of practice for state schools. This led to the anomalous position where parents of academy pupils, although using state education, potentially had neither the contractual rights of private school parents nor the full suite of statutory rights of state school parents.

As independent schools, however, academies were (and are) subject to most of the independent school standards, subject to a few exceptions,[31] which sometimes replicate or approximate to the requirements for state

---

[30] See R v Secretary of State for Education and Employment and others ex parte Williamson [2005] UKHL 15 and Beis Aharon Trust v Secretary of State for Education [2016] UKFTT 270 (HESC)

[31] The academy exceptions are found in regulation 3(2)-(3) of The Education (Independent School Standards) Regulations 2014. Exceptions include the curriculum, teaching and assessment standards and parts of the provision of information standard.

schools. As an example, the School Premises (England) Regulations 2012 only apply to maintained schools but the same provisions are replicated for independent schools and academies in the standards.

The main vehicle for regulating academies, however, is the funding agreement between the Secretary of State and the academy trust. Terms are imposed as a condition of funding. This approach was originally designed to allow state school leaders freedoms similar to those of leaders of traditional independent schools, and potentially to allow the Secretary of State scope for flexibility in response to local need. While a range of funding agreements are in use, new funding agreements tend now to be in standard form and to impose some of the statutory codes for state schools.[32] Academies are also subject to section 5 and 8 inspections by Ofsted, rather than the statutory inspection regime for independent schools which would require routine inspection against the standards.[33] This leaves little role in practice for some of the standards, except on first registration of an academy.

The White Paper: *Opportunity for all, Strong schools with great teachers for your child* (March 2022) recognises that the system that has evolved is confusing. The Schools Bill 2022 therefore proposes to bring together both new and existing requirements on academy trusts and academies (currently set out in legislation and funding agreements) into a new common set of statutory academy trust standards. The Independent School Standards would then cease to apply to academies.[34]

For the time-being, advisors of academies, or of parents whose children attend academies, should scrutinise the funding agreement for information about the obligations of the particular academy and consider also the independent school standards. The law relating to academies is beyond the remit of this book.

---

[32] See sections 2A-2D of the Academies Act 2010, inserted by section 14 of the Education and Adoption Act 2016, concerning termination of funding agreements after HMCI gives notice under section 13(3)(a) Education Act 2005.

[33] Sections 5(1) and (2)(d), section 8 of the Education Act 2005, and section 109.

[34] The DfE's briefing notes anticipate that this would take place in September 2023 at the earliest. The logical next step would be for the academy trust standards to underpin academy inspections. This would entail further legislation.

Conclusion

State schools operate within an educational system tightly controlled by the state. By contrast, independent schools are free to design and implement their own systems provided that those systems meet certain minimum standards. Parents have a right to educate their children outside the provision made by the state. The independent school standards provide a balancing mechanism which enables the Secretary of State to protect the safety of children and ensure that they receive a good education which prepares them for adult life in modern British society, while not interfering disproportionately with parental rights.

For further reading see:

- the Education Act 1944

- the Convention for the Protection of Human Rights and Fundamental Freedoms, agreed by the Council of Europe at Rome 1950

- ECtHR's Guide on Article 2 of Protocol No. 1 to the European Convention on Human Rights – Right to education 31 August 2021

- the Children Act 1989

- the UN Convention on the Rights of the Child 1989

- the Education Act 1996

- the Human Rights Act 1998

- the Education Act 2002

- the Children Act 2004

- the Safeguarding Vulnerable Groups Act 2006

- the Education and Skills Act 2008

- the Equality Act 2010

- the Children and Families Act 2014

- the Children and Social Work Act 2017

CHAPTER TWO

REGISTRATION REQUIREMENTS FOR INDEPENDENT SCHOOLS

Introduction and overview

All independent schools must be registered with the DfE, which, on behalf of the Secretary of State for Education, is the regulator and registration authority for independent schools. It is a common misconception that these functions are carried out by Ofsted.[35]

The registration process is prescribed by the Education and Skills Act 2008, sections 98 – 99. The detail and departmental policy are explained on gov.uk: _Registration of independent schools: Departmental guidance for proprietors and prospective proprietors of independent schools in England_, August 2019.

If an education provider does not meet the definition of an independent school, it cannot be registered as an independent school and does not come within the regulatory regime for independent schools.[36] If there are concerns about the education or welfare of children attending an unregistered provider, it would fall to the LA to identify the children and take action under section 436A of the Education Act 1996 and in accordance with their duties under the Children Act 1989 and 2004. These issues can be relevant to questions of when the standards apply.[37]

---

[35] HM Chief Inspector, operating through Ofsted, is the regulator of childcare. See the Childcare Act 2006.

[36] See also Chapter II, Part VI of the Education Act 1996 about Attendance Orders and also see the DfE publication: _Children missing education: statutory guidance for local authorities, September 2016._

[37] Note the Schools Bill 2022 intends to change the law to bring more institutions within the registration requirements and regulatory regime. If passed, provisions would also extend the investigatory powers of OFSTED and the DfE in relation to unregistered settings.

This chapter explains some key definitions and questions commonly arising from them, outlines the registration process and process for making material changes.

What is an independent school?

'Independent school' means:

> *'463(1) ... any school[38] at which full-time education is provided for-*
>
> *(a) five or more pupils of compulsory school age, or*
>
> *(b) at least one pupil of that age for whom an EHC plan is maintained or for whom a statement is maintained under section 324, or who is looked after by a local authority (within the meaning of section 22 of the Children Act 1989 or section 74 of the Social Services and Well-being (Wales) Act 2014)*
>
> *and which is not a school maintained by a local authority or a non-maintained special school.*
>
> *(2) For the purposes of subsection(1)(a) and (b) it is immaterial if full-time education is also provided at the school for pupils under of over compulsory school age.'[39] [40]*

The elements of the definition are considered below.

---

[38] The chain of definitions can give rise to some conceptual difficulties at the margins. The DfE has consulted on proposals to address these. https://consult.education.gov.uk/safeguarding-in-schools-team/regulating-independent-education-institutions/supporting_documents/Regulating%20IEI%20Consultation%202020%20Relaunch.pdf .

[39] Section 463 of the Education Act 1996 as substituted by section 172 Education Act 2002 and further amended by the Local Education Authorities and Children's Services Authorities (Integration of Functions) Order 2010 and the Children and Families Act 2014.

[40] The parts of section 92 Education and Skills Act 2008 which relate to part-time institutions have not yet been brought into force. Section 168(3) Education and Skills Act 2008 applies the definitions of the Education Act 1996 to the 2008 Act. See also section 138 for interpretation.

Any school …

Definitions of what is and is not a 'school' are provided in section 4 of the Education Act 1996. At its simplest level, a *'school'* is *'an educational institution which is outside the further education and the wider higher education sector'* and provides primary education, secondary education or both. *'Primary'* and *'secondary'* education are in turn defined in section 2 of the Education Act 1996. A stand-alone independent nursery is not a school.[41]

In borderline cases, the range of definitions needs to be studied carefully and the best approach may be to liaise with the independent education team at the DfE: registration.enquiries@education.gov.uk .

..at which full-time education is provided

Parents are obliged to ensure their child receives 'full-time education' and the duty to register as a school arises when an establishment provides 'full-time education'. There is, however, no legal definition of 'full-time' education.[42] The DfE has indicated that it would consider an institution to be providing full-time education

> *'…if it is intended to provide, or does provide, all, or substantially all, of a child's education.*
>
> *Relevant factors in determining whether education is full-time include:*
>
> *a) the number of hours per week that is provided – including breaks and independent study time*
>
> *b) the number of weeks in the academic term/year the education is provided*
>
> *c) the time of day it is provided*

---

[41] Section 4(1A) Education Act 1996.

[42] This is addressed in the Schools Bill 2022. See footnotes below.

d) whether the education provision in practice precludes the possibility that full-time education could be provided elsewhere.'[43]

The guidance provides a rule of thumb that a school will be considered to be providing full-time education if it is providing *'more than 18 hours per week'* during the day. This is on the basis that *'the education being provided is taking up the substantial part of the week in which it can be reasonably expected a child can be educated, and therefore indicates that the education provided is the main source of education for that child'.*[44]

.. for five or more pupils of compulsory school age

For the definition of compulsory school age see section 8 of the Education Act 1996.[45]

In summary, a child is of compulsory school age from the start of the school term after his fifth birthday until the last Friday in June in the school year in which he or she turns 16.

'8(2) A person begins to be of compulsory school age –

(a) when he attains the age of five, if he attains that age on a prescribed day, and

(b) otherwise at the beginning of the prescribed day next following his attaining that age.'

The prescribed days are currently 31st August, 31st December and 31st March.[46]

'8(3) A person ceases to be of compulsory school age at the end of the day which is the school leaving date for any calendar year –

---

43 *Registration of independent schools: departmental guidance for proprietors and prospective proprietors of independent schools in England,* DfE guidance, p. 6.

44 Ibid. The Schools Bill sets out factors to be taken into account when deciding whether a setting is providing 'full-time' education: numbers of hours, weeks and time of day of attendance.

45 Education Act 1996 section 8(1). The definition applies across all enactments.

46 The Education (Start of Compulsory School Age) Order 1998.

(a) if he attains the age of 16 after that day but before the beginning of the school year next following

(b) if he attains that age on that day, or

(c) (unless paragraph (a) applies) if that day is the school leaving date next following his attaining that age.'

The school leaving date is the last Friday in June.[47]

This means that providers who cater only for children who are not of compulsory school age, such as private nursery schools or private sixth form colleges, do not fall within the definition. These cannot be registered as independent schools but will be required to register with Ofsted as early years settings if they cater for children under compulsory school age.[48] Registered independent schools which cater for pupils under two years of age must register both with the DfE as a school and with Ofsted as an early years setting.[49] Stand-alone private further education is unregulated.[50]

'Compulsory school age' should not be confused with the 'participation age'.[51] Compulsory school age (broadly speaking ages 5-16 years) is the period for which parents are required to cause their children to receive 'suitable education'. Thereafter, young people are under a duty to

---

[47] The Education (School Leaving Date) Order 1997.

[48] See also Education Act 1996 section 4(1A) and section 4(3) and (4). Some colleges which are within the Further or Higher Education sectors are not 'schools' and therefore cannot be registered as independent schools even if they have pupils of compulsory school age.

[49] See the Ofsted publication: Registering school-based provision, February 2017, for more information about when dual registration is required.

[50] Private further education providers which sponsor students from overseas must meet Home Office/UKVI requirements in that connection. ISI provides non-statutory 'educational oversight' for those colleges.

[51] See Chapter 1, Part 1 of the Education and Skills Act 2008, and also the DfE publication: Participation of young people in education, employment or training. Statutory guidance for local authorities, September 2016

continue to participate in education or training until their 18th birthday or they attain A Levels of their equivalent,[52] whichever happens sooner.

… or one pupil of that age for whom an EHC plan is maintained

An EHC plan is an Education Health and Care plan under section 37 of the Children and Families Act 2014. LAs are under a duty to make individual plans to meet the needs of certain children. The regime is governed by the Children and Families Act 2014 and is outside the scope of this book.

… or who is looked after by a local authority …

A child is 'looked after' by a LA if he or she is in its care or is provided with accommodation for a continuous period of more than 24 hours by the authority under its social services functions.[53]

… and which is not a school maintained by a local authority or a non-maintained special school.

Understanding the term 'non-maintained special school' entails distinguishing them from other forms of independent special schools (for which see the next section below). Counterintuitively, the terms 'non-maintained special school' and 'independent special school' are not interchangeable. At one stage there were separate legal definitions of independent special school and non-maintained special school under sections 347 and 342 of the Education Act 1996, in addition to the definition of independent school in section 463.

A non-maintained special school is a school registered under section 342 of the Education Act 1996. They are regulated under the Non-Maintained Special School (England) Regulations 2015, as amended,[54] rather than the independent school standards.

---

[52] Specified as 'a level 3 qualification' – section 1(c) Education and Skills Act 2008.

[53] Section 22 of the Children Act 1989 and section 74 of the Social Services and Well-being (Wales) Act 2014.

[54] See the DfE publication: The Non-Maintained Special Schools (England) Regulations 2015: Departmental advice for non-maintained special schools, August 2015.

What is an independent special school?

There is no legal definition of 'independent special school'. The legal category and definition, formerly found in section 347 of the Education Act 1996, was repealed from 1 September 2009 for schools in England.[55]

Notwithstanding the lack of legal definition, 'independent special school' remains an administrative category for registration purposes. Independent schools are required to indicate to the DfE on first registration and annually thereafter whether they intend to admit pupils with SEN. If so, they are asked whether they will cater 'wholly or mainly' for children with SEN and are required to select a category of SEN. 'Wholly or mainly' is not defined and has not been litigated. It is essentially a process of self-identification.

This has the effect that all independent schools which are not registered under section 342 are regulated under the Education (Independent School Standards) Regulations 2014, as amended. The standards are deemed to be sufficiently broad and flexible to cover independent schools which specialise in the education of pupils with SEN.

The NMS for boarding do not apply to residential special schools. Instead, residential special schools (whether state, independent or non-maintained) must meet the NMS for Residential Special Schools. These are outside the scope of this book.

Section 41 schools

The Children and Families Act 2014 introduced a voluntary registration category of schools which enables independent and non-maintained special schools to participate in local authority SEN funding mechanisms on terms similar to those which apply to maintained schools. In exchange the schools agree to be named in EHC plans at the option of the relevant LA.

---

[55] Section 146 Education and Skills Act 2008. Regulation 3 of the Education and Skills Act 2008 (commencement no. 3) Order 2009.

Registration under section 41 of the Children and Families Act 2014 is addition to the schools' registration under section 342 and 463 of the Education Act 1996.

Participation in section 41 cannot be assumed to be a proxy indicator of the quality of provision at schools that do not choose to participate. Many independent special schools have not opted into the section 41 arrangements. This may be for good reasons, such as that their pupils tend not have EHC plans because their parents expect to self-fund like parents of pupils in other independent schools, that the needs of their pupil cohort tend not to reach the legally defined thresholds for LA intervention through EHC plans, that their provision exceeds that which LAs would expect to fund, or because the schools prefer to retain control over admission decisions.

For more information and guidance see: _Guidance for Independent special institutions applying for inclusion on the Secretary of State approved list._

How to find out the registration category of a school (non-maintained/independent special etc)

Lists of independent special schools and colleges, including their registration category, are published on gov.uk.[56] The registration category is also listed against each school on the government's online database of schools, 'Get Information About Schools' (GIAS), although because the lists are 'live' the information on the two lists is not always completely aligned.

Who is the proprietor?

The proprietor of a school is _'the person or body of persons responsible for the management of the school...(so that in relation to a community, foundation, or voluntary, community or foundation special school ... it_

---

[56] https://www.gov.uk/government/publications/independent-special-schools-and-colleges.

means the governing body)'.[57] This definition is expressed to be *'unless the context otherwise requires'.*

Notably, the definition of proprietor is not expressed in terms of ownership but of responsibility for management. The examples given in the Education Act 1996 distinguish between the owner (who might be, for example, the local authority or a foundation) and the governing body. It is not clear whether this distinction works in all contexts when applied to independent schools. The 'local governing bodies' used by some school groups may be set up as advisory only, without legal responsibilities. In other examples, it may be the same individuals on the management board and the ownership board making it difficult to draw a distinction.

The proprietor must be identified to the DfE on application to register the school. They are then registered transparently on GIAS as a matter of public record. The registered body/person is then treated as proprietor by the DfE/inspectorates. In complex cases, either before first registration or when there is a change of proprietor, the pragmatic way forward is for the school or their advisors to liaise with the DfE to ensure that the correct people or body are/is registered on GIAS before it becomes an issue during an inspection.

Application process

In outline:

- An application must be made to the DfE and approved before the school commences operation

- The application is submitted using the various online forms provided on Gov.uk: *Register an Independent school: application guidance and checklist*

- It must be accompanied by supporting documents to show how the proposed school would meet the standards, as set out in

---

[57] Section 579(1) Education Act 1996.

regulations made under the section 94 of the Education and Skills Act 2008.[58] All documentation must be available in English to facilitate inspection[59]

- It must include information about

  o the age range, sex and maximum number of students

  o the curriculum policy

  o whether the school will provide accommodation for pupils

  o whether the school will be specially organised to provide for students with special educational needs.

- The DfE commissions Ofsted to carry out a pre-registration inspection[60]

- Ofsted reports to the DfE on the extent to which the standards are likely to be met by the new school once registered

- The Secretary of State decides whether the standards are likely to be met by the proposed school once registered, taking into account

  o the Ofsted report, and

  o any other evidence relating to the standards

- The proprietor is informed of the decision by the DFE

---

[58] For full details of documentation required see p. 9 of Registration of independent schools Departmental guidance for proprietors and prospective proprietors of independent schools in England August 2019

[59] P. 6 of https://assets.publishing.service.gov.uk/government/uploads/system/uploads/attachment_data/file/800615/Independent_School_Standards-_Guidance_070519.pdf .

[60] It is always Ofsted. Independent inspectorates do not carry out pre-registration inspections.

- If the Secretary of State decides that the standards are likely to be met, the Secretary of State must register the school[61]

Making changes

Registered schools must obtain permission from the DfE before making certain material changes. 'Material changes' are defined for this purpose by section 162 of the Education Act 2002, which also governs the process. (The similar provisions included in sections 101-105 of the Education and Skills Act 2008 have not yet been brought into force.)

The following are material changes:

- A change of proprietor

- A change of school address

- A change to the age range of pupils – including nursery and sixth form

- A change to the maximum number of pupils

- A change to whether the school is for male or female pupils or both

- Adding or removing boarding accommodation for pupils

- Adding or removing provision for pupils with special educational needs

Notably changes to a school's admissions policy, religious ethos or religious character do not fall within these provisions, but consideration should be given to whether a change to these would entail a change to the school's foundational documents, such as the trust deed of a charity.[62]

---

[61] Section 95 Education and Skills Act 2008.

[62] Such changes are outside the scope of this text.

The DfE guidance: *Independent schools: making a material change – GOV.UK (www.gov.uk)* 30 June 2021 provides information about how to apply for a material change and there is more in: *Registration of independent schools: Departmental guidance for proprietors and prospective proprietors of independent schools in England.* Essentially, the school simply emails the DfE's independent schools team. The DfE may commission a 'material change inspection' from the school's usual inspectorate for advice about whether the school is likely to continue to meet 'any relevant standard' if the change were to go ahead. See Chapter Three and Chapter Twenty-Four for more about inspection.

A material change will not usually be approved at a time when a school is not meeting the standards relevant to the proposed change.[63] The DfE will only consider a material change to independent schools that do not meet the standards and are under regulatory or enforcement action if granting the change would help them to meet the standards.[64] Schools should therefore take every care to ensure they are meeting the standards before applying for a material change. This is particularly important in relation to safeguarding and welfare standards, such as anti-bullying arrangements or supervision, which may potentially be relevant to a wide range of changes.

See also Part E of : *Registration of independent schools Departmental guidance for proprietors and prospective proprietors of independent schools in England August 2019*

and : *Religious character designation: guide to applying*

Conclusion

The registration process for independent schools is simple and accessible. If in doubt, contact can be made with the DfE's independent schools team via: IndependentSchool.Applications@education.gov.uk. At the outset, schools must indicate how they will meet the standards

---

[63] See section 162(6) and (7), especially 162(6)(b).

[64] See *Independent schools: making a material change – GOV.UK (www.gov.uk)* and also Schedule 5 of the Schools Bill 2022.

and both pre-registration and ever after their statutory policies and the way they implement them are inspected to ensure they exercise their independence within the expectations for their type of setting. An understanding of the standards is therefore essential.

CHAPTER THREE

OVERVIEW OF THE INDEPENDENT SCHOOL STANDARDS

Introduction

The independent school standards take concepts of education and human behaviours and anatomise them into artificially separate components, setting standards for each for the purpose of creating accountability measures.

Many standards are principle-based to allow schools maximum discretion around how they are met while others, such as those about suitability checks, are more rule-based and allow little latitude. This approach provides a flexible framework for the regulator (DfE) and inspectorates (currently Ofsted and the Independent Schools Inspectorate) to respond to a wide range of situations, coupled with certainty on welfare issues.

The hybrid style of the standards also works well for proprietors/leaders with the confidence and ability to exercise their independence and professional discretion. It can be a source of frustration to others, including parents and potential claimants, who would prefer the certainty of clear prescription and the clarity of 'right'/ 'wrong' answers to complex scenarios. Anxiety about inspection outcomes should not be under-estimated by legal advisors. The best advice may be to start by understanding/explaining the underlying purpose of each standard and provide reassurance that all reasonable systematic approaches which consistently achieve that purpose are likely to meet the standard.

Finding the standards

The current standards are in the schedule to the Education (Independent School Standards) Regulations 2014[65], as amended.[66] They are set by the Secretary of State using powers in section 94 of the Education and Skills Act 2008. As such they form part of English law. Definitions of key terms, such as 'pupil', 'boarder', 'staff', 'supply staff', 'provided' and 'made available' are found in regulation 2 of the Education (Independent school Standards) Regulations 2014, as amended.[67]

What the standards cover

The headline issues covered by the standards are defined in the empowering legislation. The Secretary of State is required to prescribe standards for independent educational institutions about: [68]

---

[65] These are commonly known in the independent sector as the 'ISSR' or 'ISSRs' as an abbreviation for 'Independent School Standards Regulations', which is itself a misnomer. This book uses 'ISS'.

[66] The Education (Independent School Standards) Regulations 2014 have been amended by

- Regulation 9 of the Independent Educational Provision in England (Inspection Fees) and Independent School Standards (Amendment) Regulations 2018

- Regulation 11 of the Independent Educational Provision in England (Provision of Information) and Non-Maintained Special Schools (England) and Independent School Standards (Amendment) Regulations 2018

- Para. 19 of the Schedule to the Relationships Education, Relationships and Sex Education and Health Education (England) Regulations 2019

- Regulation 2 of the Education (Independent School Standards) (Coronavirus) (Amendment) Regulations 2020.

[67] For the benefit of lay readers, regulation 2 of the regulations is in the body of the regulations and not to be confused with para. 2 of the standards which are in the schedule to the regulations.

[68] Section 94 Education and Skills Act 2008.

- quality of education provided

- spiritual, moral, social and cultural development of pupils

- welfare, health and safety of pupils

- suitability of proprietors and staff

- premises and accommodation provided

- provision of information by independent schools

- manner in which complaints are handled

- quality of the leadership in and management of schools.

The standards are divided into eight parts which follow the structure set in the primary legislation. Matters not covered include for example, financial management, financial disputes with parents, staff welfare and data protection issues (with a few limited exceptions).

Other standards and regulations incorporated into the independent school standards

Although the standards themselves comprise only 14 pages, they incorporate various other statutory standards, statutory definitions and statutory guidance, some targeted to specific types of provision. These make the standards considerably more extensive than appears at first glance:

- National Minimum Standards for boarding school 2022 (29 pages)[69]

- National Minimum Standards for residential special schools 2022 (39 pages)[70]

---

[69] Made under section 87C(1) of the Children Act 1989, as amended by the Care Standards Act 2000 and the Education Act 2011. Incorporated by ISS 8.

- Statutory framework for the Early Years Foundation Stage (53 pages)[71]

- *Keeping children safe in education* (173 pages)[72]

- *Working together to safeguard children* (116 pages)[73]

- *Relationships Education, Relationships and Sex Education (RSE) and Health Education* (50 pages)[74]

- 'relevant health and safety laws' (countless)[75]

- Regulatory Reform (Fire Safety) Order 2005 (65 pages)[76]

- Education (Pupil Registration) (England) Regulations 2006 (8 pages)[77]

- Equality Act 2010: Parts 2 (key concepts), Part 6 (schools) and Schedules 10, 11, 14, 22 and 23[78]

- Section 10(2) Children Act 2004[79]

---

[70] Made under section 87C(1) of the Children Act 1989, as amended by the Care Standards Act 2000 and the Education Act 2011. Incorporated by ISS 8.

[71] Made under section 39 Childcare Act 2006, the Early Years Foundation Stage (Welfare Requirements) 2012 and Early Years Foundation Stage (Learning and Development requirements) Order 2007 each as amended from time to time. Incorporated into the standards by section 94(5)(b) Education and Skills Act 2008.

[72] Incorporated into the standards by ISS 7.

[73] Incorporated by ISS 7.

[74] Made under sections 34 and 35 Children and Social Work Act. Incorporated into the standards by ISS 2A.

[75] Incorporated by ISS 11.

[76] Incorporated by ISS 12.

[77] Incorporated by ISS 15.

[78] Incorporated by ISS2(2)(d)(ii), 3(j), 5(b)(vi).

[79] Incorporated by ISS 34(1)(c) and (2).

When the standards apply

Many independent schools operate both in and outside school terms, for example, offering children's holiday clubs or opening sports facilities to the community at large when the school is otherwise closed. The standards certainly apply when a school is operating as a school. They are generally assumed not to apply when the school is not operating as a school, or not to apply to provision that is not for pupils, but there is no case law authority on the point. When a school is not operating as a school, other relevant legislation would still apply such as the Safeguarding Vulnerable Groups Act 2006 (which defines regulated activity) and the Children Act 1989, under which local authorities would continue to have duties towards children in need or at risk in their area.

The statutory framework for the EYFS applies to early years provision at all times. The NMS for boarding schools also have a statutory status in their own right and can apply at times when the independent school standards do not.[80]

When the EYFS applies

The application of the statutory framework for the EYFS to schools can be confusing due to overlap with the standards. Depending on the age of the children, sometimes it applies instead of the independent school standards and sometimes in addition.

---

[80] This is needed because they apply also to state boarding schools. See pp 4 and 5 of the NMS for boarding for more information about when they apply.

When the statutory framework for the EYFS applies to independent school provision

Age of children	ISS apply? [81]	EYFS applies? [82]
Under 2 years	No	Yes
Age 2	For 2 year-olds, the ISS consist solely of the EYFS requirements.	Yes
Age 3-5 (end of academic year in which they turn 5)	Yes, except where the provision is a stand-alone nursery which is not part of a registered school.	Yes – although independent schools can claim exemption from the learning and development requirements. [83]

The role of the proprietor

Many standards are expressed as obligations of the proprietor, in terms of outcomes which the proprietor must ensure. See Chapter Two for the definition of proprietor and how to identify them. Proprietors carry personal legal responsibility for their schools but are not obliged to perform the duties attributed to them personally. A sole proprietor of a small school might do so but more typically in larger establishments proprietors fulfil their obligations through the leaders they appoint, good systems of governance, clear schemes of delegation, lines of accountability and effective performance management. For 'proprietor'

---

[81] Section 94(4) and 94(5)(b) Education and Skills Act 2008. The table concerns provision when a school is open.

[82] Section 40 Childcare Act 2006 makes the EYFS apply to all EY providers.

[83] For information about exemptions see: *The Early Years Foundation Stage (EYFS) Learning and Development Requirements: Guidance on Exemptions for Early Years Providers June 2017* and regulations listed there. https://assets.publishing.service.gov.uk/government/uploads/system/uploads/attachment_data/file/621771/Guidance_on_exemptions_for_Early_Years_providers.pdf .

in the standards, one can therefore read 'school' unless statutory guidance stipulates that a matter is to be dealt with at board level.

The role of inspection

The statutory purpose of inspection of independent schools, whether by Ofsted or an independent inspectorate,[84] is

- in the case of inspections at the direction of the DfE: to 'make a report to the Secretary of State on the extent to which any relevant standard is being met in relation to the institution'[85]

- in the case of material change inspections: to report to the Secretary of State on 'the extent to which, if the change is made, any relevant standard is likely to continue to be met in relation to the school'[86]

'Any relevant standard' means in each case, any of the standards specified by the Secretary of State for the purposes of the inspection or considered to be relevant by either HMCI (in the case of routine Ofsted inspections) or the person carrying out the inspection in directed inspections.[87]

---

[84] By section 106 Education and Skills Act 2008, the Secretary of State may approve independent inspectorates for inspection of independent schools. Advice about approval is found in: *Approval of Independent Inspectorates 2014*. ISI is currently the only independent inspectorate. Section 107 Education and Skills Act 2008 underpins arrangements for Ofsted to monitor the work of independent inspectorates. Letters of approval, the current MOU about monitoring and the annual monitoring letters are available on gov.uk.

[85] Section 109(2)(b) and 109(3)(b) Education and Skills Act 2008. All inspections by independent inspectorates are directed by the DfE under either section 109 or 163.

[86] Section 162(4).

[87] Section 108(2) and 109(4).

There are additional powers and provisions relating to the inspection of boarding care in section 87 et seq. of the Children Act 1989.[88]

The burden of proof is on the school to demonstrate to the inspection team that it continues to meet the standards at the time of the inspection.[89]

Inspections have been called 'the eyes and ears of the DfE'. Inspection reports enable the DfE to form a view on whether action is needed by the Secretary of State to drive improvement in particular schools against the standards. The processes and powers available to the Secretary of State following a failed inspection are set out in the Education and Skills Act 2008, starting at section 114 – 118 and the DfE's policy statement: *Independent Schools: Regulatory and Enforcement Action, April 2019.*[90] Effective enforcement action depends on clear evidence-based inspection reports which specify which standards are or are not being met.

The inspection framework of each inspectorate sets out how they will carry out their statutory duties over a period (cycle) set by the Secretary of State. Currently independent schools are routinely inspected against the standards on a three-year cycle.[91] The framework covers such matters as different types of inspections, inspection timelines, notice periods, grade descriptors and reporting against the standards. It may include reporting on additional matters after consultation with stakeholders. Inspection frameworks are designed to set a level playing

---

[88] See the MOU between DfE and Ofsted for more information: *Memorandum of understanding: independent schools.* This also covers the agreement about when Inspection of early years provision Is to be inspected as part of the whole-school inspection.

[89] Marshall v Commission for Social Care Inspection [2009] EWHC 1286 (Admin).

[90] The Schools Bill 2022 contains provisions which would extend the available enforcement powers, if passed into law.

[91] Boarding provision in residential special schools is inspected by Ofsted annually. A range of additional inspections can be triggered out of cycle.

field across schools for the period of the cycle, ensuring consistency and flexibility within parameters.[92]

Briefing schools about the requirements of the standards and any changes to them is not part of the statutory role of inspection.[93] Inspectorates may provide information as part of the 'added value' they offer but in so doing must exercise caution to avoid pitfalls such as implying limitations on the freedom of schools (where relevant) about how they meet the standards, or fettering their own discretion.

Independent school inspections are funded by the schools. In the case of Ofsted inspections, fees are regulated through the *Independent Educational Provision in England (Inspection Fees and Savings Provisions) Regulations 2019.*

Departmental guidance about the standards

The DfE has issued non-statutory advice to assist proprietors and others to understand the standards: *Independent School Standards: Guidance for independent schools, April 2019.* It advises that inspectors will take it into account when reporting to the Secretary of State on the extent to which the standards are being met, and likewise, the DfE will do so when considering regulatory action. The advice is helpful in addressing some aspects of interest particularly to faith schools and is drawn on in the chapters which follow.

Other departmental advice (whether non-statutory for all schools or statutory but only for state schools) can be helpful in relation to standards which contain little prescription except as to outcome. It indicates practice in schools generally, and therefore gives independent

---

[92] For correspondence on how covid has impacted the current cycle and frameworks see: https://www.gov.uk/government/publications/independent-schools-approved-inspectorates .

[93] Beis Aharon v Secretary of State [2016] UKFTT 270 (HESC): para.s 50, 52, 88. A criticism levelled at Ofsted for not helping a school was found to be a 'fundamental misunderstanding of the role of both Ofsted and ... the regulator.' Brayne J at para. 52.

schools a starting point when considering whether their own approach is reasonable.

Conclusion

For further reading see:

- *Independent School Standards: Guidance for independent schools, April 2019*

- *Independent Schools: Regulatory and Enforcement Action, April 2019.*

CHAPTER FOUR

KEY PROVISIONS OF THE EQUALITY ACT 2010

Introduction

Concepts from the Equality Act (EqA 2010) are woven through the standards, sometimes expressly, other times impliedly. A knowledge of the key principles of EqA 2010 is therefore important for understanding and applying many of the standards.

This short chapter cannot hope to do justice to the detail and complexity of the EqA 2010 and the case law it has generated. It aims rather to provide readers a ready reference point and high-level summary of the key concepts and definitions relevant to the standards to assist when reading this book. As such, it provides a starting point only for readers' own analysis of the EqA 2010.

Overview

The EqA 2010 prohibits certain types of conduct towards people with specified characteristics, in defined contexts. The rules are tailored to different settings (work, services, premises, associations, pension schemes, education) by extensive provisions which switch them on and off and through exceptions. This chapter summarises:

- The protected characteristics

- The prohibited conduct

- How these apply to independent schools in relation to pupils–Part 6 of the EqA 2010[94]

---

[94] Other parts of the EqA 2010 of potential relevance to schools include work (Part 5), provision of services and public functions (Part 3), contracts (Part 10)

- Exceptions

- Accessibility plans

Overview of Part 6 EqA 2010 – protected characteristics and prohibited conduct. What applies to the relationship between schools and pupils

		Prohibited conduct by schools to pupils				
Protected ch'teristics	Included in PSHE/ SMSC	Direct discrim [95]	Indirect discrim [96]	Disability Discrim ('arising from'[97] and RAs[98])	Ha'sm t[99]	Vic.n [100]
Disability[101]	Yes	Yes	Yes	Yes	Yes	Yes
Gender reass't	Yes	Yes	Yes	N/A	No[102]	Yes
Pregnancy and maternity[103]	Yes	Yes	Yes	N/A	No	Yes
Race	Yes	Yes	Yes	N/A	Yes	Yes

and the general exceptions (Part 14) including charities (sections 193 and 194) and sport (section 195), and their associated schedules. Note that section 28(2) ensures that Parts 3 and 6 do not overlap.

[95] Section 13 EqA 2010.

[96] Section 19 EqA 2010.

[97] Section 15 EqA 2010.

[98] 'RAs'(reasonable adjustments) – section 21 EqA 2010 and Schedule 13 applies.

[99] Sections 26 and 85(10) EqA 2010 – In the application of section 26 (harassment) for the purposes of section 85(3), none of the following is a protected characteristic: gender reassignment, religion or belief, sexual orientation.

[100] Section 27 EqA 2010 – Victimisation for asserting rights under the EqA.

[101] For exceptions for permitted forms of selection, see EqA 2010 Schedule 11, Part 3.

[102] Section 85(10) EqA 2010.

[103] See also section 17 EqA 2010.

Religion or belief[104]	Yes	Yes	Yes	N/A	No	Yes
Sex[105]	Yes	Yes	Yes	N/A	Yes	Yes
Sexual orientation	Yes	Yes	Yes	N/A	No	Yes
Age[106]	Yes	No	No	N/A	No	No
Marriage or civil p'ship[107]	Yes	No	No	N/A	No	No

Protected characteristics – overview

The full list of protected characteristics is:

- Disability

- Gender reassignment

- Pregnancy and maternity

- Race

- Religion or belief

- Sex

- Sexual orientation

- Age

- Marriage and civil partnership

---

[104] For exceptions relating to religious or belief-related discrimination, and schools with a religious character see Schedule 11, Part 2.

[105] For exceptions for single-sex schools and single-sex boarding see EqA 2010 Schedule 11, Part 1.

[106] Section 84 EqA 2010.

[107] Ditto.

Age and marriage/civil partnership are not protected in the context of a school's relationship to its pupils.[108]

Protected characteristics – outline definitions

The following information is in outline only.[109] There is a body of relevant case law in the education context. Where there are gaps, interpretation can also be informed by the case law developing in the context of employment.

<u>Disability</u>

A person is disabled within the meaning of the EqA 2010 if they have

- a physical or mental impairment

- which has a substantial and long-term adverse effect on their ability to

- carry out normal day-to-day activities. [110]

'Long term' means that it has lasted or is likely to last for at least 12 months, or for the rest of the life of the person affected[111]. 'Substantial' means 'more than minor or trivial'.[112]

There is guidance on 'normal day to day activities' in *Equality Act 2010: Guidance on matters to be taken into account in determining questions relating to the definition of disability*

---

[108] Section 84 EqA 2010.

[109] It is important for lawyers to read the definitions in the EqA 2010 itself. The EHRC's Technical Guidance for schools is also an invaluable accessible resource together with the growing body of case law and guidance now sits behind each of the definitions.

[110] Section 6, EqA 2010. The Children Act 1989 uses a different definition.

[111] Schedule 1, para. 2(1) EqA 2010.

[112] Section 212, EqA 2010.

A formal diagnosis of a named condition can provide helpful information but is not always conclusive that a person, such as a pupil, has a disability within the meaning of the EqA 2010. It may, for example, confirm only a degree of impairment, but not address whether the impairment has a substantial and long-term adverse effect on the pupil's ability to carry out normal day-to-day activities.

Conditions that are not impairments:[113]

- Hayfever

- Tattoos and piercings

- Addiction to alcohol, nicotine or any other substance that was not initially medically prescribed

- A tendency to set fires or to steal

- Exhibitionism

- Voyeurism

- A tendency to physical or sexual abuse of other persons[114]

Conditions which are always impairments:

- Cancer, HIV infection, and multiple sclerosis[115]

---

[113] Equality Act 2010 (Disability) Regulations 2010.

[114] But note that in the case of C & C v The Governing Body of a School, the Secretary of State for Education and the National Autistic Society [2019] AACR 10 this blanket exception was disapplied in relation to 'children in education who have a recognised condition that is more likely to result in a tendency to physical abuse. [para. 95] The disapplication of Reg 4(1)(c) means that a condition which involves violence by a child can be recognised as a disability and dealt with under normal rules for disabled children. Exclusion is therefore available after reasonable adjustments have been made and where it can be shown to be a proportionate means of achieving a legitimate aim. C &C v GB [2019] AACR 10, para. 78, and Ashdown House v JKL and MNP [2019] UKUT 259 (AAC).

[115] Equality Act 2010 Schedule 1, para. 6(1).

- Severe disfigurement (not including tattoos or body piercings that have not been removed)[116]

- Visual impairment where the person is certified blind, severely sigh impaired, sight impaired or partially sighted by a consultant ophthalmologist[117]

See also the important cases of

- PP, SP v Trustees of Leicester Grammar School [2015] ELR 86[118]

- C & C v The Governing Body of a School, the Secretary of State for Education and the National Autistic Society [2019] AACR 10 – and

- Ashdown House v JKL and MNP [2019] UKUT 259 (AAC)

Gender reassignment

A person has this protected characteristic if they are proposing to undergo, are undergoing, or have undergone a process, or part of a process, for the purpose of reassigning their sex by changing physiological or other attributes of sex.[119] Note the protected characteristic is not 'gender identity' generally and there are question marks over whether the definition of 'gender reassignment' covers the full range of trans identities.

See cases such as:

- Bellinger v Bellinger [2003] UKHL 21

---

[116] Equality Act 2010 Schedule 1, para. 3 and Equality Act 2010 (Disability) Regulations 2010, reg 5.

[117] Equality Act 2010 (Disability) Regulations 2010, reg 7.

[118] As regards whether dyslexia creates a substantial impairment for a particular pupil, the pupil should not be compared to their classmates but to their own performance without the condition.

[119] Section 7, EqA 2010.

- <u>Croft v Royal Mail [2003] EWCA Civ 1045</u>

- <u>Chief Constable of West Yorkshire Police v A (no. 2)</u> (HL) [2004] ICR 806

- <u>Taylor v Jaguar Land Rover Limited</u> (Birmingham ET 1304471/2018 14.9.20)

- <u>Forstater v CGD Europe</u> [2021] UKEAT 0105_20_1006

- <u>FDJ, R (On the application of) v Secretary of State for Justice and Sodexo [2021] EWHC 1746</u>

- <u>R (Elan-Cane) v Secretary of State for the Home Department</u> [2021] UKSC 56

See also:

- *The Cass Review: Independent review of gender identity services for children and young people: Interim report: Interim Report – February 2022*

<u>Pregnancy and maternity</u>

A woman of any age is protected if she is or has been pregnant or has given birth (including a still birth) in the last 26 weeks or are breast feeding a baby who is 26 weeks or younger.[120]

<u>Race</u>

Race includes colour, nationality, ethnic or national origins.[121]

<u>Religion or belief</u>

Religion or belief means any religion, religious or philosophical belief, or lack of religion or belief.[122]

---

[120] Section 17 (2) and (3) and 212(1). See also Technical Guidance for Schools, EHRC, para.s 5.13 – 5.16.

[121] Section 9 EqA 2010.

[122] Section 10 EqA 2010.

The House of Lords in R v Secretary of State for Education ex parte Williamson [2005] UKHL 15 set 'modest threshold requirements' for when parental beliefs qualify for protection in the education context. [123] They now appear in the EHRC Technical Guidance for Schools at 5.125: [124]

i. The belief must be genuinely held

ii. It must be a belief, not merely an opinion or viewpoint based on the present state of information available

iii. It must be a belief as to a weighty and substantial aspect of human life and behaviour

iv. It must attain a certain level of cogency, seriousness, cohesion and importance

v. It must be worthy of respect in a democratic society

vi. It must be compatible with human dignity and not conflict with the fundamental rights of others

The protection of beliefs has been discussed further in recent employment cases and the area continues to develop:

- Conisbee v Crossley Farms Limited and others [2019] UKET 3335357/2018 (6 September 2019) – the claimant's vegetarianism was not a protected belief

- Casamitjana v The League Against Cruel Sports [2020] UKET 3331129/2018 (21 January 2020)– the claimant's ethical veganism qualified as a protected belief

- Forstater v CGD Europe and others [2021] UKEAT 0105/20/1006 (10 June 2021) – the claimant's gender critical beliefs were a protected belief

---

[123] Lord Nicholls at para. 23.

[124] After being developed further in employment cases : See Grainger plc & others v Nicholson [2009] UKEAT 0219 They are often called the Grainger criteria.

Sex

A person's sex refers to whether they are female or male of any age.[125]

Sexual orientation

Sexual orientation means a person's attraction towards persons of the same sex, of the opposite sex, or of either sex.[126]

Age

Age is defined in the EqA 2010 by reference to a person's age group. An age group can mean people of the same age or a range of ages.[127]

Marriage or civil partnership

A person who is married, or in a civil partnership under the Civil Partnership Act 2004, has the protected characteristic of marriage or civil partnership.[128]

The status of being unmarried or single is not protected. People who only intend to marry or form a civil partnership, or who have divorced or had their civil partnership dissolved, are not protected on this ground.

Prohibited conduct – overview

In summary, the prohibited conduct is:

- Direct discrimination

- Indirect discrimination

- Discrimination arising from disability

---

[125] Sections 11 and 212(1), EqA 2010.

[126] Section 12, EqA 2010.

[127] Section 5 EqA 2010. See also, EHCR Employment Statutory Code of Practice, para. 2.3 and 2.4.

[128] Section 8, EqA 2010.

- Failure to make reasonable adjustments for pupils with disabilities

- Pregnancy and maternity discrimination

- Harassment

- Victimisation

Prohibited conduct – outline definitions

For a full understanding, it is important to refer to the EqA 2010 and the EHRC's *Technical Guidance for Schools*. Direct and indirect discrimination apply to all protected characteristics and there are two additional types of discrimination which are prohibited in relation to pupils with disabilities.

Types of discrimination

The distinction between types of discrimination is crucial in practice because some can be justified on grounds of proportionality or reasonableness, while direct discrimination cannot.

Direct discrimination – treating a pupil less favourably than others because of a protected characteristic. Direct discrimination is always unlawful; it cannot be justified.

- Associative discrimination – a type of direct discrimination. It means treating a pupil less favourably than others because of their association with a person with a protected characteristic

- Perceptive discrimination – again a type of direct discrimination. It means treating a person less favourably than others because they are perceived mistakenly to have a protected characteristic

- Segregation by race is direct discrimination, according to section 13(5) EqA 2010. The Court of Appeal in HM Chief Inspector of Education, Children's Services and Skills v the Interim Executive Board of Al-Hijrah School [2017] EWCA Civ 1426 held that segregation by gender in co-educational schools is also direct discrimination. For the impact of the judgment see: *Gender separation in mixed schools*, non-statutory guidance from the DfE. This explains the exceptions which may be available

Indirect discrimination – applying a provision, criterion or practice ('PCP') generally which puts pupils with a particular protected characteristic at a disadvantage compared with others, unless the school can show that the PCP was justified, that is, it was 'a proportionate means of achieving a legitimate aim'.

To paraphrase, indirect discrimination arises when aspects of the way a school is run have an unintended worse effect on pupils with protected characteristics. This will be unlawful unless that school can show that its approach is justified in terms of being proportionate and in good cause. It can be relevant to cases about issues such as behaviour and uniform.

Discrimination arising from disability – treating a pupil unfavourably because of something arising in consequence of their disability, unless the school can show that the treatment was justified, that is, that it is 'a proportionate means of achieving a legitimate aim'.

It is a defence if the school did not know and could not reasonably be expected to know that the pupil has a disability.

Failure to make reasonable adjustments for pupils with disabilities – the duty to make adjustments is set out at length in sections 20, 21 and Schedule 13 of the EqA 2010. In the context of a school's relationship to its pupils, it can arise in two ways:

- Where a PCP puts a disabled pupil at a substantial disadvantage in relation to a relevant matter in comparison with pupils who are not disabled, there is a duty to take such steps as it is reasonable to have to take to avoid the disadvantage

- Where a disabled pupil would, but for the provision of an auxiliary aid or service, be put at a substantial disadvantage in relation to a 'relevant matter' in comparison with pupils who are not disabled, there is a duty to take such steps as it is reasonable to have to take to provide the auxiliary aid or service

The 'relevant matters' are:

- Deciding who is offered admission as a pupil

- Provision of education or access to any benefit, facility or service[129]

What is 'reasonable' is a context specific and child specific judgment. For suggestions of criteria which may be taken into account in deciding what adjustments it might be reasonable for a school to have to make in a particular situation see EHRC's *Technical Guidance: Reasonable Adjustments for Disabled Pupils Guidance for Schools in England* at page 7:

- The extent to which special educational provision will be provided to the disabled pupil under Part 3 of the Children and Families Act 2014

- The resources of the school and the availability of financial or other assistance

- The financial and other costs of making the adjustment

- The extent to which taking any particular step would be effective in overcoming the substantial disadvantage suffered by a disabled pupil

- The practicability of the adjustment

- The effect of the disability on the individual

- Health and safety requirements

- The need to maintain academic, musical, sporting and other standards

- The interests of other pupils and prospective pupils

---

[129] Schedule 13, para. 2(4), EqA 2010.

<u>Pregnancy and maternity discrimination</u> – treating a pupil unfavourably because of pregnancy, maternity or because she is breastfeeding.[130] This form of discrimination is framed as 'unfavourable' rather than 'less favourable' treatment. This has the effect that it is not necessary to compare the treatment to that of other pupils.

<u>Other prohibited conduct</u>

<u>Harassment</u>

Harassment is unwanted behaviour or conduct related to a protected characteristic which has the purpose or effect of violating a pupil's dignity, or creating an intimidating, hostile, degrading, humiliating or offensive environment for that person. Sexual harassment is unwanted sexual behaviour for the same purpose or effect.

In deciding whether the conduct has had this effect, the perception of the pupil being harassed, the circumstances of the case and whether it is reasonable for the conduct to have that effect must all be taken into account.[131]

In schools, harassment only applies to the protected characteristics of disability, race and sex,[132] although harassment because of other characteristics could (depending on the facts of the particular situation) be prohibited as direct or indirect discrimination.

<u>Victimisation</u>

Bringing a claim under the EqA 2010, giving evidence in connection with such a claim, making an allegation that the school or another person has contravened the EqA 2010, or doing anything else in connection with the EqA 2010 are all 'protected acts' where they are done in good faith. A school victimises a person if it subjects them to detriment because they do a protected act.[133]

---

[130] Section 17, EqA 2010.

[131] Section 26 EqA 2010.

[132] Section 26(5) and 85(10), EqA 2010.

[133] Section 27, EqA 2010.

In the education context, protected acts are most likely to be done by parents, possibly supported by siblings. The interaction of the actions of a child, their parents and siblings, where one or other of them is not acting in good faith is covered by sections 84(5) or (5), 86 of Part 6 of the EqA 2010. Essentially, a child is protected from being victimised for the conduct of their parents (for doing a protected act) as long as the child acts in good faith.

Note that parties cannot contract out of the Equality Act 2010.[134] So even where the school/parent contract allows for the contract to be terminated for the conduct of the parents, if the conduct in question is a 'protected act' consideration will need to be given to whether termination would not only be 'victimisation' of the child but also whether the contractual term is enforceable in view of the provisions of Part 10 of the Equality Act and the implications of that for potential claims for breach of contract.

Application of the EqA 2010 to independent schools

Chapter one of Part 6 of the EqA 2010 applies the key concepts above to the education sector.

> *84 Application of this Chapter*
>
> *This Chapter does not apply to the following protected characteristics—*
>
> *(a) age;*
>
> *(b) marriage and civil partnership.*
>
> **85 Pupils: admission and treatment, etc.**
>
> *(1) The responsible body of a school to which this section applies must not discriminate against a person—*
>
> > *(a) in the arrangements it makes for deciding who is offered admission as a pupil;*

---

[134] See Part 10 of the EqA 2010.

(b) as to the terms on which it offers to admit the person as a pupil;

(c) by not admitting the person as a pupil.

(2) The responsible body of such a school must not discriminate against a pupil—

(a) in the way it provides education for the pupil;

(b) in the way it affords the pupil access to a benefit, facility or service;

(c) by not providing education for the pupil;

(d) by not affording the pupil access to a benefit, facility or service;

(e) by excluding the pupil from the school;

(f) by subjecting the pupil to any other detriment.

(3) The responsible body of such a school must not harass—

(a) a pupil;

(b) a person who has applied for admission as a pupil.

(4) The responsible body of such a school must not victimise a person—

(a) in the arrangements it makes for deciding who is offered admission as a pupil;

(b) as to the terms on which it offers to admit the person as a pupil;

(c) by not admitting the person as a pupil.

(5) The responsible body of such a school must not victimise a pupil—

(a) in the way it provides education for the pupil;

(b) in the way it affords the pupil access to a benefit, facility or service;

(c) by not providing education for the pupil;

(d) by not affording the pupil access to a benefit, facility or service;

(e) by excluding the pupil from the school;

(f) by subjecting the pupil to any other detriment.

(6) A duty to make reasonable adjustments applies to the responsible body of such a school.

(7) In relation to England and Wales, this section applies to—

(b) an independent educational institution (other than a special school)[135]

(9) The responsible body of a school to which this section applies is—

(b) if it is within subsection (7)(b) .... , the proprietor

Exceptions

<u>The curriculum</u>

The Equality Act expressly excludes the content of the school curriculum from its ambit:

Part 6, section 89(2):

Nothing in this Chapter applies to anything done in connection with the content of the curriculum.

The guidance explains that:

... schools are free to include a full range of issues, ideas and materials in their syllabuses, and to expose pupils to thoughts and ideas of all kinds, however challenging or controversial, without fear of legal challenge based on a protected characteristic. But schools will

---

[135] Defined to mean a non-maintained special school – section 89(9) EqA 2010.

need to ensure that the way in which issues are taught does not subject individual pupils to discrimination.[136]

The curriculum exception is usually considered in terms of the comments in the explanatory notes to the EqA 2010 that it would not, for example, be discrimination against a girl to include the Taming of the Shrew in the syllabus. No official guidance has addressed what it means, if anything, for curricula where the content is markedly different for boys and girls. 'Nothing' and 'anything done in connection with' seem very broad and there may be scope to explore the exception further in an appropriate case.

Positive action

The EqA 2010 allows 'positive' action to address the effects of past or present discrimination ('disadvantage') on groups of pupils who share a protected characteristic, to meet the needs of pupils or encourage their participation in activities where participation by members of their group is disproportionately low.[137] The action taken must be a proportionate means of achieving one of these three aims. An example would be taking action to encourage greater participation by girls in STEM subjects.

For extensive guidance about positive action see the EHRC's *Technical Guidance for Schools*.

Competitive sport

The EqA 2010 allows an exception for sex discrimination in relation to competitive sport, games and other competitive activity.[138] The EHRC explains in the *Technical Guidance for Schools*:

> *9.13 If the physical strength, stamina or physique of the average pupil of one sex would put him or her at a disadvantage compared to the average pupil of the other sex as a competitor in a sport, game or*

---

[136] Para, 2.9 The Equality Act 2010 and schools: Departmental advice for school leaders, school staff, governing bodies and local authorities, 2014

[137] Section 158, EqA 2010.

[138] Section 195, EqA 2010.

other competitive activity, it is not unlawful for those arranging the event to restrict participation in the activity to pupils of one sex.

A similar exception is made in respect of transgender participants but with added conditions that the restricted participation is necessary for reasons of safety or fair competition:

195 (2) A person does not contravene section 29, 33, 34 or 35,[139] so far as relating to gender reassignment, only by doing anything in relation to the participation of a transsexual person as a competitor in a gender-affected activity if it is necessary to do so to secure in relation to the activity—

(a) fair competition, or

(b) the safety of competitors.

(3) A gender-affected activity is a sport, game or other activity of a competitive nature in circumstances in which the physical strength, stamina or physique of average persons of one sex would put them at a disadvantage compared to average persons of the other sex as competitors in events involving the activity.

(4) In considering whether a sport, game or other activity is gender-affected in relation to children, it is appropriate to take account of the age and stage of development of children who are likely to be competitors.

Exceptions for schools

There are specific exceptions for schools in Schedule 11[140] to allow for:

- Single-sex admission to single-sex schools

- Single-sex boarding

- Single-sex schools turning co-educational

---

[139] These concern provision of services and management of premises. Education is a service.

[140] Schedule 11 is part pf Part 6, ie the Part of the EqA which is referenced in the standards.

- Admission by reference to religion or belief to independent schools registered with a religious ethos

- Acts of worship or religious observance in schools registered with a religious ethos

- Selection by ability independent schools

Exceptions for charities

Charity schools are permitted to provide benefits only to pupils with a shared protected characteristic if this is in accordance with the governing trust deed and either it is a proportionate means of achieving a legitimate aim or to prevent or compensate for a disadvantage linked to that protected characteristic.[141]

General exceptions

Statute – Where a school is required by statute or regulations, including the standards, to act in a particular way, then the school's action will be lawful even if it appears to breach the EqA 2010. This only applies where the statutory requirement leaves the school no option other than to act in a particular way, and applies only to disability, religion or belief, sex and sexual orientation.[142]

Communal accommodation – There are provisions relating to communal accommodation in Schedule 23 paragraph 3(1)-(8). In summary, the EHRC explains:

> *A school does not breach the prohibition of sex discrimination or gender reassignment discrimination by doing anything in relation to admitting pupils to communal accommodation, or providing any benefit, facility or service linked to the accommodation, if [certain] criteria are satisfied... it is managed as fairly as possible for both sexes and in the case of gender reassignment, a refusal to admit is a proportionate means of achieving a legitimate aim.*[143]

---

[141] Sections 193 and 194 EqA 2010.

[142] Section 191 and Schedule 22, para.1.

[143] Technical Guidance for Schools in England – 9.2 – 9.7.

For the additional detail see the EHRC *Technical Guidance for Schools*.

Contracting out – Parents and schools cannot contract out of EqA compliance. In HM Chief Inspector of Education, Children's Services and Skills v the Interim Executive Board of Al-Hijrah School,[144] the Court of Appeal stated: '*... parental choice more generally plainly cannot negate the statutory rights of a child to be educated in a non-discriminatory manner as required by the EqA 2010*'.[145]

Accessibility plans

In addition to the negative duties under Part 6 of the EqA 2010 (not to discriminate), Part 6 also introduces a positive duty on schools to make their setting more accessible over a period of time. This is done through preparing and resourcing a plan which takes into account the disabilities of pupils and any preferences expressed by them or their parents, and implementing it within a reasonable timeframe.[146]

The importance of accessibility planning and the potential strength of this requirement are often overlooked due to an over focus on physical access and underestimating the persuasive power of inspection as an enforcement mechanism. Paragraph 6.1(d) of the DfE's *The Independent School Standards: Guidance for independent schools, April 2019* explains:

> *... although the production of an accessibility plan is not part of the requirements of the independent school standards, it should be noted that there is a requirement for such a plan to be prepared, published, reviewed, revised and implemented by the proprietor of an independent school under paragraph 3 of Schedule 10 to the Equality Act 2010 and inspections may report on the performance of the duties here.*

---

[144] [2017] EWCA Civ 1426 at para. 82.

[145] Compare R (Williamson) v Secretary of State for Education and Employment [2005] UKHL 15, [2005] 2 AC 246.

[146] Schedule 10 carries over into the EqA 2010 provisions formerly in the Disability Discrimination Act 1995.

The detailed requirements are set out in Schedule 10 of the EqA 2010, paragraphs 3 and 4.

3(1) The responsible body of a school in England and Wales must prepare—

(a) an accessibility plan;

(b) further such plans at such times as may be prescribed.

3(2) An accessibility plan is a plan for, over a prescribed period – [147]

(a) increasing the extent to which disabled pupils can participate in the school's <u>curriculum</u>,

(b) improving the <u>physical environment</u> of the school for the purpose of increasing the extent to which disabled pupils are able to take advantage of education and benefits, facilities or services provided or offered by the school, and

(c) improving the delivery to disabled pupils of <u>information</u> which is readily accessible to pupils who are not disabled.

3(3) The delivery in sub-paragraph (2)(c) must be—

(a) within a reasonable time;

(b) in ways which are determined after <u>taking account of the pupils' disabilities and any preferences expressed by them or their parents</u>.

3(4) An accessibility plan must be in writing.

3(5) The responsible body must keep its accessibility plan under review during the period to which it relates and, if necessary, revise it.

---

[147] Under the Disability Discrimination Act 1995, the 'prescribed period' was prescribed by regulations: The Disability Discrimination (Prescribed Times and Periods for Accessibility Strategies and Plans for Schools) (England) Regulations 2005 as rolling three-year periods starting with 1 April – March 2006. In practice schools now prescribe their own reasonable period.

3(6) The responsible body must implement its accessibility plan.

3(7) A relevant inspection may extend to the performance by the responsible body of its functions in relation to the preparation, publication, review, revision and implementation of its accessibility plan.[148]

4(1) In preparing an accessibility plan, the responsible body must have regard to the need to allocate adequate resources for implementing the plan.

'Disabled pupils' within paragraph 3(2) refers to pupils with the full range of disabilities. In view of the current focus on adolescent mental health, schools may wish to consider whether more can be done to make participation in the curriculum more accessible to pupils with disabilities such as learning difficulties, mental health problems, eating disorders, anxiety disorders or those which give rise to behavioural challenges. Relevant measures could include such steps as strengthening staff training, communication with parents, teaching pupils about good mental health and stress management, building on existing pastoral support systems and counselling, and developing the ways pupils are supported to learn remotely when they are too unwell to attend school.[149]

Independent school parents (and others) are entitled to view the plan.[150] Paragraph 3(3) suggests that the plan should respond to the

---

[148] The duty to inspect this requirement is at para.18 of Secretary of State's approval of ISI, 27 April 2017.: https://www.isi.net/ISIapprovalletter270417.pdf

[149] The temporary provisions of the Coronavirus Act 2020 have expired. School attendance is mandatory for all pupils of compulsory school age, unless they are receiving 'education otherwise'. The priority should always be for schools to deliver high-quality face-to-face education to all pupils. For pupils of compulsory school age, remote education should only ever be considered as a short-term measure and as a last resort where in person attendance is not possible, such as when in-person attendance is either not possible or contrary to government guidance. See *Providing remote education: guidance for schools March 2022*.

[150] Para. 4(2) of Schedule 10 of the EqA 2010. State school parents can access it through the Freedom of Information Act.

needs of the pupil cohort and that their views and those of their parents should be sought.

Advising parents about accessibility plans

While accessibility plans are not directly enforceable by parents, the plans can, for example:

- be a vehicle for dialogue with the school about how/whether a child's needs are being met

- provide a legal basis for pupils and parents to express preferences about how access to the curriculum could be improved

- be the subject of a complaint under the school's complaints process

- form part of the evidence to a tribunal or court in a claim for discrimination or educational negligence

- support information provided to an inspectorate or the DfE about whether a school is meeting the standards

Conclusion

The EqA 2010 applies to independent schools as it does to other schools and services, and provides actionable rights to parents and pupils. It is also referenced in various standards and the understanding of the implications of that for compliance is still developing.

<u>Further reading</u>

Sources:

- Equality Act 2010

- *Technical Guidance for Schools* – EHRC (2014)

- *Technical Guidance: Reasonable Adjustments for Disabled Pupils* – EHRC (2015)

- *SEND code of practice* (2015)

- *Gender separation in mixed schools, non-statutory guidance* – DfE (2018)

- *Equality Act 2010: advice for schools* – DfE (2018)

Also:

- *Disability: Equality Act 2010 – Guidance on matters to be taken into account in determining questions relating to the definition of disability* – Government Equalities Office (2011)[151]

- *The Equality Act 2010 and Schools: Departmental advice for school leaders, school staff, governing bodies and local authorities* – DfE (May 2014)

---

[151] This is unlikely to be entirely up to date but it is still available at: https://www.gov.uk/government/publications/equality-act-guidance .

CHAPTER FIVE
REGULATED ACTIVITY

Introduction and overview

The Safeguarding Vulnerable Groups Act 2006 (SVGA 2006) is one of the pillars on which the standards are built alongside the Human Rights Act 1998, the Children Acts 1989 and 2004 and EQA 2010. It provides a unified scheme for regulating who can work with children and vulnerable adults, and for barring unsuitable people.[152] It replaced various disparate schemes which were criticised for being inconsistent and reactive rather than preventative.[153] It does not apply to activities carried out in the course of family relationships, and personal relationships for no consideration.[154]

Central to the SVGA 2006 is the concept of regulated activity. This is relevant to various standards and is considered separately here to provide a single reference point for key concepts on which some later parts of the text rely. Readers should be aware that the adequacy of the definition of regulated activity, and whether it is 'fit for purpose', is one of the matters which has been considered by the Independent Inquiry into Child Sexual Abuse. At the time of going to press, their report on this point may be imminent.

Regulated activity with children is: work which a barred person must not do with children. Children are people under the age of 18 years. The person who is responsible for ensuring that no one who is barred carries out regulated activity is the 'regulated activity provider'.[155]

---

[152] Vulnerable adults are not considered in this text.

[153] Bichard Report 2004.

[154] Section.6 and section.58 SVGA 2006.

[155] 'Regulated activity provider' is defined at length in section 6 SVGA 2006 essentially as the person responsible for the management and control of the activity, making or authorising the arrangements.

Regulated activity is defined in the SVGA 2006, Schedule 4, as amended by the Protection of Freedoms Act 2012. There are many activities which are regulated activity, some are defined by type of activity and the frequency with which they are done (teaching, personal care, child minding, inspection etc) and some by the establishment where they occur (hospitals, children's homes, schools etc).

A detailed technical guide is available from the DBS:

- *Disclosure and Barring Service: A guide to child workforce roles for registered bodies and employers*[156]

For summaries for non-lawyers see:

- KCSIE 2022 paragraph 235 and page 60 – focus on schools

- *Regulated activity with children in England* by the DBS[157] – goes wider than schools

- *Regulated activity in relation to children: scope* Factual note by HM Government[158] – goes wider than schools

Definitions most relevant to schools

All work in a school is likely to be regulated activity (see baseline definition, below).

In addition there are definitions which apply whether or not the work takes place in the school. These are relevant to school off-site activities when the school is the regulated activity provider.

---

[156] https://assets.publishing.service.gov.uk/government/uploads/system/uploads/attachment_data/file/804668/Child_workforce_guide_v10_0_28052019.pdf .

[157] https://assets.publishing.service.gov.uk/government/uploads/system/uploads/attachment_data/file/739154/Regulated_Activity_with_Children_in_England.pdf

[158] https://assets.publishing.service.gov.uk/government/uploads/system/uploads/attachment_data/file/550197/Regulated_activity_in_relation_to_children.pdf .

Baseline definition – all work in a school

The catch-all definition most commonly relied on in relation to work in schools is comprised of a combination of section 5 and Schedule 4, paragraphs 1(2), (2A), (2B) and 3(1)(a) SVGA 2006.

> *1(2) An activity is a regulated activity relating to children if—*
>
> *(a) it is carried out frequently by the same person or the period condition is satisfied,*
>
> *(b) it is carried out in [a school],[159]*
>
> *(c) it is carried out by a person while engaging in any form of work falling within sub-paragraph (2A) or (2B)* [explained below]
>
> *(d) it is carried out for or in connection with the purposes of the establishment, and*
>
> *(e) it gives that person the opportunity, in consequence of anything he is permitted or required to do in connection with the activity, to have contact with children.*

<u>Frequently or regularly</u>

'Frequently ... or the period condition is satisfied' – is generally summarised as 'frequently or regularly'. In the context of this school-based definition of regulated activity, it means:

- At any time on more than three days in any period of 30 days[160]

- Once a week or more often

The phrase 'Once a week or more often' appears in various of the early explanatory documents.[161] There is no separate legal authority for it and

---

[159] Actual wording: *an establishment mentioned in paragraph 3(1).* Schools are mentioned in 3(1)(a).

[160] Para. 10 of Schedule 4 Safeguarding Vulnerable Groups Act 2006.

[161] See for example: Regulated activity in relation to children: scope Factual note by HM Government.

it is no longer used in KCSIE, but it serves to emphasise helpfully that the days worked do not have to be consecutive to meet the period condition.

'At any time' means that even a short time worked counts for the purpose of the definition. So a person who works in a school for 5 minutes per day on four days in a period of 30 days would be within the period condition.

In a school

This is assumed to mean on the premises, although there is no legal authority. Where school activities take place off-site, including online, there are other definitions to rely on. (See section on teaching, care etc.)

Any form of work

This could be paid or unpaid. It covers both teaching and non-teaching work such as administration, maintenance, I.T. management, cleaning. The requirement for the activity to be 'work' distinguishes activities such as visits by parents for school events.

Carried out for or in connection with the purposes of the establishment

This arguably could exclude the activities of a hirer of school premises when the school is closed. The hirer as the proximate person/body in control is likely to be the regulated activity provider for those activities.

From 2021, KCSIE requires schools in any event to make it a requirement of any lease/hire agreement that safeguarding arrangements are in place.[162]

It gives that person the opportunity, in consequence of anything he is permitted or required to do in connection with the activity, to have contact with children

The focus here is not only on whether a person has contact with children but on whether they have the possible opportunity for contact.

---

[162] KCSIE 2022 para.s 165/6.

<u>Exceptions</u>

<u>The Tradesperson Exception – 1(2A)</u>

In brief, non-employees who provide occasional or temporary services which do not involve working with children are not in regulated activity. This enables schools to get essential maintenance done at short notice but also covers longer projects.

For the full small print underlying this summary see: paragraphs 1(2A) and 2(1) of Schedule 4 of SVGA 2006. To fall within this exception, the service provided must not entail: teaching, training, instruction of children, any form of care or supervision of children, any form of advice or guidance for children relating to physical, emotional or educational well-being, moderating a web-service for children or driving a car only for children.

<u>The Volunteer Exception – 1(2B)</u>

A supervised volunteer is not in regulated activity, unless they engage in the close contact activities described below. The supervision must be by a person in regulated activity.

Supervision means:

> *such day to day supervision as is reasonable in all the circumstances for the purpose of protecting any children concerned.*[163]

'Reasonable in all the circumstances' implies a consciously risk-based approach. 'Day to day' means that it would not be acceptable to gradually cease to supervise over a period of time.

See KCSIE 2022, Annex E for statutory guidance about supervision.

<u>The Peer Group Exception</u>

A pupil (such as a prefect) helping a teacher with other pupils, all under the supervision of the teacher, is not in regulated activity.[164]

---

[163] Para. 1(2C), Schedule 4 SVGA 2006.

[164] See para. 5 of Schedule 4, SVGA 2006.

<u>Examples</u>

School cleaners employed by the school who work regularly when pupils are on-site will be in regulated activity if there is opportunity for their paths to cross. After-school cleaners in a day school when there are no pupils on site are not in regulated activity.

A plumber who comes every afternoon for a week to fix the boiler, is not in regulated activity. The tradesperson exception applies.

A retired teacher who comes in every afternoon for a week to cover a class is in regulated activity. The parent volunteer who helps them is not in regulated activity, if they are under supervision.

Two volunteers who would be in regulated activity if unsupervised cannot supervise each other. One would have to be recognised as being in regulated activity, and vetted accordingly, to be permitted to supervise the other.

Additional definitions of regulated activity for closer contact activities

Personal care

'Relevant personal care' is always regulated activity. This is defined as:

> *1(1B) .. (a) physical assistance which is given to a child who is in need of it by reason of illness or disability and is given in connection with eating or drinking (including the administration of parenteral nutrition),*
>
> > *(b) physical assistance which is given to a child who is in need of it by reason of age, illness or disability and is given in connection with—*
> >
> > > *(i) toileting (including in relation to the process of menstruation),*
> > >
> > > *(ii) washing or bathing, or*

(iii) dressing…[165]

Additionally, prompting, supervising or training such a child is regulated activity.[166] KCSIE explains that it is not intended that personal care should include such activities as, for example, parent volunteers helping with costumes for school plays or helping a child lace up football boots.[167]

Frequency is irrelevant

The provisions above about frequency and the period condition do not apply. 'Relevant personal care' is regulated activity even if carried out only once or under supervision

Exceptions

There are no exceptions.

Examples

A supervised volunteer assists with toileting young children, as a one-off emergency. This is regulated activity. Assisting with personal care is always regulated activity. Volunteers should therefore not be used for this sort of work even once, even if supervised, unless they have been properly checked.

Health care

Health care provided by, or under the direction or supervision of, a health care professional is regulated activity. Definition:

> *1(1C) "health care" includes all forms of health care provided for children, whether relating to physical or mental health and also includes palliative care for children and procedures that are similar to forms of medical or surgical care but are not provided for children in connection with a medical condition,*

---

[165] Para. 1(1A) and (1B)(a) and (b) of Schedule 4 of SVGA 2006.

[166] Para. 1(1A) and (1B)(c)-(f) of Schedule 4 of SVGA 2006.

[167] KCSIE 2022, table on page 60, footnote 72.

"health care professional" means a person who is a member of a profession regulated by a body mentioned in section 25(3) of the National Health Service Reform and Health Care Professions Act 2002.[168]

Frequency irrelevant

The provisions above about frequency and the period condition do not apply. 'Health care' is regulated activity even if carried out only once or under supervision.

Exceptions

There are no exceptions.

Example

The work of, or under the direction or supervision of, a school nurse who is registered with the Nursing and Midwifery Council is regulated activity.

Teaching, care, supervision, advice, moderating internet chatrooms for children, driving

Certain activities, as defined at length in paragraph 2 of Schedule 4, SVGA 2006, are regulated both in and out of school. These are relevant to activities in school such as boarding and off-site situations such as school trips. When the school is the regulated activity provider, it will be responsible for ensuring that people barred from working with children are not involved.

2(1) The activities referred to in paragraph 1(1) are—

(a) any form of teaching, training or instruction of children, unless the teaching, training or instruction is merely incidental to teaching, training or instruction of persons who are not children;

---

[168] Para. 1(1A) and (1C) SVGA 2006.

(b) any form of care for or supervision of children, unless the care or supervision is merely incidental to care for or supervision of persons who are not children;

(c) any form of advice or guidance provided wholly or mainly for children, if the advice or guidance relates to their physical, emotional or educational well-being;

(d) [repealed]

(e) moderating a public electronic interactive communication service which is likely to be used wholly or mainly by children;

(f) driving a vehicle which is being used only for the purpose of conveying children and any person supervising or caring for the children pursuant to arrangements made in prescribed circumstances.

Frequently or regularly

In the context of higher risk regulated activities it means:

- At any time on more than three days in any period of 30 days[169]

- Once a week or more often

- Overnight

Overnight is defined:

10(2) In relation to an activity that falls within paragraph 2(1)(a), (b) or (c)[170]..., the period condition is also satisfied if—

(a) the person carrying out the activity does so at any time between 2 a.m. and 6 a.m, and

(b) the activity gives the person the opportunity to have face-to-face contact with children

---

[169] Para. 10 of Schedule 4 SVGA 2006.

[170] The restriction of the definition to activities within para. 2(1)(a)(b) and (c) of Schedule 4 means that it does not apply to moderating chatrooms or driving.

An overnight activity within scope is regulated activity even if it is carried out only once.

Driving

Driving a vehicle just for children or for children and their carers (such as when a disabled child is provided with accompanied transport to school) is regulated activity if it is frequent or regular.

Work experience partial exceptions

Training or supervising a child aged 16 and over in the workplace is not regulated activity, bearing in mind that 16 year olds can leave school and start work.[171]

Where pupils under 16 enter a workplace, adults who supervise them frequently or regularly could be in regulated activity unless they themselves are supervised by a person in regulated activity.[172] Consequently, employers providing work experience to pupils under 16 should arrange for vetting checks (enhanced DBS with barring information) on one member of staff who will then be able to supervise colleagues working regularly with pupils under 16. A school arranging the work experience should ask for confirmation that this has been done.

Examples

Adults supervising boarders overnight or pupils on a one-night overnight school trip are in regulated activity, even if they are unlikely to have contact with pupils overnight.

Visiting music teachers who work across several schools are in regulated activity.

---

[171] Para. 2(2) Schedule 4, SVGA 2006.

[172] Para. 2(3) and (3A) Schedule 4, SVGA 2006 and see KCSIE 2022 para. 328 et seq.

Staff of an outdoor activity centre regularly leading activities for pupils on a school trip would be in regulated activity. The regulated activity provider would be the outdoor activity centre.

Lifts for pupils to and from school arranged by parents are not regulated activity because they are personal arrangements and not in scope of the legislation.[173] Occasional lifts arranged by schools (such as when parents help to transport pupils to a sports ground or match) are not regulated activity if they are not frequent or regular. In the same example, if the same parents help the school with driving pupils every week, this would be regulated activity unless the parents are supervised volunteers.

Where schools arrange taxis for pupils, regular taxi drivers will be in regulated activity but occasional drivers will not. Those in regulated activity should be checked for suitability, by the taxi service or the school, if necessary. If the former, the school should obtain written confirmation that this has been done.

Foster care

Foster care is regulated activity.[174] This is potentially relevant when schools arrange for pupils to be accommodated with private families.

There is considerable confusion around this category of regulated activity partly because of the overlapping definitions of regulated activity but also because the SVGA encompasses but amends the definition of foster care in the Children Act 1989.

Under section 66 of the Children Act 1989, caring for and accommodating a child in one's own home is private fostering if the parties are unrelated, the child is under 16 (or under 18 if the child is disabled) and the accommodation is to be provided for 28 days or more.

The SVGA 2006 disapplies the conditions relating to age 16 and length of stay[175] with the effect that a single night home-stay, even of a 17 year

---

[173] Section 58 SVGA 2006.

[174] Section 53 and para. 1(5) of Schedule 4, SVGA 2006.

old pupil, is regulated activity for the purpose of suitability checks where it has been arranged by a school with people to whom the child is not related.

The statutory provisions are not provided here in full due to the extent and complexity of internal and external cross-referencing between sections and Acts.

> *SVGA 2006 – Section 53 ...*
>
> *(3) Subsection (4) applies if a person (P)—*
>
> > *(a) makes arrangements for another person to foster a child as a private foster parent, and*
> >
> > *(b) has power to terminate the arrangements.*
>
> *(4) P is, if he would not otherwise be, a regulated activity provider in relation to fostering carried out by the foster parent in pursuance of the arrangements.*
>
> *...*
>
> *(7) A person is a foster parent if – (c) he is a private foster parent*
>
> *(8) A person is a private foster parent if he falls within subsection (9) and looks after a child—*
>
> > *(a) for reward, or*
> >
> > *(b) in pursuance of an arrangement made by someone other than a member of the child's family.*

Who is the foster parent?

The legislation refers to 'a private foster parent'. KCSIE refers to 'responsible adults'. To bring clarity to a placement, it helps for schools arranging homestays to have a clear agreement with the householder(s) about who is responsible. That will be the person(s) in regulated activity. It is not necessary to assume that everyone in the household is responsible.

---

[175] Section 53(9) SVGA 2006.

Others who live in the household who are aged 16 or over are not in regulated activity but are eligible for an enhanced DBS check with barring information.[176]

Private arrangements

Where the child's parent(s) or a student themselves arranges their own homestay, this would be a private arrangement therefore the school or college would not be the regulated activity provider.[177]

Who is the regulated activity provider?

There is no case law to help with the interpretation of 'makes arrangements' and 'power to terminate', or to settle whether for example, foreign language exchanges set up by schools are nonetheless private arrangements between families given the element of mutuality and the practical difficulty a school might encounter in seeking to terminate the arrangement. A school would no doubt have considerable influence if it sought to terminate such arrangements but in the final analysis cannot enter a private household and remove a pupil or their exchange partner. Schools are expected to take a cautious approach – see Annex D of KCSIE 2022 for guidance.

---

[176] Reg 5C(f)(ii) Police Act 1997 (Criminal Records) (Amendment No.2) Regulations 2013/2669 as amended.

[177] Section 58 SVGA 2006.

Private fostering: comparison of thresholds for local authority involvement and regulated activity

	Length of stay	Age of child being accomm'd	Action required
Threshold for LA involvem't[178]	28 days or longer	Under 16 years (or 18 if the child is disabled)	Schools required to notify LA of such arrangements of which they are aware, whether or not arranged by the school.[179]
Threshold for regulated activity[180]	Overnight	Under 18 years	Enhanced DBS with barred list information for 'responsible adults'. Consider enhanced DBS checks for other household members aged 16 and over.[181]

Regulated activity providers

Various duties rest on regulated activity providers and they may also be subject to penalties. It is therefore important to identify the regulated activity provider.

Definitions are found in section 6, SVGA 2006

> *6.(2) A person (P) is a regulated activity provider if—*
>
> *(a) he is responsible for the management or control of regulated activity,*
>
> *(b) if the regulated activity is carried out for the purposes of an organisation, his exercise of that responsibility is not subject to*

---

[178] Section 66, Children Act 1989

[179] KCSIE. LAs are under a duty under private fostering legislation to satisfy themselves of the welfare of the child.

[180] Section 53, SVGA 2006

[181] KCSIE 2022 para.s 336-339 and pp 77 and Annex D.

supervision or direction by any other person for those purposes, and

(c) he makes, or authorises the making of, arrangements (whether in connection with a contract of service or for services or otherwise) for another person to engage in that activity.

(3) A person (P) is also a regulated activity provider if section 53(4) (fostering) so provides.

...

(5) P is not a regulated activity provider if he is an individual and the arrangements he makes are private arrangements.

'Private arrangements' are arrangements for the benefit of the organiser or a child who is a family member or a friend.[182]

In complex cases when it is difficult to identify who is responsible, it can help to consider who is funding the arrangements as that tends to be the party who is in control.

Responsibilities and offences of regulated activity providers

The regulated activity provider must ensure that a barred person does not carry out the activity. It is an offence to knowingly allow a barred person to engage in regulated activity or supply a person for that purpose. This includes using or supplying that person when the regulated activity has reason to believe that they are barred and may be asked to engage in regulated activity.[183]

Duty to refer to the DBS

Regulated activity providers and personnel suppliers have a legal duty to provide information about individuals to the DBS where certain conditions are met. This applies even when a referral has also been made to a local authority safeguarding team or professional regulator. The DBS will then consider whether to bar the person.

---

[182] Section 6(5)-7) and (11) SVGA 2006

[183] Section 9 SVGA 2006.

The duty is set out in section 35 SVGA 2006. It is triggered when two conditions are met:

- The provider/supplier has removed the individual from regulated activity with children, or would have done so if they had not already ceased

- The provider/supplier thinks the individual has engaged in 'relevant conduct', satisfied the 'harm test' or been convicted or cautioned for a relevant offence (meaning one which incurs automatic barring either with or without the right to make representations).

For guidance covering the detail of the tests and the mechanics and timing of making a referral, see:

- *Making barring referrals to the DBS*[184]

- KCSIE 2022

Conclusion

Determining whether a person is in regulated activity

There are various situations when it is vital to determine whether a person is or will be working in regulated activity. While it will often be clear, sometimes it will be necessary to think through the application of each of the definitions one by one:

- Does the individual work regularly in a school with opportunity for contact with children?

  o If so, does one of the exceptions apply? (Tradesperson, supervised volunteer, peer.)

---

[184] https://www.gov.uk/guidance/making-barring-referrals-to-the-dbs#what-is-a-referral .

- Do they perform one of the close contact functions? (Personal care, health care.)

- Do they teach, train, supervise, provide care frequently or overnight?

- Is it private foster care?

If the answer to any of these is 'yes' and there is no relevant exception, the person is in regulated activity. The next consideration will be whether the school or another is the regulated activity provider and consequently to determine the role of the school under the standards in keeping children safe, particularly when it comes to checking suitability.

PART TWO

THE STANDARDS

CHAPTER SIX

THE QUALITY OF
EDUCATION STANDARDS

Introduction and overview

Part one of the standards covers the Quality of Education provided, including

- the Curriculum – ISS paragraph 2

- Relationships education, and Relationships and Sex education – ISS paragraph 2A

- Teaching – ISS paragraph 3, and

- Assessment – ISS paragraph 4.[185]

The chapters which follow consider each of the standards individually. In practice these separate standards interact closely with each other and other standards, particularly those in Part two[186] of the standards which concern non-academic development of pupils. Various themes run through several standards to ensure that the issue is addressed from all sides.

Themes

The Quality of Education standards include themes such as:

- Pupil progress – academic

---

[185] The standards in Part one do not apply to academies as curricular matters are covered separately in their funding agreements. The notation used from here on is as follows: ISS 2 means paragraph 2 of the schedule to the Education (Independent School Standards) Regulations 2014, as amended, etc.

[186] Spiritual, moral, social and cultural development of pupils (SMSC).

- Subjects and skills

- Fundamental British values

- Respect for others

- Equality/anti-discrimination requirements on schools

- Preparation for adult life

The ways the standards can be combined around a topic are open-ended; the table below is intended to help readers to begin to see the themes and work with the standards. Some wording from the standards has been shortened in the table. Notation: ISS 4 means paragraph 4 of the independent school standards etc.

Academic progress	
The curriculum[187] must take into account the ages, aptitudes and needs of all pupils, including those with an EHC plan	ISS 2(1)(i)
The curriculum must provide all pupils the opportunity to learn and make progress	ISS 2(2)h)
The teaching must enable pupils to acquire new knowledge and make good progress	ISS 3(a)
There must be a framework for regular assessment which is used to plan teaching so that pupils can progress	ISS 3(g)
A framework must be in place to evaluate pupil performance by reference to the school's own aims as provided to parents and/or national norms	ISS 4
Academic subjects	
For pupils of compulsory school age: the curriculum must provide experience in linguistic, mathematical, scientific, technological, human and social, physical and aesthetic and creative education.	ISS 2(2)((a)

---

[187] Where 'curriculum' is referenced, this includes both the curriculum documentation (policy, and the supporting plans and schemes of work) and effective implementation of all of these. This is explained further in the next chapter.

For pupils <u>below</u> compulsory school age: the curriculum must provide a programme of activities which is appropriate to their educational needs in relation to personal, social, emotional and physical development and communication and language skills. In practice this is met by implementation of the statutory framework for the EYFS.	ISS 2(2)(f)
For any pupils <u>over</u> compulsory school age: the curriculum must provide a programme of activities which is appropriate to their needs	ISS 2(2)(g)
Skills	
The curriculum must provide for (all) pupils to acquire speaking, listening, literacy and numeracy skills.	ISS 2(2)(b)
For any pupils below compulsory school age, the curriculum must provide a programme of activities which is appropriate to their educational needs in relation to personal, social, emotional and physical development and communication and language skills needs. In practice this is met by implementation of the statutory framework for the EYFS.	ISS 2(2)(g)
The teaching must enable pupils to acquire new knowledge and make good progress according to their ability so that they increase their understanding and develop their skills in the subjects taught.	ISS 3(a)
The school must actively promote principles which enable pupils to develop their self-knowledge, self-esteem and self-confidence.	ISS 5(b)(i)
Fundamental British Values (FBV)	
The curriculum must not undermine FBV: • democracy • the rule of law, • individual liberty • mutual respect and tolerance of those with different faiths and beliefs	ISS 2(1)(b)(ii)
The teaching must not undermine the FBV.	ISS 3(i)
The proprietor/school must actively promote the FBV.	ISS 5(a)

The proprietor/school must actively promote principles which enable pupils to distinguish right from wrong and to respect the civil and criminal law of England.	ISS 5(b)(ii)
The proprietor/school must encourage respect for democracy and support for participation in the democratic process, including respect for the basis on which the law is made and applied in England.	ISS 5(b)(vii)
Respect for others	
The curriculum (PSHE) must encourage respect for other people, paying particular regard to the protected characteristics set out in the Equality Act.	ISS 2(2)(d)(ii)
Relationships and Sex Education – entails teaching respect for others. This is included in the statutory guidance to which schools must have regard.	ISS 2A(d)
The curriculum and teaching must not undermine … values of individual liberty, mutual respect and tolerance of those with different faiths and beliefs.	ISS 2(i)(b)(ii) and 3(i)
The proprietor/school must actively promote … values of individual liberty, mutual respect and tolerance of those with different faiths and beliefs.	ISS 5(a)
The proprietor/school must actively promote principles which - further tolerance and harmony between different cultural traditions by enabling pupils to acquire an appreciation of and respect for their own and other cultures - encourage respect for other people, paying particular regard for the protected characteristics set out in the Equality Act.	ISS 5(b)(v) ISS 5(b)(vi)
Equality/anti-discrimination requirements on schools	
The teaching must not discriminate against pupils contrary to Part 6 of the Equality Act 2010.	ISS 3(j)
The curriculum, plans and schemes of work must take into account the needs of <u>all</u> pupils.	ISS 2(1)(i)
The curriculum must provide for <u>all</u> pupils to make progress.	ISS 2(2)(h)
The proprietor/school must ensure <u>every</u> registered pupil …is provided with RE/RSE.	ISS 2A

The teaching must enable all pupils to acquire new knowledge and make good progress according to their ability so that they increase their understanding and develop their skills in the subjects taught.	ISS 3(a)
Other parts of the teaching standard concerning planning, effective teaching methods, having a good understanding of the needs of pupils and a good range of good quality classroom resources will also be relevant to meeting the needs of all pupils.	ISS 3(c)(d)(g)
The proprietor/school must actively promote principles which enable pupils to develop their self-knowledge, self-esteem and self-confidence.	ISS 5(b)(i)
Preparation for adult life	
The curriculum must provide for effective preparation of pupils for the opportunities, responsibilities and experiences of life in British society.	ISS 2(2)(i)
The curriculum must include personal, social, health and economic education, encouraging respect for others paying particular regard for those with protected characteristics.	ISS 2(2)(d)
The curriculum must provide secondary pupils access to accurate, up-to-date careers guidance that– (i) is presented in an impartial manner; (ii) enables them to make informed choices about a broad range of career options; and (iii) helps to encourage them to fulfil their potential.	ISS 2(2)(e)
See also all sections on FBV above – which includes individual liberty	
RSE – Every registered pupil must be provided with RE/RSE.	ISS 2A
The teaching must foster in pupils the ability to think and learn for themselves.	ISS 3(b)
The proprietor/school must actively promote principles which enable pupils to develop their self-knowledge, self-esteem and self-confidence.	ISS 5(b)(i)
The proprietor/school must actively promote principles which enable pupils to distinguish right from wrong and to respect the civil and criminal law of England.	ISS 5(b)(ii)

The proprietor/school must promote principles which encourage pupils to accept responsibility for their behaviour, show initiative and understand how they can contribute positively to the lives of those living and working in the locality in which the school is situated and to society more widely.	ISS 5(b)(iii)
The proprietor/school must enable pupils to acquire broad knowledge of public institutions and services in England.	ISS 5(b)(iv)
See also all parts of ISS 5 regarding respect for others, respect of the democratic process and balanced presentation of any political issues brought to the attention of pupils.	ISS 5(b)(vi) ISS 5(b)(vii) ISS 5(c) and (d)

CHAPTER SEVEN

THE CURRICULUM STANDARD – ISS PART 1

Introduction

The applicable guidance is *The Independent School Standards: Guidance for independent schools, April 2019,* which should be read in full. What follows is an overview.

ISS paragraph 2(1)

> *2(1)   The standard in this paragraph is met if—*
>
> *(a)   the proprietor ensures that a written policy on the curriculum, supported by appropriate plans and schemes of work, which provides for the matters specified in sub-paragraph (2) is drawn up and implemented effectively; and*
>
> *(b)   the written policy, plans and schemes of work–*
>
> *(i) take into account the ages, aptitudes and needs of all pupils, including those pupils with an EHC plan; and*
>
> *(ii) do not undermine the fundamental British values of democracy, the rule of law, individual liberty, and mutual respect and tolerance of those with different faiths and beliefs.*

Overarching requirements of the curriculum – ISS paragraph 2(1)

This requires schools to **have** and **effectively implement** the following paperwork:

- a policy

- plans

- schemes of work

These documents should be available in English.

<u>The policy</u>

In the absence of an obligation to use the national curriculum, independent schools must draw up their own curriculum and implement it effectively.

The overarching approach (subjects taught and approach to other matters in ISS paragraph 2(2)) must be recorded in a curriculum policy which is made available to parents of pupils and prospective pupils.[188] It is acceptable, in principle, to base the curriculum on a commercially available scheme if it meets the requirements.[189] Independent schools may opt to use the national curriculum and if so state that in the curriculum policy.

<u>Plans</u>

The DfE describes 'plans' as *proposals for how the curriculum policy will be implemented*.[190]

<u>Schemes of work</u>

The curriculum policy must be supported by appropriate schemes of work. The DfE has described these as *detailed specifications for each subject of what is to be taught throughout the year for each year group taking that subject*.

ISS paragraph 2 prescribes a range of educational areas that pupils must experience. The plans and schemes of work must illustrate how each

---

[188] The publication requirement is in the Provision of Information Standards explained in Chapter Fifteen.

[189] See <u>Beis Aharon v Secretary of State</u> [2016] UKFTT 270 (HESC).

[190] P. 6 of the Independent School Standards: Guidance for independent schools, April 2019.

prescribed area is to be covered by the school curriculum, although it is not a requirement to separate each area out for the purpose of teaching it. Where schools teach thematically rather than subject by subject, it is particularly important for documentation to be clear about how each area is being covered.

There is a presentational point here for advisors. Given the lack of detailed prescription in the standard, the curriculum policy is an important source of information for parents about what they are buying into. When preparing for registration or inspection, schools would be well advised to present information in ways that ensure the necessary regulatory elements are clearly identifiable rather than relying on readers to be able to unpick and identify regulatory information from complex documentation. The burden of proof to show that it meets the standards is on the school.

Take into account ... the needs of all pupils

The policy, plans and schemes of work must meet the needs of <u>all</u> pupils taking into account their ages, aptitudes and needs.[191] This standard is closely linked to the requirement in ISS paragraph2(2)(h) that all pupils have the opportunity to learn and make progress.

This is in effect a requirement for the curriculum to cater for needs and aptitudes such as

- special educational needs (of pupils with or without EHC plans)

- disabilities

- English as an additional language

- particular strengths and aptitudes

- other additional needs

Age – The requirement for the curriculum to be age-appropriate underpins the standards on quality of education. So, for example, the

---

[191] Para. 2(1)(b)(i).

requirement to provide RSE, to introduce the protected characteristics and teach children how to stay safe, are all to be done by means which are age-appropriate.

SEN – Independent schools are not required to have a SEN policy separate from the main curriculum policy but many do so. The process of writing a separate policy and reviewing it from time to time along with the corresponding plans and schemes of work can support schools to think through how they are meeting the needs of pupils with SEN and can assist to demonstrate clearly to stakeholders how the school meets this element of ISS paragraph 2(1)(b)(i). It can also help identify how the statutory accessibility plan should be developed.

The curriculum policy, plans and schemes of work must also meet the needs of pupils with an EHC plan. The detail of SEN law is outside the scope of this text but see Chapter Twenty for an introduction. Even in the case of a well-drafted EHC plan which names the independent school, the plan is unlikely to provide curriculum detail so that responsibility sits with the school.

'Fundamental British values'

There are four fundamental values named in the standards:

- democracy

- the rule of law

- individual liberty

- mutual respect and tolerance of those with different faiths and beliefs.

'Those with different faiths and beliefs' should be assumed to include those with no faith.[192]

---

[192] Section 10(2) EqA 2010.

'Fundamental British values' appear three times in the standards. There are

- negative duties to ensure that the curriculum and teaching do not undermine the fundamental British values in ISS paragraphs 2(b)(ii) and 3(i), and

- a positive duty to actively promote the values in ISS paragraph 5(a).

Fundamental British value IV overlaps with provisions under the curriculum, teaching and SMSC standards requiring schools to encourage respect for other people both generally and '*paying particular regard to the protected characteristics*', and not to discriminate against pupils contrary to the Equality Act 2010 (ISS paragraphs 2(2)(d)(ii), 3(j) and 5(b)(vi)).

The idea of a set of shared values to underpin a multi-cultural society may have first emerged in the context of the Prevent strand of the counter-terrorism strategy. The four value formulation which is now part of the standards was used by the independent reviewer of terrorism legislation in his May 2011 report to the Home Secretary.[193] The Prevent Strategy presented to parliament by the Home Secretary in June 2011 listed a range of slightly different 'core' values, such as 'democracy, rule of law, equality of opportunity, freedom of speech and the rights of all men and women to live free from persecution of any kind', 'human rights, democracy and the rule of law' and also 'support for individual liberties within the law, equality, mutual tolerance and respect'. However, it did use the formulation now known as 'fundamental British values' as part of its definition of 'extremism':

> '*Extremism is vocal or active opposition to fundamental British values, including democracy, the rule of law, individual liberty and mutual respect and tolerance of different faiths and beliefs. We also*

---

[193] Report to the Home Secretary of Independent Oversight of Prevent Review and Strategy – May 2011 – Lord Carlile of Berriew Q.C.

include in our definition of extremism calls for the death of members of our armed forces, whether in this country or overseas.'[194]

The inclusion of the fundamental British values in the standards aligns the expectations on independent schools with those placed on state schools through the Teachers' Standards which came into effect on 1 September 2012.[195] The Teachers' Standards define the minimum level of practice expected of trainees and teachers in state funded schools. Part two of the Teachers' Standards, which concerns professional and personal conduct, is also used to assess cases of serious misconduct of teachers in independent schools.

'Teachers uphold public trust in the profession and maintain high standards of ethics and behaviour, within and outside school, by ... :

- *Not undermining fundamental British values, including democracy, the rule of law, individual liberty and mutual respect, and tolerance of those with different faiths and beliefs'*

The introduction of fundamental British values also reflected the commitment in the Prevent strategy that *'there should be no "ungoverned spaces" in which extremism is allowed to flourish without firm challenge and, where appropriate, by legal intervention.'*[196] Subsequently a more positive narrative has developed around the role and importance of common values in the Integrated Communities Strategy Green Paper, March 2018:[197]

'This is what true integration looks like – communities where people, whatever their background, live, work, learn and socialise together, based on shared rights, responsibilities and opportunities. Communities where many religions, cultures and opinions are

---

[194] https://assets.publishing.service.gov.uk/government/uploads/system/uploads/attachment_data/file/97976/prevent-strategy-review.pdf .

[195] https://www.gov.uk/government/publications/teachers-standards

[196] Para. 3.39 of the prevent strategy 2011.

[197] Integrated Communities Strategy Green Paper: https://assets.publishing.service.gov.uk/government/uploads/system/uploads/attachment_data/file/696993/Integrated_Communities_Strategy.pdf .

celebrated, underpinned by a shared set of British values that champion tolerance, freedom and equality of opportunity.'

See also, the Integrated Communities Action Plan, February 2019:[198]

'Educational settings should prepare all children, young people and adults to participate fully in life in modern Britain. They should be inclusive environments which enable students to mix and build positive relations with those from different backgrounds, and equip learners with the skills, knowledge and values to become active citizens.'

And corresponding action point:

'We will work with Ofsted to ensure there continues to be strong coverage of integration through schools' promotion of fundamental British values within their new inspection handbook due to be consulted on in 2019.'

The DfE's guidance *The Independent School Standards: Guidance for independent schools, April 2019* explains that the aim is to ensure that the planned curriculum is not in conflict with, or inconsistent with, any of the four values. This applies to the curriculum for any subject. The guidance provides practical examples concerning lesson materials which would be at odds with fundamental British values, such as those which promote non-democratic political systems, whether for reasons of faith or otherwise. Teaching that some or all religions or beliefs, including atheism/agnosticism, are wrong does not conflict with fundamental British values, so long as it is made clear that adherents of those belief systems should be treated with respect. If schools teach about religious law, the distinction between religious and state law should be explored and it should be made clear to pupils that all people living in England are subject to its law.

---

[198] https://assets.publishing.service.gov.uk/government/uploads/system/uploads/ attachment_data/file/778045/Integrated_Communities_Strategy_Govt_Ac tion_Plan.pdf.

Content of the curriculum – ISS paragraph 2(2)

> 2(2)   *For the purposes of paragraph (2)(1)(a), the matters are—*
>
> (a) *full-time supervised education for pupils of compulsory school age (construed in accordance with section 8 of the Education Act 1996), which gives pupils experience in linguistic, mathematical, scientific, technological, human and social, physical and aesthetic and creative education;*
>
> (b) *that pupils acquire speaking, listening, literacy and numeracy skills;*
>
> (c) *where the principal language of instruction is a language other than English, lessons in written and spoken English, except that this matter does not apply in respect of a school which provides education for pupils who are all temporarily resident in England and which follows the curriculum of another country;*
>
> (d) *personal, social, health and economic education which–*
>
> > (i) *reflects the school's aim and ethos; and*
> >
> > (ii) *encourages respect for other people, paying particular regard to the protected characteristics set out in the 2010 Act(a);*
>
> (e) *for pupils receiving secondary education, access to accurate, up-to-date careers guidance that–*
>
> > (i) *is presented in an impartial manner;*
> >
> > (ii) *enables them to make informed choices about a broad range of career options; and*
> >
> > (iii) *helps to encourage them to fulfil their potential;*
>
> (f) *where the school has pupils below compulsory school age, a programme of activities which is appropriate to their educational needs in relation to personal, social, emotional and physical development and communication and language skills;*

(g) where the school has pupils above compulsory school age, a programme of activities which is appropriate to their needs;

(h) that all pupils have the opportunity to learn and make progress; and

(i) effective preparation of pupils for the opportunities, responsibilities and experiences of life in British society.

These paragraphs describe the range of matters which must be covered in the curriculum policy, plans and schemes of work and implemented effectively for each stage of study by pupils of compulsory school age. Beyond this very high-level prescription the content and details of delivery are left entirely to the school.

Interpreting the standard in the context of the ECHR, UNCRC and the other legislation and standards, we can deduce that the education provided must be 'efficient', 'effective', enable pupils to make 'good progress', prepare the child for 'responsible life in a free society' and actively promote their well-being as defined in section 10(2) of the Children Act 2002.[199] The latter entails consideration of pupils' long term social and economic well-being and ability to contribute to society.

The role of inspectorates or the regulator as regards filling the gaps in the standard with school-specific guidance was considered in Beis Aharon v Secretary of State [2016] UKFTT 270 (HESC):

Freedom to do things the way it [the school] thinks fit is not compatible with the regulator providing prescriptive guidance and support.[200]

---

[199] See chapter one for the ECHR, UNCRC, Education Act 1996 section 7, ISS 3(a) and ISS 34(1)(c) and 34(2). Many other articles and standards may be relevant to the interpretation.

[200] Beis at para.s 88 and 52 – See more below.

'Full-time, supervised education'

The curriculum policy and supporting plans and schemes of work required by ISS paragraph 2(2)(a) must cater for 'full-time' supervised education'. 'Full-time' is not defined in law. See Chapter Two above for how the DfE has addressed this most recently in guidance. The rule of thumb given is 18 hours. 'Supervised' implies that there will be recognition of teacher/adult involvement in the policy, plans and schemes of work. See also the separate standard about supervision in ISS paragraph 14.

The question of how much time should typically be devoted to the prescribed areas in each school week or school day in order to meet the standard was considered by the First-tier Tribunal in Beis Aharon Trust v Secretary of State for Education [2016] UKFTT 270 (HESC). The school in question was said to devote about five hours per week, in effect one hour per day, to its secular curriculum which included 'English (literacy, reading, handwriting, spelling, grammar, comprehension, creative writing and developing skills), mathematics, science, geography, history, PE, PSHE and Citizenship'.[201] The remainder of the curriculum was based on studies of religious texts and commentaries. It was suggested on behalf of the school that if enough time was not allocated to the secular curriculum, the inspectorate or regulator should state what is the right amount of time. The First-tier tribunal explained:

> *It is clear that the thinking behind the standards for independent schools is that schools should be able to determine for themselves what are their priorities, how they organise the curriculum, who they employ to teach it (to the extent that no minimum qualifications are specified), how they assess achievement, and what else pupils do while at school. It would be impossible and inconsistent with this approach if Ofsted were at the same time expected to specify how the teaching is organised. We agree with the evidence of Ms Ward, which was to the effect that the school has responsibility for deciding how to arrange its timetable and resources to meet the standards.[202]*

---

[201] Beis at para. 20.

[202] Beis at para. 52.

In the same case, the school submitted that some requirements of the standards were met through the religious element of the curriculum *'in which Hebrew, Aramaic and Yiddish were studied and [which] also included 'reading, speaking, listening and writing skills, mathematics, science and technological, human and social sciences (especially law, philosophy, political science, geography and history) creative and aesthetic, personal and social education'.* It appears that this submission came too late in the proceedings to be taken into account; it was also unevidenced and inspectors had not been invited to consider it on any of the inspections. There was no suggestion by the tribunal, however, that the suggestion was untenable in principle and indeed the possibility is now covered in the DfE guidance.[203]

Required subjects – ISS paragraph 2(2)(a)

The following information weaves together the DfE's 2011 information pack about *Registration of Schools*,[204] with the current guidance in the *Independent School Standards: Guidance for independent schools, April 2019.* Dates are provided by each quote to distinguish the 'live' guidance from the previous information which though moribund remains helpful.

> *Linguistic: this area is concerned with developing pupils' communication skills and increasing their command of language through listening, speaking, reading and writing. In all schools, except for foreign national schools whose pupils are all temporarily resident in this country, there must be lessons in written and spoken English. Many schools will also teach other languages and some will use a language other than English as the main medium of instruction.* 2011
>
> *Mathematical: this area helps pupils to make calculations, to understand and appreciate relationships and patterns in number and*

---

[203] *The Independent School Standards: Guidance for independent schools, April 2019 –* para. 2.7.

[204] Archived version still available online: https://dera.ioe.ac.uk//2965/ .

space and to develop their capacity to think logically and express themselves clearly. Their knowledge and understanding of mathematics should be developed in a variety of ways, including practical activity, exploration and discussion. 2011

Scientific: this area is concerned with increasing pupils' knowledge and understanding of nature, materials and forces and with developing the skills associated with science as a process of enquiry: for example, observing, forming hypotheses, conducting experiments and recording their findings. 2011

If there is no practical element in the teaching of science …, the school should be able to show how it compensates for this in a way which allows pupils to reach an appropriate overall level of understanding of the subject in question. 2019

The DfE guidance explains that independent schools may teach creationism

as part of a belief system but it should not be presented as having a similar or superior evidence base to scientific theories. On the other hand, schools should not suggest that those who hold creationist beliefs are not worthy of respect. 2019[205]

Technological: Technological skills can include the use of information and communication technology (ICT); developing, planning and communicating ideas; working with tools, equipment, materials and components to produce good quality products; and evaluating processes and products. 2011

Schools which discourage or ban the use of IT/electronic media, or whose pupils cannot use them due to disability, may legitimately reflect this in their approach to technological education, but should still ensure that pupils have conceptual familiarity with digital skills and technology which will be encountered in everyday life, e.g. cars, cash machines and mobile phones. 2019

---

[205] Para. 2.8 of *The Independent School Standards: Guidance for independent schools, April 2019.*

Human and social [humanities]: *this area is concerned with people and with their environment, and how human action, now and in the past, has influenced events and conditions. In most schools the subjects of history and geography make a strong contribution to this area.* 2011

Physical: this area aims to develop the pupils' physical control and co-ordination as well as their tactical skills and imaginative responses, and to help them to evaluate and improve their performance. Pupils should also acquire knowledge and understanding of the basic principles of fitness and health. 2011

PE should be a timetabled lesson, not just an extended break. Clothing requirements are not a good reason for limiting the amount of pupils' participation in PE although they can legitimately influence which activities are undertaken. Although not stated specifically in Part 1, the requirement in Part 5 for outdoor space for PE strongly implies that at least some PE should take place outdoors rather than just using school halls. In addition, schools should be aware that if they take advantage of the exception in section 195 of the Equality Act 2010 which permits single sex sports in mixed sex schools under certain circumstances, a school still has to allow girls, or boys as the case may be, equal opportunities to participate in comparable sporting activities. Guidance on gender separation in mixed schools has been published by the department. 2019

Aesthetic and creative: this area is concerned with the processes of making, composing and inventing. There are aesthetic and creative aspects of all subjects, but some make a particularly strong contribution including art, music, dance, drama and the study of literature because they call for personal, imaginative, and often practical, responses. 2011

There is no requirement for aesthetic and creative education to cover any specific art form, such as music. 2019

Similarly to scientific education: *if there is no practical element in the teaching of aesthetic and creative education, a school should be able to show how it compensates for this in a way which allows pupils to reach an appropriate overall level of understanding of the subject in question.* 2019

Relationships Education and Relationships and Sex Education (RSE): These are covered below under ISS paragraph 2A.

Acquiring speaking, listening and numeracy skills - ISS paragraph 2(2)(b)

This part of the standard requires little explanation. It should be interpreted in the context of the overarching requirement that the materials must take account of the ages and aptitudes and need of all pupils (ISS paragraph 2(b)(i)) and later standards, such as that pupils are enabled to make good progress (ISS paragraph 3(a)). Rote learning will not suffice.[206]

Inclusion of lessons in written and spoken English – ISS paragraph 2(2)(c)

If pupils are taught principally in a language other than English, those schools must include some lessons in written and spoken English. These must be available to all pupils in all year groups with the expectation that all pupils will be able to read, write and speak English with sufficient fluency for everyday life in England by the time they leave school.[207]

This does not apply where all the pupils are only temporarily resident in England and the school follows the curriculum of another country. An example of a school which might fall within this exception would be a small school connected to an embassy for the children of embassy staff who are only temporarily resident in England.

---

[206] Ibid. at para. 2.8.

[207] Ibid. at para. 2.10.
https://assets.publishing.service.gov.uk/government/uploads/system/uploads/attachment_data/file/800615/Independent_School_Standards-_Guidance_070519.pdf
.

If the school intends to claim the exemption, it should keep good records to show that it applies.

Personal, social, health and economic education (PSHE) - ISS paragraph 2(2)(d)

PSHE has been a statutory requirement for independent schools since the standards were first introduced in 2003. Meanwhile PSHE was a non-statutory 'expectation' for state schools until the aspects relating to health and RSE were put onto a statutory footing for all schools from September 2020. There is now overlap between PSHE and RSE.

The PSHE policy, plans and schemes of work must cover personal, social, health and economic education. In principle, PSHE need not be timetabled as a separate subject of that name as long as all four elements of the standard are covered and clearly identifiable in the documentation and implemented. However, this flexibility does not apply to Relationships and Sex Education. KCSIE 2022 stipulates that RSE will be delivered in regularly timetabled lessons.[208]

<u>Reflecting the school's ethos and encouraging respect – paying particular regard to the protected characteristics</u>

The departmental dedicated PSHE advice[209] provides little substantive guidance about the content of PSHE and makes clear that it is largely up to schools to determine what is taught, with teachers *best placed to understand the needs of their pupils*. There are only two stipulations for PSHE in the standards:

- It *'reflects the school's aims and ethos'*. This has been part of the PSHE standard since the introduction of the standards in 2003. 'Aims and ethos' would include any faith ethos.

---

[208] Para. 130, KCSIE 2022

[209] https://www.gov.uk/government/publications/personal-social-health-and-economic-education-pshe/personal-social-health-and-economic-pshe-education .

- It must *'encourage respect for other people, paying particular regard to the protected characteristics set out in [the Equality Act 2010]'*.

The second requirement (respect) was introduced in the 2014 standards and should be seen as updating the original standard to reflect the Equality Act 2010, and as such qualifying the original standard. In short, schools cannot avoid teaching respect for other people, including those with protected characteristics, on the basis that this is at odds with their 'aims and ethos'.

The requirement to encourage respect for others includes and pays particular attention to those with protected characteristics but is not limited to those groups. Regarding the interplay of the requirements to encourage respect and in so doing to pay particular regard to the protected characteristics, the DfE guidance advises:

> *It is not sufficient for a school to say that it meets this standard because its curriculum encourages respect for all people in a general way; that is not paying particular regard to protected characteristics, of which pupils must be made aware (although only to the extent that it is considered age appropriate). However, a school does not necessarily have to address all of the characteristics in every year group because in drawing up its policy, plans and schemes of works relating to the PSHE curriculum, a school is to take account of (amongst other things) the ages of pupils and their learning abilities and deliver the curriculum appropriately.*

Although the DfE has said that a school does not necessarily have to address all protected characteristics with all age groups, it also explains that events may intervene to make it important for an issue to be covered sooner to help children to understand a situation, in an age-appropriate way, and to ensure they respect all those with protected characteristics.

The protected characteristics

The protected characteristics are: age, disability, gender reassignment, marriage and civil partnership, pregnancy and maternity, race, religion or belief, sex, sexual orientation.[210] These should all be referenced in curriculum documentation.[211]

Some of the protected characteristics (age, marriage and civil partnership) are not protected when it comes to the conduct of schools towards pupils. This means that it remains lawful, for example, for schools to treat children of different ages differently. But pupils must be taught the concept of protected characteristics and what they all are in an age-appropriate way.[212]

The DfE guidance[213] gives practical examples of PSHE which would not meet the standard, such as encouraging pupils to see people of particular races or religions as inferior, suggesting to male pupils that women and girls should be treated with less respect than males or that a woman's role is subservient to that of a man.

In Beis, the tribunal went further, suggesting a proactive duty to challenge discriminatory attitudes in school:

> The school failed to challenge an 'extremely restricted view of the role of women' and [continued] to avoid discussion of some protected characteristics under the Equality Act.' [para.s 32 and 30 of Beis]

The tribunal criticised the school for not covering all the protected characteristics in its PHSE curriculum and pointed out that

> ... there may be pupils in the school who themselves have, or may have, such characteristics (or in the case of gender reassignment, a need to understand such characteristics because of their own gender

---

[210] See section 4 of the Equality Act 2010 – see also Chapter Four above.

[211] Para. 2.14 – *Independent School Standards: Guidance for independent schools, April 2019.*

[212] See the table in Chapter Four.

[213] Para. 2.15 – *Independent School Standards: Guidance for independent schools, April 2019.*

confusion). Such pupils could themselves be denied respect, because neither they, their peers nor their teachers will be able to acknowledge the protected characteristic. [pp. 22/23 of Beis]

<u>'Personal' and 'social' education</u>

There is no specific guidance for independent schools on what 'personal' and 'social' education means or should cover, as distinct from respect, as above, health education (discussed below), and RSE which has been subject to a separate standard since September 2020 (see ISS paragraph 2A, also below). Personal resilience is a theme common to several pieces of guidance, such as those on *Prevent, Character Education, Mental Health and behaviour in schools* and RSE. The DfE advises that the education should be tailored to reflect the needs of pupils and *'we expect schools to use their PSHE education curriculum to equip pupils with a sound understanding of risk and with the knowledge and skills necessary to make safe and informed decisions'.* [214]

The following is a small selection of the available DfE resources:

- *Character Education Framework Guidance* (2019)[215]

- Review of sexual abuse in schools and colleges (Ofsted June 2021)[216]

- *KCSIE* (statutory) – signposts various resources to be used for PSHE such as <u>*Every Mind Matters and effective PSHE provision*</u> by Public Health England and the PSHE association

- *The Prevent duty Departmental advice for schools and childcare providers* (2015)[217]

---

[214] <u>Personal, social, health and economic (PSHE) education – GOV.UK (www.gov.uk)</u> .

[215] <u>https://www.gov.uk/government/publications/character-education-framework</u>

[216] <u>https://www.gov.uk/government/publications/review-of-sexual-abuse-in-schools-and-colleges/review-of-sexual-abuse-in-schools-and-colleges</u>

[217] <u>https://www.gov.uk/government/publications/protecting-children-from-radicalisation-the-prevent-duty</u>

- *Preventing and tackling bullying* (2017)[218]

- *Teaching online safety in school: Guidance supporting schools to teach their pupils how to stay safe online, within new and existing school subjects* (2019)[219]

- DfE and ACPO *Drugs: advice for schools* (2012)[220]

<u>Health education</u>

Health education includes both physical and mental health and wellbeing. A school which is not introducing mental health in the curriculum will not be meeting the standards.

New materials and guidance about health education were produced by the DfE to support the introduction of mandatory health education into the maintained sector from 2020. The section on health opens by explaining the aim of health education:

> *The aim of teaching pupils about physical health and mental wellbeing is to give them the information that they need to make good decisions about their own health and wellbeing. It should enable them to recognise what is normal and what is an issue in themselves and others and, when issues arise, know how to seek support as early as possible from appropriate sources. Physical health and mental wellbeing are interlinked, and it is important that pupils understand that good physical health contributes to good mental wellbeing, and vice versa. It is important for schools to promote pupils' self-control and ability to self-regulate, and strategies for doing so.*

These materials are not statutory for independent schools (although the subject is) but may be a helpful resource. See for example the following documents which set out what pupils should be taught about physical health and mental wellbeing and when:

---

[218] https://www.gov.uk/government/publications/preventing-and-tackling-bullying

[219] https://www.gov.uk/government/publications/teaching-online-safety-in-schools

[220] https://www.gov.uk/government/publications/drugs-advice-for-schools

- *Relationships Education, Relationships and Sex Education (RSE) and Health Education Statutory guidance for governing bodies, proprietors, head teachers, principals, senior leadership teams, teachers,* pages 31-35[221]

Other materials place teaching about mental health and wellbeing in the context of a whole school approach to mental health, such as:

- *Mental health and behaviour in schools 2018* which advises that that prevention will include teaching pupils about mental wellbeing through the curriculum and reinforcing this teaching and promoting resilience through school activities and ethos[222]

- *PSHE Teacher Guidance: Preparing to teach about mental health and emotional wellbeing* – Has been produced by the PSHE Association. It provides guidance for schools on teaching about mental health and emotional wellbeing as part of PSHE and signposts to organisations that can provide support for specific mental health conditions[223]

For a further understanding of the purpose of the standard see Annex C of the guidance on RSE and health education which explains how it links to various cross government strategies such as those relating to mental health, drugs, internet safety, childhood obesity, physical activity, loneliness.[224]

---

[221] https://assets.publishing.service.gov.uk/government/uploads/system/uploads/ attachment_data/file/908013/Relationships_Education__Relationships_and_Sex_ Education__RSE__and_Health_Education.pdf

[222] https://assets.publishing.service.gov.uk/government/uploads/system/uploads/ attachment_data/file/755135/Mental_health_and_behaviour_in_schools__.pdf

[223] https://www.pshe-association.org.uk/curriculum-and- resources/resources/guidance-teaching-about-mental-health- and?ResourceId=570&Keyword=&SubjectID=0&LevelID=0& ResourceTypeID=3&SuggestedUseID=0

[224] https://www.gov.uk/government/publications/relationships-education- relationships-and-sex-education-rse-and-health-education/annex-c-cross- government-strategies-for-relationships-education-relationships-and-sex- education-rse-and-health-education

Economic education

There is no guidance prescribing the content of 'economic education'. The vision of the Integrated Communities Strategy provides useful context:

> *We want [everyone] to play a full part in our society and to make the most of the economic and social opportunities available to them.*[225]

Economic education has also been referred to from time to time as 'financial education'.[226] The RSE guidance references preparing pupils to take their place in society as responsible citizens, manage their money well and make sound financial decisions.[227] In the context of the standard on PHSE, economic education is about personal finances/economics and financial inclusion.

Economic education will help ensure that pupils are equipped to make their own choices when they become adults. They will understand that in England their 'individual liberty' is a fundamental value which is respected and that accordingly they have the right to have a career of their own choosing and some knowledge of how they would approach that; they will also have a broad basic understanding of the existence of banks and bank accounts, perhaps credit cards and the welfare state. The content is wide open for schools to choose and implement but, as with other standards, it must meet the needs of their pupils and prepare them for adult life.

Careers education – ISS paragraph 2(2)(e)

Careers education plays a part in several strands of government policy: ensuring all children are prepared for the opportunities of adult life, that they can make informed choices about their future[228] which are not

---

[225] Integrated Communities Strategy Green Paper, at p. 20.

[226] Personal, social, health and economic (PSHE) education – GOV.UK (www.gov.uk).

[227] RSE guidance para. 105 – referring to the national curriculum for state schools.

[228] Opening doors, Breaking barriers: A strategy for Social Mobility 2011: *We will make schools responsible for securing access to independent , impartial careers guidance*

based on stereotypes,[229] that children are supported to reach their potential and are not held back by their background, that they will be able to achieve economic independence and make a positive contribution.[230]

This standard applies to pupils receiving secondary education. 'Secondary education' is defined in section 2 of the Education Act 1996. In practice this applies to pupils aged at least 12 years (or at least 10 and a half if being educated with senior pupils).[231] This means that prep schools which cater for pupils aged up to 13 are required to start to introduce age-appropriate careers guidance.

The standard echoes the requirement on state schools in section 42A of the Education Act 1997, as explained in the DfE guidance: Careers guidance and access for education and training providers *Statutory guidance for governing bodies, school leaders and school staff* July 2021.[232] While this legislation and guidance do not apply to independent schools, they may help advisors of independent schools to identify safe harbours. For example,

- 'Independent' is defined as

   external to the school. External sources of careers support could include employer visits, mentoring, website, telephone and helpline access and personal guidance provided externally to the school.

---

for all their pupils.'
https://assets.publishing.service.gov.uk/government/uploads/system/uploads/attachment_data/file/61964/opening-doors-breaking-barriers.pdf .

[229] Careers strategy: making the most of everyone's skills and talents December 2017: *Careers services must play a key role in encouraging people of all ages and backgrounds to consider the value of STEM qualifications and careers, dispelling stereotypes and making sure people have up-to-date information about the skills employers will need.* Para. 40.

[230] This links to the definition of 'well-being' in section 10(2)(d) and (e) of the Children Act 2004.

[231] See para. 2.17 of *The Independent School Standards: Guidance for independent schools, April 2019.*

[232] https://www.gov.uk/government/publications/careers-guidance-provision-for-young-people-in-schools

Taken together, the external sources must include information on the range of education and training options, including apprenticeships. Personal guidance does not have to be external – it can be delivered by school staff, if trained. Where this advice or any other element of the careers programme is internal, it must be supplemented by external sources of support to ensure compliance with the legal duty.

- For what constitutes 'careers' guidance, the 'Gatsby benchmarks' may be helpful[233]

- 'Impartial' is defined as *'showing no bias or favouritism towards a particular institution, education or work option'*[234]

The standard requires a written policy and supporting materials. The careers guidance should *'expand horizons'*, ensure *'that pupils have a broad view of the careers options open to them'* and cover a *'opportunities ... available to school leavers generally'* and enable pupils to make informed choices of the *'to enable them to succeed in adult life'*. Work experience is good practice.[235]

The guidance identifies some pitfalls to be avoided if the standard is to be met:

- Advice based on gender stereotypes

- Undermining the messages of the careers guidance through other teaching, materials and other parts of the curriculum

- Limiting horizons – presenting a restrictive view

- Discouraging further or higher education[236]

---

[233] Ibid. p. 9.

[234] Ibid. p. 13.

[235] Para. 2.17 of *The Independent School Standards: Guidance for independent schools, April 2019* .

[236] Ibid. at para 2.17

Activities for pupils below compulsory school age – ISS paragraph 2(2)(f)

This standard is essentially for reception classes and below.[237] The EYFS applies to this age group and is part of the standards. See the Table in Chapter Three for how the EYFS and standards work together.

Exemptions are available from the learning and development requirements of the EYFS but not from the welfare requirements. For information about exemptions see: *The Early Years Foundation Stage (EYFS) Learning and Development Requirements: Guidance on Exemptions for Early Years Providers June 2017* and regulations listed there.[238] This standard fills a gap in regulation which might otherwise appear where a school has obtained a dispensation from part of the EYFS. It entails drawing up and effectively implementing the required curriculum policy and other documents.

Activities for pupils over compulsory school age – ISS paragraph 2(2)(g)

In colloquial terms this standard relates to sixth forms which are part of a school.[239] There is no requirement for as broad a range of subjects at this level when pupils often start to specialise, but there should be an element of enrichment available for pupils beyond the subject specialisms.

Opportunity for all pupils to learn and make progress – ISS paragraph 2(2)(h)

This requirement underpins the entire curriculum. It must be appropriate to the age, ability and aptitude of pupils, neither under nor over demanding but enabling each to progress. The DfE guidance adds:

---

[237] See Chapter Two for the detailed definitions of compulsory school age.

[238] Careers guidance and aGuidance on exemptions for Early Years providers.pdf .

[239] See Chapter Two for the detailed definition of above compulsory school age.

A key word in this standard is 'all'; a school should not be seeking to cater only for the majority of pupils – if there are pupils of exceptional ability they should be enabled to make progress, and if there are pupils with special needs or who come from a disadvantaged background and in consequence have delayed attainment, inspectors will wish to see that the needs of these pupils are appropriately taken into account in the policy on curriculum and in supporting documents.

As ever, the curriculum plans and schemes of work must be effectively implemented.

Effective preparation for the opportunities, responsibilities and experiences of life in British society – ISS paragraph 2(2)(i)

This is a broad standard aimed at *'ensuring that all pupils can function properly as adult citizens'*. As such it is closely linked to those about the academic curriculum and also careers education, PSHE, RSE, protected characteristics and others. The comments of Munby LJ in Re G (children) [2012] EWCA Civ 1233 may be relevant, about keeping a child's options open for them:

… our objective must be to bring the child to adulthood in such a way that the child is best equipped both to decide what kind of life they want to lead – what kind of person they want to be – and to give effect so far as practicable to their aspirations. Put shortly, our objective must be to maximise the child's opportunities in every sphere of life as they enter adulthood.

In Beis it was said that if pupils were not informed about protected characteristics they would *'not be equipped to enter modern British society which accepts as part of its diversity civil partnerships, gay marriage, families with same sex parents and transgender persons'*, or indeed equipped with understanding they might need on their own account.[240]

---

[240] Brayne J in Beis, p. 23.

Children who live within particular communities must be prepared for contact with wider society at both national and local level and for engagement with public institutions.

The practice of segregating pupils by sex in co-educational schools, apart from potentially being discriminatory has been found in some cases also to be a failure to prepare pupils for life in British society where it is common for people of different genders to mix. See the case of HM Chief Inspector v Interim executive board of Al Hijrah school [2017] EWCA Civ 1426 and the DfE's non-statutory guidance: *Gender separation in mixed schools 2018*. Schools need to ensure that any such practices come within the limited lawful grounds afforded by the Equality Act 2010 for separating pupils by gender. DfE guidance[241] suggests that segregation could be lawful for sex education, for example, and adds:

> *Schools will also have to be able to show that the children ... understand and respect that any gender can fulfil almost any role in society, with very few exceptions (such as ministers in some religions).*

Additional reading

- *Report to the Home Secretary of Independent Oversight of Prevent Review and Strategy* – May 2011 – Lord Carlile of Berriew Q.C.

- The Prevent Strategy – June 2011

- Hansard: Commons debate 9 June 2014 and statements by the Home Secretary and Secretary of State for Education

- *Hansard : Volume 754: Education: British values debated on Thursday 26 June 2014 House of Lords*

- *Extremism in schools: the Trojan Horse affair* – HoC Education Select Committee – 11 March 2015

---

[241] Para. 2.22 of *The Independent School Standards: Guidance for independent schools, April 2019.*

- *The Casey Review: A review into opportunity and integration* – Dame Louise Casey DBE CB – 2016

- *Select Committee on Citizenship and Civic Engagement The Ties that Bind: Citizenship and Civic Engagement in the 21st Century* – April 2018[242]

- *Civil society strategy: Building a future that works for everyone* – August 2018

- *Integrated communities strategy action plan* – February 2019[243]

---

[242] See para.s 69 and 70 for the recommendation to move to away from fundamental British values as a means to counter-extremism towards a tool to encourage positive citizenship. See also Chapter Three about the role of education.

[243] See for example, p. 11.

CHAPTER EIGHT

RELATIONSHIPS EDUCATION AND RELATIONSHIPS AND SEX EDUCATION (RSE)

Introduction

RSE was placed onto a statutory footing for all schools in England from 1 September 2020. The statutory curriculum takes a broad view of the information today's children and young people need to stay safe and healthy and manage their personal and social lives on and offline. Implementation was initially hampered by the pandemic. In the meantime the importance of the new curriculum was confirmed by a review of sexual abuse in schools by Ofsted, published June 2021. Implementation of this standard in its statutory form is relatively new and is a focus of attention.

ISS paragraph 2A

(1) The standard in this paragraph is met if the proprietor—

(a) ensures that every registered pupil who is provided with primary education at the school is provided with relationships education,

(b) ensures that every registered pupil who is provided with secondary education at the school is provided with relationships and sex education, except in so far as the pupil is excused as mentioned in sub-paragraph (2),

(c) … [about academies]…,

(d) in making arrangements for the purposes of paragraphs (a), (b) or (c), has regard to any guidance under section 80A of the Education Act 2002 that applies in relation to the provision of education by maintained schools,

(e) makes and keeps up to date a separate written statement of its policy with regard to the provision of education as required by each of paragraphs (a) and (b),

(f) consults parents of registered pupils at the school before making or revising a statement under sub-paragraph (e), and

(g) publishes a copy of the statement on a website and provides a copy of the statement free of charge to anyone who asks for one.

(2) Arrangements made by the proprietor for the purposes of sub-paragraph (1)(b) must ensure that where a pupil's parent requests that the pupil is wholly or partly excused from sex education provided as part of relationships and sex education, the pupil is so excused until the request is withdrawn, unless or to the extent that the head teacher considers that the pupil should not be so excused.

(3) Sub-paragraph (1)(a) and (c) do not apply to a pupil who is under compulsory school age.

The requirements of paragraph 2A have been inserted into the standards by the Relationships Education, Relationships and Sex Education and Health Education (England) Regulations 2019 which are made under the Children and Social Work Act 2017, section 34 and 35. [244]

Summary

In short:

- Every primary pupil (reception and above) must be provided with relationships education.

- Every secondary pupil must be provided with RSE, unless they are lawfully excused.

---

[244] An attempt at legal challenge failed on the basis that it was out of time.

- From September 2022, it has been clarified that it should be delivered as a planned programme in regularly timetabled lessons reinforced throughout the whole curriculum.[245]

- This standard appears to be outcome focused:
  the proprietor ensures that every pupil[246].... is provided with....
  This suggests that schools should ensure the requirements are met for all pupils, subject to the right to be excused covered below.

	Primary	Secondary	Standard	Statutory guidance
Relationships education	Required – no opt out	Required – no opt out	ISS 2A(1)(a)	Yes
Relationships and sex education	Not a requirement* – opt out should be allowed	Required – limited legal opt out available	ISS 2A(1)(b)	Yes
Health	Required	Required	PSHE – ISS (2)(d)	No

*Primary schools may teach sex education although it is not a requirement. The DfE recommends that all primary schools have a sex education programme tailored to the age and the physical and emotional maturity of the pupils – see paragraphs 67 and 68 of the RSHE guidance.

For definitions of 'primary education', 'secondary education' and 'pupil' see the Education Act 1996, sections 2 and 3.

---

[245] Para. 130, KCSIE 2022.

[246] Except those under school age – ISS 2A(3).

Legal force of the guidance

The Secretary of State's power to issue guidance about RSHE is found in section 80A of the Education Act 2002, as inserted by paragraph 8 of the schedule to the Relationships Education, Relationships and Sex Education and Health Education (England) Regulations 2019.

The guidance is currently: *Relationships Education, Relationships and Sex Education (RSE) and Health Education Statutory guidance for governing bodies, proprietors, head teachers, principals, senior leadership teams, teachers*, as updated in 2021. This is the same guidance that applies to state schools.

Proprietors/schools are required to have regard to it, meaning that they must follow it in the absence of a good reason not to.

The guidance relating to health education is not statutory for independent schools, although health education is compulsory.[247]

RSE curriculum content

Concerning the content of the statutory guidance, the empowering legislation stipulates:

> *Section 34 (3) The regulations must provide that guidance given by virtue of subsection (2)(a) is to be given with a view to ensuring that when relationships education or relationships and sex education is given—*
>
> > *(a) the pupils learn about—*
> >
> > > *(i) safety in forming and maintaining relationships,*
> > >
> > > *(ii) the characteristics of healthy relationships, and*
> > >
> > > *(iii) how relationships may affect physical and mental health and well-being, and*

---

[247] ISS 2(2)(d). See also footnotes 1 and 2 of *Relationships Education, Relationships and Sex Education (RSE) and Health Education Statutory guidance for governing bodies, proprietors, head teachers, principals, senior leadership teams, teachers* 2019.

(b) the education is appropriate having regard to the age and the religious background of the pupils.[248]

The statutory guidance sets out at a high level the core content which all pupils should receive. The headlines are given below but there is no substitute for reading the guidance in full.

By the end of primary education[249] pupils should know about:

- families and people who care for me

- caring friendships

- respectful relationships

- online relationships

- being safe

Pupils should be taught the knowledge they need to recognise and to report abuse, including emotional, physical and sexual abuse. Pupils should know how to seek advice or report concerns when they suspect or know that something is wrong.[250]

At secondary level, schools should continue to develop knowledge on topics specified for primary and, building on these, by the end of secondary pupils should know about:

- Families

- Respectful relationships including friendships

- Online and media safety

- Being safe

---

[248] Children and Social Work Act 2017.

[249] 'Primary' and 'secondary' are defined in the Education Act 1996.

[250] Para. 62 of *Relationships Education, Relationships and Sex Education (RSE) and Health Education Statutory guidance for governing bodies, proprietors, head teachers, principals, senior leadership teams, teachers 2019.*

- Intimate and sexual relationships

Pupils should be made aware of the law relating to topics when they are taught them, including for example:

- marriage

- consent, including the age of consent

- violence against women and girls

- online behaviours including image and information sharing (including 'sexting', youth-produced sexual imagery, nudes, etc.)

- pornography

- abortion

- sexuality

- gender identity

- substance misuse

- violence and exploitation by gangs

- extremism/radicalisation

- criminal exploitation (for example, through gang involvement or 'county lines' drugs operations)

- hate crime

- female genital mutilation (FGM)

There is a wide range of helpful, non-statutory, teaching materials available on Gov.uk.[251] These provide a governmental perspective on how the teaching of these issues could be approached.

Protected characteristics and equality matters

Neither the primary nor secondary legislation concerning RSE overtly reference teaching about the protected characteristics. To do so would create duplication as they are already expressly covered in the PHSE standard, and SMSC standard. The statutory RSE guidance is clear, however, that:

> *Pupils should be taught the facts and the law about sex, sexuality, sexual health and gender identity in an age-appropriate and inclusive way. All pupils should feel that the content is relevant to them and their developing sexuality. Sexual orientation and gender identity should be explored at a timely point and in a clear, sensitive and respectful manner.[252]*

Further, schools should:

> *be alive to issues such as everyday sexism, misogyny, homophobia and gender stereotypes and take positive action to build a culture where these are not tolerated, and any occurrences are identified and tackled.[253]*

RSE should be accessible to all pupils, including those with SEN/D.[254] The Independent Inquiry into Child Sexual Abuse (IICSA) heard evidence about a tendency of adults to infantilise pupils with SEN/D and therefore sometimes to provide less effective sex education for this

---

[251] https://www.gov.uk/guidance/teaching-about-relationships-sex-and-health#train-teachers-on-relationships-sex-and-health-education

[252] Para. 75, RSE statutory guidance.

[253] Para.31, RSE statutory guidance.

[254] Para. 130, KCSIE 2022.

group whereas their additional vulnerabilities may make sex education all the more important.[255]

Faith perspectives

The Children and Social Work Act 2017 is clear that the education must be *appropriate having regard to the age and the religious background of the pupils*. The guidance would suggest that this is about how the required core content is taught, that is, providing a faith perspective on it, rather than avoiding elements of core content. Importantly it is recognised that there is a range of opinions regarding RSE. The applicable law should be taught in a factual way so that pupils are clear on their rights and responsibilities as citizens and schools may explore faith and other perspectives in other subjects such as Religious Education.[256]

Of interest, in <u>Birmingham City Council v Afsar & others</u>,[257] the court granted an injunction to restrict street protests about the teaching of LGBT issues in a state school. The case may be instructive although it pre-dates the current statutory RSE curriculum. It was found that the teaching had been misunderstood, misinterpreted and grossly misrepresented by protestors. The matters which had actually been taught were limited and lawful. Warby J was not persuaded that '*the School's decision to provide its pupils with limited instruction in relation to sexual orientation ..., notwithstanding objection from some parents on cultural, religious or philosophical grounds, involve[d] direct or indirect discrimination against the pupils or their parents on grounds of race, religion or belief*'. He found it '*hard to detect any real conflict between*

---

[255] See expert evidence on harmful behaviours from Professor Hackett – Durham University https://www.iicsa.org.uk/key-documents/14669/view/EWM000469.pdf in Part B at para. 11.11). See also: IICSA's Victims and Survivors Forum Consultation on Protected Characteristics: Summary Report February 2021 which records the views of victims about the bearing their protected characteristics had on their experiences.

[256] Para.s 76 and 77 of RSE statutory guidance 2019. See also comments on children's rights to education in Chapter One.

[257] [2019] EWHC 3217 (QB)

what the school is teaching, and the beliefs identified'. But found that if, contrary to his views, the limited instruction provided did represent indirect discrimination, it was justified by the need to comply with the legal requirements.[258] The case could be seen as demonstrating the importance of parental engagement which is now a legal duty, see below.

Assessment

There is an expectation in the RSE statutory guidance, reflected in the current inspection approach, that teaching will be assessed and assessments used to identify where pupils need extra support, and that pupil progress will be assessed: *For example, tests, written assignments or self-evaluations, to capture progress.*[259]

Parental rights in relation to RSE

Parent engagement

The regulations require 'consultation' with parents.[260] A reading of the guidance suggests that this is about informing parents, listening to the parent voice and explaining the approach that the school will take. Ultimately, however, schools must have regard to the guidance and parents do not have the right to veto it. There is non-statutory guidance from the DfE about parental engagement: *Parental Engagement on Relationships Education.*[261]

---

[258] Birmingham judgment at para.s 62 and 63. These were state school duties which find equivalence in the ISS, such as the duty to safeguard and promote the welfare of pupils. The duties to promote FBV and prepare pupils for adult life.

[259] Para.s 123-125, RSE statutory guidance.

[260] ISS para. 2A(1)(f).

[261] https://www.gov.uk/government/publications/engaging-parents-with-relationships-education-policy

Right to request that a child be excused

Parents have a right to request that their children be excused or partly excused from the sex education element of RSE, as set out in the standard above. Such a request must be acceded to *'unless or to the extent that the headteacher considers that the pupil should not be so excused'*.

The guidance notes that it would be good practice to discuss such a request with the parents, and advises what the discussions should cover. Once those discussions have taken place, the guidance directs schools to respect the parental request as follows:

> *... except in exceptional circumstances, ... up to and until three terms before the child turns 16. After that point, if the child wishes to receive sex education rather than be withdrawn, the school should make arrangements to provide the child with sex education during one of those terms.'*[262]

Complex questions arise around ISS paragraph 2A(2) if a Gillick competent pupil asks to receive sex education in contravention of a parental request prior to the third term before turning 16, especially if the child does not want their parents to be informed. It could be argued on behalf of a child that the parental right as formulated is at odds with their own rights under provisions such as Article 10 of the ECHR and Article 13(1) of the UNCRC. Presumably such a dispute might be considered a situation which could be an 'exceptional circumstance' within the guidance. [263]

What can pupils be excused from?

The right to be excused applies only to the sex education element of RSE. There has been no determination by a court yet as to exactly what that means given that the guidance does not separate the elements of RSE into distinct categories of 'sex' and 'relationships'. Pending guidance from a court, determining the reach of the 'right to withdraw'

---

[262] Para. 47, RSE statutory guidance. It Is not clear that this direction sits entirely comfortably with the notion of the headteacher's discretion under ISS 2A(2).

[263] For a recent discussion about Gillick competence see for example, Bell v Tavistock [2021] EWCA Civ 1363.

may be largely a matter for reasonable professional discretion and discussion with parents, perhaps based on the tables and advice in paragraphs 81 and 82 of the RSE guidance. A few points may assist:

- The duty to teach about the protected characteristics and respect stands apart from RSE, being covered in both the curriculum standard (ISS paragraph 2(2)(d)(ii)) and the SMSC standard (ISS paragraph 5(b)(vi)). A school will therefore still be under a duty to convey that information to pupils whose parents exercise the right to request withdrawal.

- *Keeping children safe in education* is clear that pupils should be taught how to stay safe and links this duty to RSE.[264] Child-on-child abuse is known to be so prevalent that all schools should assume it is a live issue for their pupils.[265] **New** for 2022, KCSIE provides an indicative list of the aspects of RSE which might be considered part of the safeguarding standard.[266] This text suggests that these issues (set out below) could, therefore, not be encompassed in the right to withdraw from sex education, although there is no authority on the point. Child-on-child abuse is covered again in Chapter Eleven and Chapter Nineteen.

- In LA maintained schools, reproduction is covered in the national curriculum for science. So a child in a LA maintained school who is withdrawn from RSE would still acquire that basic information elsewhere in the curriculum. However, the national curriculum is not compulsory for independent schools, so this is an area where there is potentially a difference for secondary age pupils in the two sectors.

If all parents at a school indicate a wish to withdraw their children from sex education, it seems likely that a school may still meet the standard

---

[264] Para. 128 et seq., KCSIE 2022.

[265] See Ofsted's Review of sexual abuse in schools and colleges, June 2021.

[266] Para. 130, KCSIE 2022.

in ISS paragraph 2A as long as it is clear that the school stands ready to provide sex education if any parent, or pupil of the relevant age, wishes.

Making a policy statement

The statutory guidance contains considerable advice about the content coverage of the policy statement.[267] Here 'policy statement' means policy. While there is no express requirement to consult teachers and pupils, as there is for parents, the guidance advises that the policy should reflect their views and that listening to the views of young people *will strengthen the policy, ensuring that it meets the needs of all pupils'*. The policy statement (i.e. the policy) must then be published on the school website, if any, and kept up to date.

Cross-over with other standards

The RSE guidance is also incorporated into KCSIE, the statutory guidance on safeguarding. It plays a crucial part in preventative education through teaching children how to behave, how to treat other people and how to keep themselves safe.[268] In appropriate cases failure to follow it could be deemed a failure to meet the safeguarding standard in ISS paragraph 7, covered in Chapter Eleven below.

New for 2022, KCSIE provides more information about which parts of the RSE curriculum can be considered crucial to safeguarding. The list should be seen as indicative only:

- Healthy and respectful relationships

- Boundaries and consent

- Stereotyping, prejudice and equality

- Body confidence and self-esteem

---

[267] RSE guidance at para.s 13–18.

[268] Para. 130, KCSIE 2022.

- How to recognise an abusive relationship

- Concepts and laws relating to:

    - domestic abuse,

    - so-called honour-based violence such as forced marriage and FGM

    - how to access support,

- What constitutes sexual harassment, sexual violence and why these are always unacceptable.[269]

Additional reading

House of Commons Library – Relationships and sex education in schools (England) by Robert Long – 16 July 2021

IICSA: Victims and Survivors Forum Consultation on Protected Characteristics: Summary Report February 2021

Ofsted: Review of sexual abuse in schools and college – June 2021

---

[269] Para. 130, KCSIE 2022.

CHAPTER NINE

THE TEACHING STANDARD

Introduction

Qualifications are not prescribed for those who teach in independent schools, except where the EYFS applies. Where this works well it enables schools to access a wide range of expertise to teach pupils such as ex-professional sports players and coaches, therapists, university professors, professional musicians, ministers of religion. The teaching standard ensures that, whatever the qualifications of staff, in practice teaching is delivered to a standard that enables pupils to make good progress. While the focus is on the teaching rather than the individual teacher, many elements of the standard chime with those in the Teachers' Standards made under the Education (School Teachers' Appraisal) (England) Regulations 2012.

ISS paragraph 3(j) prohibits discrimination contrary to the Equality Act 2010 and as such may be argued to import the law of discrimination into the standards. This is discussed below.

Essential guidance about the teaching standard is found in the DfE's non-statutory advice: *The Independent School Standards: Guidance for independent schools, April 2019*. Key points are quoted below as an indication of the type of content but advisors should access the advice direct for full information. The case of *Beis Aharon v Secretary of State* [2016] UKFTT 270 (HESC) which concerned the quality of education is also instructive although only a first instance decision.

ISS paragraph 3

> *The standard in this paragraph is met if the proprietor ensures that the teaching at the school—*

(a) enables pupils to acquire new knowledge and make good progress according to their ability so that they increase their understanding and develop their skills in the subjects taught;

(b) fosters in pupils self-motivation, the application of intellectual, physical and creative effort, interest in their work and the ability to think and learn for themselves;

(c) involves well planned lessons and effective teaching methods, activities and management of class time;

(d) shows a good understanding of the aptitudes, needs and prior attainments of the pupils, and ensures that these are taken into account in the planning of lessons;

(e) demonstrates good knowledge and understanding of the subject matter being taught;

(f) utilises effectively classroom resources of a good quality, quantity and range;

(g) demonstrates that a framework is in place to assess pupils' work regularly and thoroughly and use information from that assessment to plan teaching so that pupils can progress;

(h) utilises effective strategies for managing behaviour and encouraging pupils to act responsibly;

(i) does not undermine the fundamental British values of democracy, the rule of law, individual liberty, and mutual respect and tolerance of those with different faiths and beliefs; and

(j) does not discriminate against pupils contrary to Part 6 of the 2010 Act.

What is 'the teaching'?

'Teaching' is not expressly defined in the standards, the interpretation regulation (regulation 2) of the Education (Independent School Standards) Regulations 2014, or in the empowering legislation.

On one view 'teaching' could refer to almost everything done in a school. Vital skills are acquired by school pupils outside the formal curriculum, such as socialisation and communication. If the girls in a school cannot eat until after the boys have finished, what is that 'teaching' them about their expectations for adult life? If pupils with disabilities are not always included in all trips or after-school activities, if children with protected characteristics are not protected from bullying, what does that experience teach them about their value in society?

On another view, the 'teaching' refers only to the matters mentioned in the teaching standard itself, such as lesson planning and behaviour management. On yet another, the matters covered by the Teachers' Standards[270] could be relevant, particularly in Part 2 which applies to teachers in independent schools. Dictionary definitions could also be consulted.

The meaning of 'teaching' could be a consideration in the context of, for example, regulatory action or an adverse inspection finding about 'the teaching' which appeared to relate to actions or decisions which had not been taken at classroom level but by managers and governors. Examples could include exclusions, policy matters such as uniform or meals, or matters relating to fees.

Remote and online teaching

The standards do not prescribe how teaching is delivered. During and since the pandemic, remote education in various forms has become commonplace and has sometimes been mandated. However, now that the temporary provisions of the Coronavirus Act 2020 have expired, the DfE's stated policy position is that the priority should always be for schools to deliver high-quality face-to-face education to all pupils. School attendance is mandatory for all pupils of compulsory school age. For pupils of compulsory school age, remote education should only ever

---

[270] https://assets.publishing.service.gov.uk/government/uploads/system/uploads/attachment_data/file/1007716/Teachers__Standards_2021_update.pdf.

be considered as a short-term measure and as a last resort where in person attendance is not possible, such as when in-person attendance is either not possible or contrary to government guidance. See *Providing remote education: guidance for schools March 2022.*

The teaching standard applies to whichever mode is used although, according to current DfE policy, schools whose educational provision is delivered entirely remotely are not governed by the independent school standards. [271]

What are 'good progress', 'good understanding', 'good knowledge' and 'good quality'?

The term 'good' in the 2014 standards can cause confusion in the context of inspection reports because the inspection frameworks also use 'good' as a grade descriptor. There is no automatic read-across between meeting the minimum standards of the standards and achieving the grade 'good' in an inspection. The criteria for inspection grades, including 'good', are set out in grade descriptors of the relevant inspectorate.[272]

---

[271] See the 2019 consultation about online schooling:

https://consult.education.gov.uk/independent-education-division/online-schools-accreditation-scheme/supporting_documents/Online%20Schools%20Consultation.pdf.

The current DfE position is that an online school cannot be registered as an independent school, even if the education is full-time and for more than five children of compulsory school age. This is because an online school which has no building where pupils are taught full-time cannot, by definition, meet Part 5 of the ISS, which relates to premises. The DfE also considers that other standards, particularly in relation to welfare, could be difficult to inspect under existing frameworks for either maintained or independent schools.

See also the subsequent policy paper published 24 June 2021: Accreditation for online education providers.
https://www.gov.uk/government/publications/accreditation-for-online-education-providers/accreditation-for-online-education-providers .

[272] The Ofsted grade descriptors are publicly available. The ISI grade descriptors are available to schools inspected by ISI.

There are conflicting views which have not yet been litigated as to whether, in view of parental rights of choice and privacy, the minimum standard can mean more than that the education is good enough to meet the child's right to education under Article 2, Protocol 1 (see Chapter One). The counter-argument would be that states are entitled to set a higher expectation.

Parts of the teaching standard

These comments highlight key points from *The Independent School Standards: Guidance for independent schools, April 2019.*

Enabling good progress in knowledge understanding and skills, and according to ability– ISS paragraph 3(a)

The guidance distinguishes a child who is making good progress from one who is 'just getting by'. 'Good' is judged according to the ability of the individual pupils. To meet the standard, the teaching must

- Actively push pupils towards increased achievement

- Do this according to the ability of the pupils[273]

Fostering motivation – ISS paragraph 3(b)

The guidance explains:

> *As well as the basic requirement to encourage pupils to work hard and achieve, and take a positive attitude towards learning, schools should also feel able to encourage open discussion by pupils and staff of problems and themes which arise from the curriculum or everyday life. Schools which suppress debate and do not encourage questioning and individual opinion are not likely to meet this standard.*[274]

---

[273] *The Independent School Standards: Guidance for independent schools, April 2019*

[274] Ibid. at para. 2.26

Planning, methods and management of class time – ISS paragraph 3(c)

No particular pedagogic methods are required, instead but schools are expected to be able to show that their particular approach is based on sound principles and orderly. The guidance confirms that

> *The overall quality of teaching is what matters and a single poor lesson observed during an inspection would not constitute a failure against this standard.*

Good understanding of aptitudes, needs and prior attainments taken into account in lesson planning – ISS paragraph 3(d)

This means that teachers should know their pupils and plan their lessons accordingly. An effective system to track pupils' progress can help to provide evidence for meeting this standard.

Good knowledge and understanding of the subject matter being taught – ISS paragraph 3(e)

This standard will not be met if the school's teaching staff do not have a good understanding and knowledge of the subject(s) which they teach.

Effective use of good quality, quantity and range of classroom resources – ISS paragraph 3(f)

This standard is designed to ensure pupils are exposed to a wide range of stimulating material. There must be enough books and other teaching resources and they must be of good quality. This standard also encompasses resources for supporting particular groups of pupils such as those with SEN/D or young children.

The guidance explains that inspection entails the examination of learning resources, whether in libraries and online, for materials which *'espouse values which conflict with any of the standards'* and if so questioning how they are used. (See also the comments about ISS paragraph 5(c) and (d) below, about the need to provide appropriate context for some resources in order to meet other standards.) It also entails consideration of how the school uses filters to monitor pupil access to online materials online which may breach the standards.

<u>Assessment to support planning of teaching – ISS paragraph 3(g)</u>

The guidance explains:

> *This requirement is designed to ensure that schools use pupil assessment actively to inform the planning of teaching, rather than simply as an end in itself or simply to demonstrate progress – important though the latter is. Teaching achieves more where it takes full account of individual pupils' real progress to date, for instance by being flexible enough to undertake more work on areas where progress has been poor. A written record of the assessment of pupils' progress will help demonstrate that the standard is met.*

This standard, and that in ISS paragraph 4, does not require schools to use nationally standardised tests.

<u>Effective strategies for managing behaviour – ISS paragraph 3(h)</u>

Good teaching can be undermined where pupil behaviour is poor. Behaviour management is therefore part of good teaching. As explained in the guidance: '... *that includes putting the school's behaviour management policy into operation from day to day'*.

This standard links to the Behaviour Standard (ISS paragraph 9) and also ISS paragraph 3(b) which concerns fostering self-motivation because *'pupils' behaviour will be assisted where they are interested in their work and encouraged to think and learn for themselves'*.

<u>Fundamental British values – ISS paragraph 3(i)</u>

The teaching must not undermine the fundamental British values of:

- Democracy

- The rule of law

- Individual liberty

- Mutual respect and tolerance of those with different faiths and beliefs.

The DfE's guidance notes that teachers must not

... convey in their teaching that either the values are wrong, or that they do not apply to the community served by the school. Evidence of such teaching would lead to this standard not being met. In order to assess compliance with the standard inspectors will check pupils' understanding, in an age-appropriate way, of the concepts listed.

Prohibition on unlawful discrimination – ISS paragraph 3(j)

This standard in effect imports much of the Equality Act 2010 in a few words:

The teaching ... does not discriminate against pupils contrary to Part 6 of the [EqA] 2010 Act.

It would allow the DfE to take regulatory action against a school which discriminates unlawfully in its teaching. As ever, whether action would be appropriate in a particular case, following from an adverse tribunal or court finding, would depend on all the facts at the time including whether, notwithstanding past failings, the school had remedied its teaching practices by the time the proposed action.

Part 6 of the EqA 2010 is about the duties of schools towards pupils. Schools also have duties under other parts of the EqA 2010, for example, as employers but these are not part of the standards. For what it means to *'discriminate against pupils contrary to Part 6 of the [EqA] 2010'*, see the synopsis of the EqA 2010 at Chapter Four.

The implications of this standard have yet to be litigated. Possible meanings of 'the teaching' are discussed above. At its widest, it could encompass almost anything that happens in a school. At its narrowest, it must cover at least all the matters covered in the teaching standard at ISS paragraph 3. In view of the developing body of case law and other reports involving schools, schools should be proactive about ensuring that pupils with protected characteristics are fully included in the life of the school and do not experience unlawful discrimination.

Inclusive teaching practices

The focus should start with inclusive teaching practices, with thought being given to each of the characteristics which are protected in schools in relation to pupils: disability, gender reassignment, pregnancy and maternity, race, religion or belief, sex and sexual orientation. Equality does not mean always treating everyone the same; on the contrary, differentiation (reasonable adjustments in the case of pupils with disabilities) may be essential to ensure equality of provision or opportunity. Direct discrimination is always unlawful whereas indirect discrimination is permissible where it is a proportionate means of achieving a legitimate aim, as explained in more detail in Chapter Four.

It is not uncommon for parents to be concerned that schools discriminate unlawfully in areas such as:

- marking academic work

- awards (prizes, appointment of prefects etc)

- application of the behaviour policy to pupils

- responses to incidents of bullying between pupils

- failing to recognise the additional needs and/or vulnerabilities of some pupils and provide appropriate support

- access to sport, facilities and coaching

- kudos accorded to sporting endeavours

- pupil participation in performing arts

- boarding accommodation.

To ensure the school meets the standard, it can help leaders to consider questions such as

- how they can use record-keeping to monitor whether the teaching discriminates

- whether training for staff would raise awareness, particularly in relation to the areas above

- the potential impact of new policies and practices on pupils with various protected characteristics, while the policies are in development

- how they can enable pupils to provide honest feedback about their experiences of discrimination

- whether the school is proactive about creating a welcoming environment where all pupils can thrive and where discriminatory attitudes, including by pupils, are challenged appropriately.

For pupils with disabilities, teaching should ensure that adjustments are made both in the classroom and to procedures and policies (such as behaviour management) so far as reasonable, to ensure they are not put at a substantial disadvantage. This standard will often link to the requirements to assess pupils, plan lessons and ensure that all make good progress according to their ability (ISS paragraphs 3(a), 3(c) and 3(g)), and to implement effective behaviour management strategies (ISS paragraph 3(h)). It encompasses all aspects of school life such as school trips, performances and after-school clubs. Various pieces of DfE guidance, while non-statutory for independent schools, contain advice which could be viewed as reasonable steps/adjustments for pupils with disabilities. See for example:

- *Supporting pupils at school with medical conditions* 2014

- *Mental health and behaviour in schools* 2018

Exceptions

Chapter Four explains the exceptions in the EqA 2010 for the curriculum, competitive sport, communal accommodation, single sex boarding, positive action, selection and so on.

<u>Segregation</u>

Segregation of pupils by race is always direct discrimination.[275] Strict segregation by any other protected characteristic is also likely to be direct discrimination, following the case of <u>HM Chief Inspector v Al Hijrah School</u> [2017] EWCA Civ 1426.

Views are divided on where this leaves co-educational schools which provide education on a so-called 'diamond' model,[276] with the weight of views among lawyers being that the model does not sit easily with the EqA 2010. Some see outstanding questions about the impact of <u>Al Hijrah</u> such as:

- whether all forms of segregation by sex in co-educational schools should now be seen as discriminatory or only 'strict' segregation

- whether the case means that inspectorates must always take the view that segregation by sex in co-educational schools is discriminatory (subject to the exceptions In the EqA), whether or not it improves academic outcomes.

These and other questions may only be settled by further litigation. In the meantime, the DfE has provided guidance and indicated that co-education on a 'diamond' model could potentially be considered 'positive action' where a school makes a clearly evidenced case. [277]

This text would suggest that diamond schools which wish to argue that their model of segregation falls within the 'positive action' exception should consider working with their legal advisors to structure their inspection preparation around the obvious questions which might arise, such as:

---

[275] Section 13(5), EqA 2010.

[276] In 'Diamond' models, girls and boys are educated together in junior and senior schools but apart for certain years in between. The details of the model, such as the extent and timing of the segregation, can vary from school to school and year group to year group within some schools.

[277] See: *Gender separation in mixed schools.* Section 158, EqA 2010 and Chapter Four of this text.

- how, when and where are pupils segregated by sex (which lessons, arrangements for breaktimes, mealtimes, trips, events etc)

- times when pupils of different sexes have opportunities to interact

- the disadvantage(s) the model seeks to address, with an emphasis on educational disadvantage (but not necessarily to the exclusion of other aspects)

- any evidence to support the view that the model is a valid means of addressing the identified disadvantage

- how and how often the effectiveness of the model is monitored and reviewed

- how the school ensures pupils' preparation for life in British society is not compromised

- arrangements for listening to the views of pupils about this issue

Interaction with other standards

Where teaching discriminates unlawfully against pupils, the standard in ISS paragraph 3(j) will not be met and this will often impact compliance with other standards also.

For example:

- Teaching which does not meet the educational needs of pupils with disabilities may be discriminatory contrary to ISS paragraph 3(j), and may also engage standards such as curriculum (ISS 2(1)(b)(i)) and pupil progress (ISS 3(a))

- Teaching which tackles some forms of bullying effectively but dismisses others as 'banter', such as racist remarks or sexual harassment of girls, could be discriminatory within ISS paragraph 3(j). This could also engage standards such as safeguarding (ISS paragraph 7(a) and (b)), behaviour (ISS 9), behaviour management (ISS 3(h)) and bullying (ISS 10)

- Arrangements for teaching sport which do not assure privacy for transgender pupils when changing, could be discriminatory[278] within ISS paragraph 3(j) and could also engage the premises standard, ISS 23(1)(c) and NMS 4.1 (boarding accommodation, privacy)

- Strict segregation by sex could be discriminatory within ISS paragraph 3(j) and might also limit pupils' preparation for adult life in British society and impact the development of self-esteem (ISS paragraphs 2(2)(i) and 5(b)(i))

- In all cases, the leadership and management standard would be engaged. It could be questioned whether leaders had the understanding and commitment to ensure the other standards were met and were actively promoting the well-being of pupils (ISS 34).

Whole school approach to inclusion

Teachers and leaders need to be proactive about inclusion throughout their practice and policies. Listening to pupils with a view to understanding their needs, perspective and experience of school will support schools to meet this standard. Teachers and leaders should consistently challenge behaviours and interactions (whether staff/pupil or pupil/pupil) which could create or allow a hostile environment for pupils with protected characteristics and intervene through appropriate action, be it disciplinary, educative and/or pastoral as the situation requires. The aim should be to create a positive, inclusive culture in which every pupil feels valued and can flourish.

The following sources are important reading:

- the Part 6 of the Equality Act 2010

- *The Independent School Standards: Guidance for independent schools, April 2019*

---

[278] See para 3.20 EHRC *Technical guidance for schools* for discussion

- the DfE's non-statutory advice: *Equality Act 2010 and Schools*

- the EHRC's non-statutory advice:

  o *Technical guidance for schools in England*

  o *Reasonable adjustments for disabled pupils* – Guidance for schools in England

- *Disability: Equality Act 2010 – Guidance on matters to be taken into account in determining questions relating to the definition of disability 2011* – Government Equalities Office[279]

- the SEND Code of Practice: 0-25 years – paragraphs 9.91-9.92 about reasonable adjustments

- <u>HM Chief Inspector of Education, Children's Services and Skills -v- Interim Board of Al-Hijrah School and others</u> [2017] EWCA Civ 1426 about segregation by sex

- DfE non-statutory guidance: *Gender separation in mixed schools*

- Ashdown House <u>Ashdown House v JKL and MNP</u> [2019] UKUT 259 (AAC) about reasonable adjustments, proportionality, behaviour management and exclusion

- the Ofsted Review of sexual abuse in schools and colleges 2021

The Assessment Standard

Introduction

This standard is self-explanatory. Independent schools are not obliged to use the nationally accredited testing systems used by the state sector, although they typically do so to some extent, but must have some way of evaluating pupil performance and progress.

---

[279] This is unlikely to be entirely up to date but it is still available at: https://www.gov.uk/government/publications/equality-act-guidance .

ISS paragraph 4

> *The standard in this paragraph is met where the proprietor ensures that a framework for pupil performance to be evaluated, by reference to the school's own aims as provided to parents or national norms, or to both, is in place.*

Key points

The DfE guidance[280] makes three points:

- Schools should assess the progress of individual pupils for the purpose of lesson planning

- Whatever system the school uses must also enable it to provide parents a detailed and clear assessment of their child's performance, including the annual written report on progress and attainment in each main subject area, as required by ISS paragraph 32(1)(f)

- The framework adopted must also enable parents to judge the child's performance in the context of the school's aims, or national norms, or both.

EYFS

For the separate assessment requirements for pupils in the EYFS, see Section 2 of the statutory framework for the EYFS:

- Progress check at age 2

- Assessment at the start of reception year – the Reception Baseline Assessment (RBA). This is optional for independent schools

---

[280] *The Independent School Standards: Guidance for independent schools, April 2019:*

- Assessment at the end of the EYFS – The Early Years Foundation Stage Profile (EYFSP)

- Information to be provided to the LA on request.

CHAPTER TEN

THE SMSC STANDARD (SOCIAL, MORAL, SPIRITUAL AND CULTURAL DEVELOPMENT OF PUPILS) – ISS PART 2

Introduction

This standard focuses on the values and principles which are to be inculcated in pupils through the ethos and provision of the school.

The purpose of the standard is to ensure that pupils' development in non-academic terms will enable them to play a confident, informed role in society, have a fully developed values system and be able to interact with other people in a positive way.

And also

To prevent political indoctrination of pupils through the curriculum.

The standard echoes the duties on the governing bodies for maintained schools.[281]

There is extensive guidance about the meaning of the SMSC standard, what is required and examples of how to meet it, in the DfE's non-statutory: *The Independent School Standards: Guidance for independent schools, April 2019.*

---

[281] For SMSC see section 78(1), Education Act 2002, included in inspections under section 5(5B), Education Act 2005. For duties concerning political impartiality, see sections 406 and 407 Education Act 1996.

ISS paragraph 5

5. The standard about the spiritual, moral, social and cultural development of pupils at the school is met if the proprietor—

(a) actively promotes the fundamental British values of democracy, the rule of law, individual liberty, and mutual respect and tolerance of those with different faiths and beliefs;

(b) ensures that principles are actively promoted which—

(i) enable pupils to develop their self-knowledge, self-esteem and self-confidence;

(ii) enable pupils to distinguish right from wrong and to respect the civil and criminal law of England;

(iii) encourage pupils to accept responsibility for their behaviour, show initiative and understand how they can contribute positively to the lives of those living and working in the locality in which the school is situated and to society more widely;

(iv) enable pupils to acquire a broad general knowledge of and respect for public institutions and services in England;

(v) further tolerance and harmony between different cultural traditions by enabling pupils to acquire an appreciation of and respect for their own and other cultures;

(vi) encourage respect for other people, paying particular regard to the protected characteristics set out in the 2010 Act; and

(vii) encourage respect for democracy and support for participation in the democratic process, including respect for the basis on which the law is made and applied in England;

(c) precludes the promotion of partisan political views in the teaching of any subject in the school; and

(d) takes such steps as are reasonably practicable to ensure that where political issues are brought to the attention of pupils—

(i) while they are in attendance at the school,

(ii) while they are taking part in extra-curricular activities which are provided or organised by or on behalf of the school, or

(iii) in the promotion at the school, including through the distribution of promotional material, of extra-curricular activities taking place at the school or elsewhere,

they are offered a balanced presentation of opposing views[282].

Schools are not required to have a separate SMSC policy, although the process of creating, implementing, monitoring and reviewing a policy provide visibility to governors/proprietors and a useful accountability structure. The principles should be infused through all parts of the curriculum, policies and ethos of the school.

'Actively promote'

Active promotion of fundamental British values entails having a clear strategy for embedding them and proactively challenging opinions and behaviours to the contrary. That does not mean discouraging debate around the issues. See Chapter Seven above for more about fundamental British values.

The duty to promote respect for those of other faiths and beliefs, does not mean that schools must promote faiths and beliefs which conflict with their own. The DfE guidance does however encourage schools to use teaching resources from a wide variety of sources to help pupils understand and be familiar with a range of faiths.

Active promotion of democracy might entail, for example, not only studying the different forms it can take and debating the advantages and disadvantages but also enabling pupils to experience democracy in

---

[282] 5(d) is modelled on section 407 of the Education Act 1996 which applies to maintained schools.

school through a school council, mock elections, and votes which enable their voice to be heard.

<u>Self-knowledge, self-esteem and self-confidence</u> – ISS paragraph 5(b)(i)

> *The purpose of this paragraph of the standard is to ensure that schools actively help their pupils develop into self-assured, confident, happy, positive young people. Schools should help pupils to learn to articulate their feelings and justify them in both informal and formal settings and be given responsibility and trust to develop their confidence. Schools can develop the traits listed in the standard by celebrating achievement and encouraging pupils to have the confidence to undertake difficult tasks and have a wide range of experiences. Pupils should also be encouraged to question things which prevent them developing into confident adults – for example, lack of aspiration and unfair 21 discrimination. Pupils are likely to be helped in their development if adults and older pupils in the school act as appropriate role models for younger pupils.*

<u>Distinguishing right from wrong and respecting the civil and criminal law of England</u> – ISS paragraph 5(b)(ii)

Pupils should understand that while people may hold different views about what is right and wrong, in England we are all subject to the law. Where pupils are taught religious law, they should be made aware of the differences between the religious law and the law of the land and the implications of living in England.

<u>Accepting responsibility for behaviour, showing initiative and making a positive contribution to local and wider society</u> – ISS paragraph 5(b)(iii)

To meet this standard pupils must have contact with communities other than their own. The aim if for pupils to become responsible independent adults who can make a positive impact on the lives of other people. The DfE guidance suggests group activities which teach co-operation and initiative, giving pupils responsibilities within the school setting and enabling pupils to serve other people in the wider community.

<u>Acquiring broad general knowledge of and respect for public
institutions and services in England</u> – ISS paragraph 5(b)(iv)

The services and institutions mentioned in the DfE guidance include
Parliament, the police force, civil service, health, welfare and education
services. Pupils should understand and respect their importance to daily
life in a modern society, Educational visits and work experience can
enhance pupils' understanding.

<u>Furthering tolerance and harmony between cultural traditions
through appreciation and respect for pupils' own and other cultures</u> –
ISS paragraph 5(b)(v)

Culture is about the factors that are common to communities, such as
customs, traditions, music, dress and food. It is often interlinked with
faith. Pupils should be encouraged to regard all cultures with respect
and teaching should aim to prepare them to interact positively with
people of other cultures and faiths. The DfE guidance suggests doing
this both through the curriculum and links with other schools and
organisations. The curriculum may have a particular emphasis on the
culture and achievements of England but must allow for pupils to learn
about the achievements of other cultures in and outside Europe.

<u>Respecting others, paying particular regard to the protected
characteristics</u> – ISS paragraph 5(b)(vi)

The duty to promote respect for others, paying particular regard to the
protected characteristics, should be seen as having two parts, relating
firstly to respect of others generally and secondly to respect for those
with protected characteristics. Both must be met and, to do this, pupils
be informed of the protected characteristics in an age-appropriate way.
See also Chapter Seven and Chapter Eight about PSHE and RSE.

<u>Encouraging respect for democracy and the law-making process, and
participation in the democratic process</u> – ISS paragraph 5(b)(vii)

Closely connected to ISS 5(a), the DfE guidance makes three points.
This standard requires schools to

- *understand why democracy is perceived within the UK as the fairest
  form of political organisation*

- *understand why taking part in democracy is a good thing and*

- *understand why law-making on the basis of representation in Parliament is seen as better than alternatives.*

Preclusion of political indoctrination

<u>Preclusion of promotion of partisan political views in any subject</u> and <u>requirement for balanced presentation</u>– ISS paragraphs 5(c) and (d)

These standards aim to prevent political indoctrination of pupils through the curriculum. It echoes section 406(1)(b) Education Act 1996 which applies to maintained schools.

This standard is relevant also to after-school clubs and events and associated literature and promotional materials. The DfE guidance documents are both essential reading:

- *The Independent School Standards: Guidance for independent schools, April 2019*[283]
- *Political impartiality in schools*, February 2022.

There is no prohibition on the teaching, discussion and debate of political issues, indeed, the latest guidance, *Political impartiality in schools*, February 2022, sees this as an important part of preparing young people for life in modern Britain.

> *Teaching about political issues, the different views people have, and the ways pupils can engage in our democratic society is an essential part of a broad and balanced curriculum. It is an important way in which schools support pupils to become active citizens who can form their own views, whilst having an understanding and respect for legitimate differences of opinion.*[284]

---

[283] See para.s 3.20 – 3.29

[284] This encouragement is taken from the Secretary of State's introduction to *Political impartiality in schools*, February 2022. It is not a requirement.

However, pupils should not be actively encouraged to support particular viewpoints. The 2022 guidance explains the rationale:

Legal duties on political impartiality ultimately help schools command the confidence of our whole diverse and multi-opinioned society. Parents and carers want to be sure that their children can learn about political issues and begin to form their own independent opinions, without being influenced by the personal views of those teaching them. ...

... nothing in this guidance limits schools' freedom to teach about sensitive, challenging, and controversial political issues, as they consider appropriate and necessary.

Schools should also continue to reinforce important shared principles that underpin our society, whether that be upholding democratic rights or more generally promoting respect and tolerance. Understanding where views and opinions go further than this and where the legal duties on political impartiality may be relevant, is an important part of doing this effectively.

The dedicated guidance on *Political impartiality in schools*, gives advice about the meaning of 'political', how to choose resources, and also provides practical guidance in the context of a wide range of scenarios and topics.

There are two helpful cases. The case of <u>Dimmock v Secretary of State for Education and Skills</u> [2007] EWHC 2288 (Admin) concerned the distribution to secondary schools by the Secretary of State for Education of a film about global warming, 'An inconvenient truth' by ex-Vice President, Al Gore. The judgment confirmed:

- 'Political' is not limited to party political. The film was agreed to be political as it promoted a vision which would be used to influence a range of political policies.

- 'Partisan' meant one-sided. Detailed criteria are provided in the guidance.[285]

- 'Balanced presentation' means 'fair and dispassionate'. It may not mean 'equal air time'. Building on this, the guidance for schools now confirms that they do not need to take a mechanistic approach to balance and that balance can be achieved over a period of time.[286] Schools also do not need to present misinformation to achieve balance. [287]

Burton J held that a school does not necessarily 'irremediably' promote materials simply by using them. What amounted to 'promotion' would depend largely on the context and how they were used.

> *The statute cannot possibly mean that s406 is breached whenever a partisan political film is shown to pupils in school time. ... ... What is forbidden by the statute is, as the side heading makes clear, "political indoctrination".*

> *If a teacher uses the platform of a classroom to promote partisan political views in the teaching of any subject, then that would offend against the statute.*

> *If on the other hand a teacher, in the course of a school day and as part of the syllabus, presents to his pupils, no doubt with the appropriate setting and <u>with proper tuition and debate</u>, a film or document which itself promotes in a partisan way some political view that cannot possibly in my judgment be the mischief against which the statute was intended to protect pupils. It would not only lead to bland education, but to education which did not give the opportunity to pupils to learn about views with which they might, vehemently or otherwise, either agree or disagree.*

---

[285] Para. 3.21 *The Independent School Standards: Guidance for independent schools, April 2019*

[286] Para. 3.26 of *The Independent School Standards Guidance for independent schools, April 2019.*

[287] Scenario A in *Political impartiality in schools, 2022.*

In the particular case, following changes consequent on an earlier hearing, the film was to be distributed for use alongside a guidance note and information pack which would support teachers to contexualise the themes of the film through questions to stimulate discussion and help pupils examine the evidence critically. The court approved the note which explained the legal requirement to avoid promotion of partisan political views, that there were climate-change sceptics but where the balance of scientific views lay, and added *'the High Court has made clear the law does not require teaching staff to adopt a position of neutrality between views which accord with the great majority of scientific opinion and those which do not'.*

More recently, <u>R (on the application of A) v Hampshire CC</u> [2022] EWHC 49 a claimant challenged the lawfulness of local authority advice to schools about how to support transgender pupils It was confirmed that merely explaining a protected characteristic was lawful: *'there is no "indoctrination' involved in explaining the meaning of 'intersex/transgender/agender, etc" or in teaching that respect Is owed to all individuals regardless of gender issues.*

<u>Political activity by pupils</u>

The DfE has confirmed:

> *Although not explicitly prohibited in the Independent Schools Standards, it is unlikely it would ever be appropriate for pupils of this age to engage in political activity at any school. Given their developmental stage, this would typically be seen as a school promoting partisan political views, in breach of legal duties which apply to all schools.*[288]

---

[288] *Political impartiality in schools, 2022.*

Visiting speakers

Exposure of pupils to a range of views is positive and it is permissible for pupils to hear from representatives of political parties and campaigning organisations. The DfE guidance, *Political impartiality in schools 2022,* contains advice about working with and choosing external agencies. Where it is intended to use external agencies or speakers, schools are advised to draw up and implement a clear policy about the school's approach.

Visiting speaker policy, suggested contents:

- how speakers are chosen and by whom

- who must be informed

- records to be kept

- how a balance of opposing views is to be achieved and the timeframe for this

- how speakers will be vetted and by whom

- that the content of presentations should be agree beforehand, and how this is to be achieved

- the options for how the school will respond to events that 'go wrong', such as the following, and who will manage that

    o   immediate challenge

    o   arranging alternative speaker with opposing views for a later date

    o   presenting opposing views through class teaching

    o   communications to the school community. [289]

---

[289] Based on para.s 327 – 329, *The Independent School Standards Guidance for independent schools, April 2019.*

Conclusion

The SMSC standard is one that is rarely failed alone. A failure to promote the relevant principles is likely to find echoes in in other standards such as those relating to the curriculum, the teaching, pupil behaviour, safeguarding and leadership and management.

CHAPTER ELEVEN

THE SAFEGUARDING STANDARD – ISS PART 3

Overview

A full explanation of safeguarding duties of schools, with practical guidance and case studies, could fill a book on its own. For lawyers new to the area this book can only hope to summarise key points and signpost further reading.

In contrast to the wide latitude given to independent schools compared to state schools in relation to their educational provision, the expectations for safeguarding pupils are tightly defined and are the same for independent and state schools.[290] 'Safeguarding' goes much wider than 'child protection', which tends to be used to refer to post-event responses to harm. The overarching safeguarding principle is that schools should act in the best interests of their pupils.[291]

> *Safeguarding and promoting the welfare of children is everyone's responsibility. Everyone who comes into contact with children and their families has a role to play. In order to fulfil this responsibility effectively, all practitioners should make sure their approach is child-centred. This means that they should consider, at all times, what is in the best interests of the child.*[292]

> *This means involving everyone in the school … and ensuring that safeguarding and child protection are at the forefront and underpin all relevant aspects of process and policy development. Ultimately, all*

---

[290] The legal roots differ but the guidance is the same.

[291] Echo-ing the paramountcy principle of section one of the Children Act 1989. See also the UN CRC Art 3.

[292] Para.2 KCSIE 2022.

systems, processes and policies should operate with the best interests of the child at their heart.[293]

All practitioners should follow the principles of the Children Acts 1989 and 2004 – that state that the welfare of children is paramount ...[294]

While legal advisors will always want to ground their advice on a thorough understanding of the distinction between what is required or advisable, the line between the two is often blurred when it comes to safeguarding. A school is as likely to fail an inspection for not paying sufficient regard to guidance without good reason as it is for not fulfilling a legal requirement. So this is an unusual situation where it may not necessarily benefit schools to take an overly legalistic view if that were to result in giving the impression that the school takes a minimalistic approach to the safety of pupils. The standards require leadership and management to 'actively promote the well-being of pupils' and this may entail taking a broad and generous view of their duties.[295]

The starting place for reading into safeguarding requirements for schools is the statutory guidance for schools: *Keeping children safe in education* (KCSIE). Definitions of safeguarding are provided at paragraph 4. Further guidance, *Working together to safeguard children* (WT) describes how the safeguarding arrangements for schools and other organisations fit into the wider safeguarding system alongside the duties of statutory agencies such as LAs, the police, probation service, health and others.

Information published by the relevant inspectorates is also vital reading for those advising schools, such as 8

- Ofsted's: Inspecting safeguarding in early years, education and skills settings: Guidance for Ofsted inspectors to use when

---

[293] Para. 94 KCSIE 2022.

[294] Para. 11, p.9 of WT 2018.

[295] ISS 34(1)(c).

inspecting safeguarding under the education inspection framework.[296]

ISS paragraph 7

7. The standard in this paragraph is met if the proprietor ensures that—

(a) arrangements are made to safeguard and promote the welfare of pupils at the school; and

(b) such arrangements have regard to any guidance issued by the Secretary of State

Preliminary points of interpretation

Arrangements to safeguard and promote welfare

The safeguarding standard requires schools to put in place systems and processes as described in KCSIE and WT (see later). Having appropriate arrangements in place, as required, which are operated by well-trained people in the context of an institutional culture which supports good safeguarding practice, helps schools to pick up matters affecting the welfare of pupils both in and outside school and to prevent safeguarding issues arising in school. When issues do arise, it should ensure schools respond to them immediately, effectively and transparently in partnership with external agencies.

There is a school of thought that the mere occurrence of any safeguarding incident in school shows that arrangements are either not in place or not effective, and that this has automatic implications for the school's next inspection. This view arguably ignores the fact KCSIE itself anticipates that incidents will happen and gives guidance on processes to ensure schools respond effectively when they do (such as those in parts four and five of KCSIE). These are a central part of the

---

[296] https://www.gov.uk/government/publications/inspecting-safeguarding-in-early-years-education-and-skills

'arrangements'. If a need to follow KCSIE's procedures, such as external reporting, were to be evidence of failure to meet the safeguarding standard, this could risk creating perverse incentives for schools to conceal abuse. It could also reduce the effectiveness of the required post-incident process of reflection and learning lessons.[297] The view also does not address the difference between a direct requirement to 'safeguard and promote welfare' and a once-removed requirement to 'make arrangements to safeguard and promote welfare'.[298]

It should not, therefore, be assumed that the occurrence of a safeguarding incident in a school is evidence *per se* of a failure to have regard to KCSIE. In any event, whether or not a school was following the guidance at the time of an incident, any deficiencies may have been put right before the next inspection. On this view, the impact of an event on a school's next inspection report is not automatic but a matter of judgment for the inspection team in the context of all the evidence at that time. [299]

Have regard to …

The DfE guidance[300] explains:

> *4.14 The phrase 'have regard to' does not mean that the statutory guidance must always be followed to the letter but any departure from the requirements set out in the documents must be considered and based on appropriate reasons, and proprietors will therefore want to <u>record</u> the justification behind any departure.[301]*

---

[297] Para. 419 — 420, KCSIE 2022.

[298] Compare the duties on others under the Children Act 1989, such as the LA in section 17, a non-parent with care of a child (section 3(5)) or the police in section 46(9)(b), Children Act 2004 section 11, section 175 Education Act 2002.

[299] See Part H, para. 23 et seq. of *The IICSA Residential Schools Investigation Report, March 2022*, for a discussion of 'Inspection as a snapshot'.

[300] *The Independent School Standards: Guidance for independent schools, April 2019.*

[301] For cases about the meaning of a duty to have regard to guidance, and how it may apply to guidance which has been through different processes, see:

- <u>W v Blaenau Gwent</u> [2003] EWHC 2880, [2004] ELR 152

Putting this together with the overarching principle in KCSIE that schools prioritise the welfare of the pupils, it would be expected that any departure from guidance would be based on the best interests of the pupils.

... any guidance

The safeguarding standard is deceptively short but the requirement for arrangements to have regard to 'any guidance' issued by the Secretary of State in effect incorporates hundreds of pages of guidance.

The DfE's approach in practice is that 'any guidance' refers specifically to:

- *Keeping children safe in education 2022* (KCSIE) (173 pages)

- *Working together to safeguard children 2018* (WT) (116 pages)[302]

and also

- Revised *Prevent Duty guidance: for England and Wales* 2021

- *The Prevent Duty: Departmental advice for schools and childminders* (non-statutory).[303]

KCSIE also incorporates further statutory guidance such as

- *Relationships education, relationships and sex education (RSE), and health education – September 2021*

- R (Khatun) v Newham London Borough Council [2005] QB 37

- Munjaz v Mersey NHS Trust [2005] UKHL 58, [2006] 2 AC 148.

- R (London Oratory School Governors) v Schools Adjudicator [2015] EWHC 1012 (Admin)

[302] A companion document to WT sets out relevant legislation: Working Together to Safeguard Children Statutory framework: legislation relevant to safeguarding and promoting the welfare of children July 2018.

[303] See para.s 4.12 and 4.14 of the departmental advice: *Independent School Standards: Guidance for independent schools, April 2019.*

- *Disqualification under the Childcare Act* 2006.

KCSIE also signposts copious quantities of essential non-statutory advice. Of these, the following are the most crucial as a starting point:[304]

- *What to do if you're worried a child is being abused – advice for practitioners* – 2015

- *Information sharing Advice for practitioners providing safeguarding services to children, young people, parents and carers* – July 2018

- *When to call the police: guidance for schools and Colleges* – by the National Police Chiefs Council (NPCC) – 2020.

From September 2021, it is advisable to also read the following for an up to date understanding of the context in which schools are operating and current policy priorities:

- Ofsted Review of sexual abuse in schools and colleges (10 June 2021)

- Relevant IICSA publications.

In terms of practical advice to lawyers, it can be helpful to download and keep an archive of the key guidance and advice to help with tracing changes as they are updated over time and with ascertaining what was in force at any particular time when problems come to light in later years.

<u>Cross-over with the risk assessment standard</u>

The safeguarding standard often works in conjunction with the risk assessment standard in ISS paragraph 16, for which see later.

16. …

---

[304] Note that *Sexual Violence and Sexual Harassment Between Children in Schools and Colleges* 2021 has been withdrawn from September 2022, and relevant information incorporated into KCSIE.

(a) the welfare of pupils at the school is safeguarded and promoted by the drawing up and effective implementation of a written risk assessment policy; and

(b) appropriate action is taken to reduce risks that are identified.

Risk assessment is a methodical means by which schools can tailor KCSIE-based safeguarding arrangements to reflect their own circumstances and identify any exceptional reason to depart from the guidance or the need to put in place any additional measures beyond KCSIE.

Cross-over with the NMS for boarding

The safeguarding standard also works with the NMS for boarding. See section about boarding towards the end of this chapter.

KCSIE and WT

Statutory status of KCSIE and WT

KCSIE explains:

> *This is statutory guidance from the Department for Education ('the Department') issued under ... the Education (Independent School Standards) Regulations 2014,...*
>
> *Schools and colleges in England must have regard to it when carrying out their duties to safeguard and promote the welfare of children. For the purposes of this guidance children includes everyone under the age of 18.*

WT contains a similar assertion.

While the statutory status of KCSIE and WT has not been questioned in litigation, it is not clear that the statutory chain is as complete as for some other statutory guidance.[305] For example, while the Secretary of

---

[305] For comparison, in each of the cases referenced above about the meaning of the requirement to 'have regard', the relevant Secretary of State had a clear power to issue the relevant guidance or code of practice in primary legislation. See also, for

State is empowered to set standards by regulations (which must be laid before parliament), the power to issue a sub-document, such as KCSIE, is not clear in either the primary or secondary legislation. No guidance is named in the *Education (Independent School Standards) Regulations 2014* and the departmental advice which names the relevant guidance is not binding. Major changes to KCSIE are subject to public consultation although it is not clear whether it is laid before parliament or what level of scrutiny it receives. WT also, for example, asserts confusingly that it 'applies in its entirety to <u>all</u> schools', page 7, although large parts are without obvious application to schools. However, so far the arrangement works in practice and provides the Secretary of State flexibility to adapt KCSIE in response to emerging issues and as the understanding of safeguarding grows.

<u>'Must' and 'should'</u>

KCSIE explains:

> *We use the terms "must" and "should" throughout the guidance. We use the term "must" when the person in question is legally required to do something and "should" when the advice set out should be followed unless there is good reason not to.*

WT echoes:

> *This document should be complied with unless exceptional circumstances arise.*

The guidance also provides advice which is informative and not directive, using phrases such as 'will want to' and 'need to'.

'Should' is normally best treated as synonymous with 'must' when advising schools. The DfE's advice on the standards advises that '*any departure from the requirements set out in the documents must be considered and based on appropriate reasons, and proprietors will therefore want to record the justification behind any departure*'.

---

comparison, the clearer statutory underpinning of the EYFS. The Childcare Act 2006 grants a power to make regulations which can refer to 'a document' and underlying regulations, name the document and give it force.

There are certain 'should' duties where it is almost impossible to envisage a 'good reason' to depart from the guidance. One such is the duty to report allegations of abuse of trust externally.

Working together

The value of WT for schools is largely in the information about the roles and duties of other agencies, particularly the LA, and what to expect after a referral to children's social care or the LADO.

LA duties – Children's services/children's social care

While parents and carers are the primary carers for children, local authorities have specific duties to safeguard and promote the welfare of all children in their area. The Children Acts of 1989 and 2004 set out specific duties:

- section 17 of the Children Act 1989 puts a duty on the local authority to provide services to children in need in their area, regardless of where they are found

- section 47 of the Children Act 1989 requires local authorities to undertake enquiries if they believe a child has suffered or is likely to suffer significant harm.[306]

Definition of 'harm'

'Harm' is defined in section 105 of the Children Act 1989, referring back to section 31(9) and 31(10):

(9) In this section—

- ...

- *"harm" means ill-treatment or the impairment of health or development including, for example, impairment suffered from seeing or hearing the ill-treatment of another;*

---

[306] Introduction to WT.

- *"development"* means physical, intellectual, emotional, social or behavioural development;

- *"health"* means physical or mental health; and

- *"ill-treatment"* includes sexual abuse and forms of ill-treatment which are not physical.

(10) Where the question of whether harm suffered by a child is significant turns on the child's health or development, his health or development shall be compared with that which could reasonably be expected of a similar child.

The LADO(s)

Local authorities must designate a particular officer or team of officers to deal with allegations against people who work with children, usually referred to as the 'LADO' or 'DO'.[307] The LADO does not investigate the allegations themselves but involves the police or children's social care. Where the LADO has reasonable cause to suspect that a child Is suffering, or is likely to suffer significant harm, they must call a multi-strategy meeting. [308]

Allegations must be passed to the LADO(s) without delay. The LADO(s) is a source of advice and guidance on dealing with allegations. While there is no specific legal duty on schools to follow or have regard to the advice of the LADO in those terms, an omission to do so could be seen as a failure to co-operate with statutory processes in accordance with duties set out in KCSIE and WT.

Local safeguarding partners (LSP/LSCP)[309]

The safeguarding partners for a local authority area are:

- the local authority

---

[307] WT p. 60, para 5.

[308] See para. 12 of Part E of *The IICSA Residential Schools Investigation Report, March 2022* , for more on the role of the LADO.

[309] LSCP: local safeguarding children partners. Both abbreviations are common.

- Integrated Care Systems (previously known as clinical commissioning groups) for an area any part of which falls within the LA area[310]

- the chief officer of police for a police area any part of which falls within the LA area.

They are required to make arrangements to work together with each other and with 'relevant agencies' to safeguard and promote the welfare of local children including identifying and responding to their needs. [311] Independent schools are relevant agencies.[312] As such they are under a legally enforceable duty to act in accordance with arrangements published by the safeguarding partners.[313] The system is described in WT.

Organisational safeguarding duties

An overarching structure for organisational safeguarding requirements is provided in a bulleted list in paragraph 3 of chapter two of WT. It is worth thinking the list through in the context of school clients. [314]

> *... organisations and agencies should have in place arrangements that reflect the importance of safeguarding and promoting the welfare of children, including:*
>
> - *a clear line of accountability for the ... provision of services designed to safeguard and promote the welfare of children*

---

[310] See Health and Care Act 2022.

[311] Section 16E of the Children Act 2004 as inserted by the Children and Social Work Act 2017 and para. 1 of WT. See section 16E(1) and (3) for 'relevant agencies'.

[312] Para. 7 of the Schedule to the Children Safeguarding Practice Review and Relevant Agency (England) Regulations 2018.

[313] Section 16G(2),(4)-(6).

[314] The list is intended for section 11 organisations. Although independent schools are not section 11 institutions, WT asserts that the whole document applies to all schools – para.4, p.7 WT.

- *a senior board level lead with the required knowledge, skills and expertise or sufficiently qualified and experienced to take leadership responsibility for the organisation's ... safeguarding arrangements*

- *a <u>culture of listening to children and taking account of their wishes and feelings</u>, both in individual decisions and the development of services*

- *clear whistleblowing procedures, which reflect the principles in Sir Robert Francis' Freedom to Speak Up Review and are suitably referenced in staff training and codes of conduct, and <u>a culture that enables issues about safeguarding and promoting the welfare of children to be addressed</u>*

- *clear escalation policies for staff to follow when their child safeguarding concerns are not being addressed within their organisation or by other agencies*

- *arrangements which set out clearly the processes for sharing information, with other practitioners and with safeguarding partners*

- *a designated practitioner ... for child safeguarding. Their role is to support other practitioners in their organisations and agencies to recognise the needs of children, including protection from possible abuse or neglect. Designated practitioner roles should always be explicitly defined in job descriptions. Practitioners should be given sufficient time, funding, supervision and support to fulfil their child welfare and safeguarding responsibilities effectively*

- *safe recruitment practices and ongoing safe working practices for individuals whom the organisation or agency permit to work regularly with children, including policies on when to obtain a criminal record check*

- *appropriate supervision and support for staff, including undertaking safeguarding training*

- *creating <u>a culture of safety, equality and protection</u> within the services they provide*

In addition:

- *employers are responsible for ensuring that their staff are competent to carry out their responsibilities for safeguarding and promoting the welfare of children and creating an environment where staff feel able to raise concerns and feel supported in their safeguarding role staff should be given a mandatory induction, which includes familiarisation with child protection responsibilities and the procedures to be followed if anyone has any concerns about a child's safety or welfare*

- *all practitioners should have regular reviews of their own practice to ensure they have knowledge, skills and expertise that improve over time*

KCSIE

Coming to KCSIE from scratch, there is no substitute for reading and re-reading it in full, noting not only the advice but the musts/shoulds (perhaps colour coding these) and timescales for action.

<u>Scope of the requirements of KCSIE</u>

The broad range of matters which school safeguarding arrangements should cover are set out in part two of KCSIE along with considerable guidance about each:

- The legal context: Human Rights Act, Equality Act 2010

- A whole school approach to safeguarding under board level leadership

- Safeguarding policies and procedures, including

    o A safeguarding policy

    o A pupil behaviour/anti-bullying policy

- A staff code of conduct

- Arrangements for responding to children missing education

- Record keeping systems for child protection files

- Safer recruitment processes

- Emergency contact numbers for pupils (more than one where reasonably possible)

- The appointment of a designated safeguarding lead (DSL) and any deputies needed

- Participation in multi-agency working

- Information sharing and the impact of the Data Protection Act

- Staff training

- Opportunities to teach pupils to stay safe

- Online safety, including policy, filters, monitoring and review

- What staff should do if they have a concern about another member of staff, covering both allegations and low-level concerns

- Arrangements for dealing with child on child abuse

- For boarding schools and residential special schools, implementation of the NMS for boarding or NMS for residential special schools

- Use of reasonable force

- Use of school premises for non-school activities

- Arrangements for children potentially at greater risk of harm

Key roles in KCSIE

<u>The designated safeguarding lead (DSL)</u>

Every school should (read as 'must' for compliance purposes) designate a named senior member of staff from the leadership team to take lead responsibility for safeguarding and child protection.[315] The role must be explicitly part of their job description and should also cover on-line safety. They must have sufficient status, authority, training and resource (especially time) to carry out the role.[316] Imagine, for example, a situation where staff have to be rapidly redeployed or urgent changes made to a timetable to enable a member of staff to liaise with social services, or where a person has to be asked to leave the premises. The DSL should have the status or levers to ensure the safety of children within the school's procedures.

In smaller schools the DSL is commonly the head or deputy head. In schools colloquially known as 'proprietorial schools', where the school has a sole proprietor or is a family enterprise, the DSL must be able to discharge the role with sufficient independence particularly in relation to any allegations involving the proprietor or members of the proprietor's family.[317]

There must be sufficient cover for the role at all times so the DSL typically has one or more deputies (DDSLs) who must be trained to the same level as the DSL.[318]

New for 2022

- KCSIE confirms it is not appropriate for the proprietor to be the DSL.[319]

---

[315] Para. 10 KCSIE 2022 and Annex C.

[316] Para. 103 and Annex C, KCSIE 2022.

[317] Footnote 29, KCSIE 2022.

[318] Annex C, KCSIE.

[319] Para. 102 KCSIE 2022. When this was first mentioned by IICSA it referred specifically to a 'sole proprietor' – para. 16 of Part K of the IICSA residential schools report.

- DSLs should be aware of the requirement for children ('juveniles' in the language of the criminal law) to have an 'appropriate adult' in the context of detention, treatment and questioning of suspects by police, including searches and strip searches.[320] Detailed advice about the lawful processes around police strip searches, including school duties in relation to issues such as after-care, record-keeping and informing parents, can be found in *Searching, Screening and Confiscation Advice for schools July 2022.* [321]

The safeguarding governor

Every institution should have a 'board level lead' to champion safeguarding at board level[322] although the legal responsibility is shared by the whole board.

Concerns have been expressed about the efficacy of safeguarding in schools without a governing body to challenge safeguarding practice and hold the executive to account, such as 'proprietorial schools' (see above).[323] It is good practice for such schools to arrange regular (at least annual) external reviews of their safeguarding policy and practices. One way this is commonly approached to ensure that safeguarding arrangements are robust at all times is through appointment of an advisory board to provide guidance, scrutiny and challenge to the proprietor.

Until 2022, safeguarding training for governors and even for the safeguarding governor was not prescribed by the DfE, although

---

[320] See PACE Code C 2019. The Code is made under the Police and Criminal Evidence Act 1984. The role of the appropriate adult is to safeguard the rights and welfare of juveniles. They are expected, among other things, to support and advise the young person and observe whether the police are acting properly to respect their rights and inform a senior office if they are not.

[321] Takes effect September 2022.

[322] Para. 80 and p. 59, WT 2018.

[323] See evidence to IICSA from the inspectorates, such as: https://www.iicsa.org.uk/key-documents/24181/view/public-hearing-transcript-fri-27-november.pdf p. 67.

governors were expected to ensure that they had the skills and knowledge needed for their work. While many governing bodies undertook regular training together on a voluntary basis, and some governors bring safeguarding expertise from their day jobs, IICSA expressed concern that there were no formal training requirements for governors given their responsibility to oversee safeguarding in their schools.[324] **New** for September 2022, KCSIE requires governors to receive safeguarding training.[325] This text would add that the training for the safeguarding governor will need to equip them for their particular role.

Formulating the school's safeguarding arrangements

A written safeguarding policy

A written policy is considered the bedrock of good practice.[326] The purpose of a school's safeguarding policy is to summarise its approach to key issues so that members of the school community (staff, a supply teacher who is perhaps only around for a day or two, a concerned parent or member of the public, a pupil) have a ready reference point and are enabled to take action quickly if necessary. Some potential readers will not be trained in safeguarding or familiar with KCSIE. The policy therefore needs to be simple, clear and focused, in accessible language and format, and to cover all the necessary ground whilst shaping it to the provision of the particular school. It is best to avoid operational detail and direct the reader to further information, if necessary. It is possible for a school to be judged not to meet the safeguarding standard on the basis of an inadequate safeguarding policy alone, although that is more commonly an evaluation of the combined effectiveness of policy and practice and school culture.

---

[324] The IICSA Residential Schools Investigation Report, March 2022, para. 23 on page 182.

[325] See para.s 81-82, KCSIE 2022 and the section below on Safeguarding Policy Content, under Training.

[326] See : para. 4.5 of *The Independent School Standards: Guidance for independent schools, April 2019* and para. 97, KCSIE 2022.

Safeguarding policy content

KCSIE sets out non-exhaustive contents for policies in various places, such as paragraphs 98, 156 and 198. Some inspectorates publish a checklist used by inspectors for reviewing policies with the caveat that it is a starting point only given that policies must always be tailored to the circumstances of each school. If a checklist is not available on the inspectorate open website it is worth checking with the client school whether they have access.

The following are suggested generic content for a school safeguarding policy:

Contact details – The names and contact details of key people or agencies:

- the school's designated safeguarding lead for the school (and early years provision, where relevant), any DDSLs[327]

- the LADO

- the local children's social care team

- the chair of governors

- the safeguarding governor

Principles – The school's commitment to keeping all pupils safe, to listening to children and to acting in their best interests. The school's commitment to anti-discriminatory practice.

The guidance which the school is following – The policy should currently be based on KCSIE 2022, WT 2018 (2022) and Prevent 2021.

References to the further guidance (see above).

Local arrangements – The name of the local safeguarding children partnership for the area in which the school is situated.

---

[327] It is good practice to include the DSL's job title to demonstrate that they have the required seniority for the role.

A statement that the school follows the local procedures, including the local criteria for action and protocols for assessments, and participates in local multi-agency working.

<u>Types and signs of abuse and neglect</u> – Types of abuse should be named in line with the definitions in KCSIE: physical, emotional, sexual abuse and neglect. Suggestions of signs of these can be found in: *What to do if you're worried a child is being abused Advice for practitioners March 2015.*[328]

There should be sufficient consideration of the list of specific safeguarding issues listed in Annex B of KCSIE – typically listing them and/or signposting KCSIE for further detail. Serious violence should be included where relevant to the school.

<u>Vulnerable groups</u> – Recognition that some pupils are more vulnerable to abuse, such as children who need a social worker, children missing education, looked after children, care leavers, those with SEND.[329] In the case of pupils with SEND, there can be additional barriers to communication and recognising abuse such as assumptions that indicators of possible abuse (mood, behaviour, injury) relate to the child's condition. These pupils may be more vulnerable to child-on-child abuse and bullying.[330]

Recognition that mental health issues can be an indicator of abuse, neglect or exploitation.

The safeguarding or other policy should provide that, if staff have a mental health concern about a child that is also a safeguarding concern, immediate action should be taken, following the procedures in the safeguarding policy and speaking to the DSL.[331]

---

[328] https://assets.publishing.service.gov.uk/government/uploads/system/uploads/attachment_data/file/419604/What_to_do_if_you_re_worried_a_child_is_being_abused.pdf .

[329] Para. 169 et seq of KCSIE 2022.

[330] For SEND guidance see KCSIE para.s 198 – 201.

[331] KCSIE para.s 45 – 47.

New for 2022, KCSIE states that LGBT is not itself a risk factor for abuse although children can be targeted by others but risks can be compounded when children who are LGBT lack a trusted adult. Schools are asked to endeavour to reduce the additional barriers faced and provide a safe space to speak and share concerns with members of staff.[332]

<u>Teaching pupils to stay safe</u> – Confirmation that the school teaches children to stay safe, including online, referencing when and how that is done, for example, through PSHE and RSE lessons.

<u>Arrangements for listening to children</u> – The policy should confirm that the school recognises the importance of hearing the voice of the child and reference their arrangements for listening to children.

<u>Additional arrangements for safeguarding disabled pupils</u>, where relevant – Signpost any additional policies for issues such as intimate care and communication

<u>Child-on-child abuse</u> – This section should describe a whole school approach to child-on-child abuse and include:[333]

- Reference to part five of KCSIE. (The additional guidance: *Sexual Violence and Sexual Harassment between children in schools and colleges* has been withdrawn from 30 August 2022.)

- Recognition that children can abuse and that this can happen in and outside school or online

- Indicators and signs of peer abuse and how to respond (all concerns or disclosures to be relayed to the DSL)

- Procedures to minimise the risk of child-on-child abuse

- The systems in place for children to confidently report abuse, knowing their concerns will be treated seriously

---

[332] KCSIE para. 202 – 204.

[333] KCSIE para.s 32-35, and 156.

- How allegations of child-on-child abuse will be recorded, investigated and dealt with

- Clear processes for supporting victims, perpetrators and any other children affected by child-on-child abuse

- Recognition that even if there are no reported cases of child-on-child abuse, such abuse may still be taking place and is simply not being reported

- A statement which makes clear there should be a zero-tolerance approach to abuse, and it should never be passed off as "banter", "just having a laugh", "part of growing up" or "boys being boys" as this can lead to a culture of unacceptable behaviours and an unsafe environment for children

- Recognition that it is more likely that girls will be victims and boys perpetrators, but that all child-on-child abuse is unacceptable and will be taken seriously; evidence shows pupils with SEND pupils are also at greater risk of child-on-child abuse[334]

- The different forms child-on-child abuse can take, such as: bullying (including cyberbullying, prejudice-based and discriminatory bullying); abuse in intimate personal relationships between peers (also known as teenage relationship abuse); physical abuse which can include hitting, kicking, shaking, biting, hair pulling, or otherwise causing physical harm; sexual violence and sexual harassment; causing someone to engage in sexual activity without consent, such as forcing someone to strip, touch themselves sexually, or to engage in sexual activity with a third party; up-skirting (which is a criminal offence), and initiation/hazing type violence and rituals

- The school's response to consensual and non-consensual sharing of nude and semi-nude images and/or videos (also known as

---

[334] Para. 448 KCSIE 2022.

sexting or youth produced sexual imagery), should be outlined, referencing guidance such as: *Searching Screening and Confiscation Advice for schools* and *Sharing nudes and semi-nudes: advice for education settings working with children and young people* (UKCIS Education Group)

- For boarding schools, the policy should reflect the unique nature of boarding accommodation and the risks associated with children sharing overnight accommodation

<u>Governance and review</u> – Arrangements for oversight and challenge of safeguarding policy and practice should be described, bearing in mind the need for creative solutions where there is no governing body (see above).

A statement that the efficacy of the policy and arrangements are reviewed at least annually and updated to reflect changes to national guidance and lessons learned in school.[335]

<u>Training</u> – The arrangements for safeguarding training:

- Staff induction – All staff must read and understand part one (or Annex A) of KCSIE as determined by the governing body (indicate which, or which groups, read which part or the criteria for differentiating). Annex B is read by school leaders and those who work directly with children. The following are explained and provided to staff: the safeguarding policy (including procedures to deal with child-on-child abuse), the role and identity of the DSL and DDSLs, the staff code of conduct, the pupil behaviour and anti-bullying policy/policies (which should include measures to prevent bullying, including cyberbullying, prejudice-based and discriminatory bullying), the school's safeguarding response to children missing education, the school policy on online safety (if separate), part one of KCSIE and/or Annex A/B.

Arrangements to check understanding.[336]

---

[335] KCSIE 2022, para. 98.

- Staff ongoing regular updates – at least annual and with informal updates, in line with LSP advice, covering topics such as: recognising abuse, the importance of vigilance and professional curiosity, the importance of building trusted-relationships which facilitate communication, how to receive a disclosure of abuse, exploitation, neglect and what to do next, reassuring the pupil that they are being taken seriously, will be supported, record keeping, internal processes, awareness of the process for making referrals to children's social care, the role of staff in the local early help process, Prevent training – in effect drip-feeding and a continual cycle of reflection and development.

- DSL and DDSLs – DSL training, including inter-agency working, local protocols and thresholds, participation on child protection conferences, supporting children in need, promoting a culture of listening to children, record keeping, Prevent, identifying children at risk of radicalisation and any local issues – 2 yearly plus informal updates

- Others – how the school trains others. This is a matter for the discretion of the school. Regular volunteers and contractors for example should at least know the identity of the DSL, how and when to contact them and understand expectations of their own behaviour

- **New** for 2022 – Governor training – Induction training, regularly updated, to equip them to provide strategic challenge to test and assure themselves that the safeguarding policies and procedures are effective and strategic and support a robust whole school approach to safeguarding (including online). Also, to cover their obligations under the HRA, EqA (and PSED for public authorities).[337] In principle, this applies to governors, trustees and proprietors.

---

[336] See for example, KCSIE para. 13 and p. 5 re checking understanding.

[337] KCSIE para. 81-82.

<u>Staff code of conduct</u> – This can be part of the safeguarding policy or sign-posted elsewhere. See section below.

<u>Reporting procedures</u> – Clear guidance on how to respond to and report concerns about a child's welfare, about a child in need or at risk, in line with KCSIE

Essentially:

- concerns about a **child in need** must be acted on immediately, reported to the DSL who will assess the need for and arrange for pastoral or other in-school support, 'early help' or onwards referral to children's social care, in accordance with local protocols, as appropriate

- concerns about a **child at risk** must be reported at once to the DSL for immediate onwards referrals to children's social care and the police if a crime has been committed.

It must be clear that anyone can make a referral if necessary and that parental consent is not required for referrals to statutory agencies, particularly where to do so would put the child at risk of harm.

<u>Reporting procedures for allegations against staff, including the Head and the DSL, supply staff, volunteers and contractors</u> – A statement that the school follows the procedures in part four of KCSIE 2022.

A statement of the 'harm threshold' (see KCSIE 2022, paragraph 355).

Concerns and allegations which meet the harm threshold about:

- Staff, the DSL, supply staff, volunteers and contractors – should be referred to the head and thence to the LADO

- The head – should be referred to the chair and from there to the LADO, without informing the head at that stage

- A sole proprietor – should be referred direct to the LADO

- Where there is a conflict of interest in reporting a matter to a head, it should be reported to the LADO direct

- Where an allegation relates to supply staff, the agency should be fully involved.

Confirmation that the school would not conduct a full investigation before making the referral but gather only the basic details which the LADO will require.[338]

Referrals – Acknowledgement of the duty to refer to the DBS and duty to consider referring to the TRA in appropriate cases. [339]

Low-level concerns – A statement of how the school deals with concerns about staff behaviour which do not meet the harm test ('low level concerns') including:

- any deviations from the staff code of conduct

- internal reporting procedures such as those above, including for self-referral

- responsive, sensitive and proportionate handling of concerns raised

- keeping records and reviewing them periodically for patterns of behaviour or institutional cultural issues which may need to be addressed

- keeping records of decisions.[340]

Recruitment procedures – A statement that the school uses safer recruitment procedures in line with KCSIE part three, and either a summary or a signpost to another document.

Internet safety – This can be part of the overarching safeguarding policy or signposted separately.

---

[338] Para. 362, KCSIE 2022.

[339] See para. 346 – 350, KCSIE 2022 for detail.

[340] See para.s 423 – 444 KCSIE 2022.

<u>Additional matters for boarding schools</u> – The NMS 2022 specify requirements for the coverage boarding school safeguarding policies:

- the school's policy on sexual relationships between children (and the Importance of boarders understanding the policy)

- additional risks in boarding relating to child-on-child abuse

- the approach to protecting children where there is a significant gender imbalance in the school

- the approach to harmful online content and how boarders' devices are managed in terms of bringing a device into the school, and harmful content that may already be downloaded on to it, and the opportunity to download harmful content via 3,4 and 5G that will bypass the school's filtering and monitoring systems.[341]

<u>Matters relating to the particular school</u> – The policy should reference the arrangements relevant to safeguarding risks matters peculiar to the particular school, which have not been covered. For example, safeguards relating to other institutions using the same site.

Associated policies

<u>School values</u>

Schools should have a *clear set of values and standards upheld and demonstrated throughout all aspects of school life*. These will underpin many of the other policies below and be reinforced throughout the curriculum, including RSE.[342]

<u>Pupil behaviour policy</u>

This is covered under Chapter Twelve below because for independent schools it is the subject of a separate standard. But the reference in

---

[341] NMS 8.4

[342] KCSIE 2022, para. 130.

KCSIE is a reminder that the behaviour policy should cover the overlap between pupil behaviour and safeguarding (such as child-on-child abuse).

The staff code of conduct

A statement of values and the staff code of conduct set the standards and professional boundaries for staff behaviour. Reinforced rigorously in relation to all staff through the low-level concerns policy, the staff code of conduct helps to maintain standards by ensuring unprofessional behaviour is addressed at an early stage. This in turn can help to disrupt or prevent attempts at organisational grooming such as those which have been a pattern in many safeguarding scandals.[343]

KCSIE advises that the staff code of conduct should cover among other things: *acceptable use of technologies (including the use of mobile devices), staff/pupil relationships and communications including the use of social media.* It is an offence (breach of trust) under section 16 of the Sexual Offences Act 2003, for a person aged 18 or over (e.g. teacher, youth worker) to have a sexual relationship with a child under 18 where that person is in a position of trust in respect of that child, even if the relationship is consensual. A situation where a person is in a position of trust could arise where the child is in full-time education and the person looks after children under 18 in the same establishment as the child, even if s/he does not teach the child.[344]

Both the staff code of conduct and safeguarding policies should set out the approach to low-level concerns and also cover expectations in respect of allegations and whistle-blowing. (See above under 'policy content'.)[345] This potentially makes non-reporting of concerns a

---

[343] See the expert evidence EWM0000471on the IICSA website for further explanation – available online: https://www.iicsa.org.uk/key-documents/15771/view/EWM000471.pdf .

[344] KCSIE 2022, para. 98 and footnote 27.

[345] KCSIE 2022, para.s 13, 98 and 429.

disciplinary matter, in appropriate cases – which could be seen as a soft form of 'mandatory reporting'.[346]

For guidance about other content for staff codes of conduct see: *Guidance for Safer Working Practices for those working with children and young people in education settings,* which is published by the Safer Recruitment Consortium. In addition to issues relevant to all schools, it is important for the code to cover matters relevant to any distinctive features of the particular school.

Whistleblowing

Whistleblowing procedures should be in place which enable staff to raise concerns about people or practices.[347] Their content is likely to be largely covered by the reporting lines in the safeguarding and low-level concerns policies. See the *Freedom to speak up* report, by Sir Robert Francis, which is referenced in WT, for more information.

Children missing education

The relevant guidance is: *Children missing education: statutory guidance for local authorities.*[348] Although directed at LAs, this guidance also explains the legal duties of schools in accessible language. These cover recording and monitoring attendance (see the Registration Standard at Chapter Twelve below), investigating unexplained absences, making reasonable enquiries about the whereabouts of missing children and informing the LA. See the guidance for the detail.

Recruitment and selection procedures

Schools should have robust processes to ensure the suitability of those who work with pupils. This topic will be dealt with in greater detail in Chapter Thirteen about the Suitability Standards.

---

[346] At the time of updating this text, the recommendation of IICSA concerning mandatory reporting is still awaited.

[347] WT p. 59.

[348] The Common Transfer Files system is not available to independent schools usually.

A recruitment procedure can be set out as a checklist/table rather than a narrative.

Online safety policy

Schools should take a whole school approach to online safety. KCSIE divides the risks into four categories: content, contact (harmful interactions), conduct and commerce (gambling, scams, inappropriate advertising etc). Online safety should be a running theme through all safeguarding training, responsibilities and policies. Schools should have a clear policy on the use of mobile and smart technology while at school. It should cover safety when pupils are learning remotely. There should be adequate filters and monitoring systems in place to protect pupils when using the school's IT system, without disproportionate interference with privacy. Schools should also have appropriate cyber security in place to safeguard their systems and users. The UK Safer Internet Centre has published guidance as to what 'appropriate' might look like: *UK Safer Internet Centre: appropriate filtering and monitoring*. Guidance on e-security is available from the National Education Network (NEN). Systems should be renewed regularly in view of the fast pace of technological change. KCSIE suggests schools consider an annual review.[349]

Reasonable force policy

A reasonable force policy is not a requirement for all schools. Schools with a 'no contact' policy, should record that in the staff code of conduct. Those which allow staff to use reasonable force should be clear what that means in the particular school, (such as, which staff can use it, when and type of intervention), should ensure relevant staff are suitably trained, that it is only used for legitimate purposes (such as, keeping children safe), keep thorough records and review them regularly for patterns which may need to be addressed.

Force cannot be used as a punishment because corporal punishment by schools is unlawful and its use would constitute a criminal offence.

---

[349] KCSIE 2022, para. 134 – 147 and Annex B.

Encouraging parents to use it for misbehaviour in school would be a breach of the safeguarding standard.

For resources about use of force see: KCSIE, paragraph 162 – 164 and the DfE's: Use of reasonable force in schools, Reducing the need for restraint and restrictive intervention, and Ofsted's: *Positive environments where children can flourish.*

Practical tips for policy writing

- If a checklist of policy contents is available from the relevant school inspectorate, consider structuring the policy in line with that, while being sure to tailor the content to the particular school (such as early years provision, boarding or single sex, specialist performance school)

- Keep the contact details up to date

- Put all contact details into one prominent place such as the front page

- Keep the policy succinct. But, where this is not feasible, include an index and sub-headings to clearly signpost the reader's eye

- Use clear language which would be accessible to a child or a person in a panic

- Review the policy and how well it is working at least once a year or as soon as the next iteration of KCSIE is available. Take the opportunity at the same time to check and update references to guidance and delete references to obsolete guidance

- Ensure the policy is approved by governors, dated and placed on the school website, if any. If there is no website it must be provided to parents on request[350]

---

[350] ISS 32(1)(c).

Prevent

<u>Legislation and guidance</u>

The Prevent duty arises under section 26 of the Counter-Terrorism and Security Act 2015. The legislation was brought forward against a background of 'severe' national threat of terrorism. Its provisions are intended to *strengthen the legal powers and capabilities of law enforcement and intelligence agencies to disrupt terrorism and prevent individuals from being radicalised in the first instance.*[351]

The Act provides:

General duty on specified authorities

26 (1) A specified authority must, in the exercise of its functions, have due regard to the need to prevent people from being drawn into terrorism.

(2) A specified authority is a person or body that is listed in Schedule 6.

Power to issue guidance

29 (1) The Secretary of State may issue guidance to specified authorities about the exercise of their duty under section 26(1).

(2) A specified authority must have regard to any such guidance in carrying out that duty.

Proprietors of independent schools are among those listed in Schedule 6 of the Act. Schools must have regard to the *Revised Prevent Duty guidance for England and Wales* 2021 (statutory) and will also be assisted in carrying out the duty by: *The Prevent Duty: Departmental advice for schools and childminders (non-statutory).*

The risk of radicalisation presents a risk of harm to young people, quite apart from the risks it may present to the wider community. As such it has been incorporated into KCSIE so that preventing young people being drawn into terrorism is now part of a school's safeguarding duties

---

[351] Explanatory Notes to the Counter-Terrorism and Security Act 2015.

under ISS paragraph 7. KCSIE here provides a bridge from the Counter-Terrorism and Security Act 2015 to the independent school standards with the effect that the Prevent duty on schools can be enforced if necessary through the provisions of the Education and Skills Act 2008.[352]

Contents of the duty

In outline, the four themes of the strategy are:

- Risk assessment, both general for the school and area, and specific for particular pupils

- Working in partnership with LSCPs, the police, parents and families

- Staff training – certain prescribed courses are available for DSLs and others

- IT policies, to ensure pupils are safe from terrorist and extremist material when accessing the internet in schools through teaching internet safety and us of appropriate filters[353]

Links to other standards

The duty links to parts of the Curriculum, Teaching and SMSC standards (ISS 2, 3 and 5 respectively), particularly the duty to ensure a balanced presentation of political matters but also the duties to teach shared values and respect for others, internet safety and to introduce democracy and the world of work as peaceful means of engaging with issues and generating change.

---

[352] Section 108 et seq. for inspections and 114 et seq. for action plans and enforcement action and Part Four of the Schools Bill 2022 for the direction of travel.

[353] *The Prevent duty Departmental advice for schools and childcare providers*, June 2015.

Conclusion: Compliance and culture

Having prepared and published a policy, as above, the safeguarding work of a school is only just beginning. The matters described must be put into effect rigorously if they are to have any value. Schools should also be aware that the safeguarding standard links to almost every other standard.

It is said of many parts of the standards that compliance is composed of three parts: policies, policy implementation and culture. This is nowhere truer than in relation to the safeguarding standard. IICSA's final public hearing in 2020 considered the role of leadership and organisational culture in safeguarding and how appropriate values can be embedded throughout an institution.[354] WT provides markers for safeguarding structures but also references the role of culture: a *'culture of listening to children'* and a *'culture of safety, equality and protection'.* Likewise, the headlines in the *Freedom to Speak up Report* by Sir Robert Francis, cited in WT, are about cultural issues: the importance of:

- *A culture of safety and learning in which all staff feel safe to raise concerns. Raising concerns should be part of the normal routine business of any well-led ... organisation*

- *A culture free from bullying. Freedom to speak up about concerns depends on staff being able to work in a culture which is free from bullying and other oppressive behaviours.*

- *A culture of visible leadership. All employers ... should demonstrate, through visible leadership at all levels in the organisation, that they welcome and encourage the raising of concerns by staff.*

- *A culture of valuing staff. Employers should show that they value staff who raise concerns, and celebrate the benefits for [service users] from the improvements made in response to the issues identified.*

---

[354] https://www.iicsa.org.uk/investigation/effective-leadership-child-protection. Report expected Autumn 2022.

- *A culture of reflective practice. There should be opportunities for all staff to engage in regular reflection of concerns in their work.*

In terms of pupil experience, the inspectorates take into account not only the public culture of a school and daily experience of most pupils but also the hidden culture, that is, the perspective of pupils who struggle with school and are negatively impacted by the environment for whatever reason.

There are many theories about why people comply with the law, including deterrence/fear and reward/recognition theories, but studies in a variety of contexts have found that 'compliance' is most effectively achieved when stakeholders are motivated by a proper understanding of the reason for particular rules, are fully behind their purpose and believe in their efficacy. That is one explanation of what a culture of safeguarding looks like. IICSA is due to report on cultural issues in 2022. Meanwhile the evidence the Inquiry heard is available on the IICSA website.

Additional reading

Wider reading:

- Sections 1-3, 17, 31, 47, 87-87D, and part one of Schedule 2 Children Act 1989

- Sections 10,11 and 16E Children Act 2004 as amended by sections 16 – 23 Children and Social Work Act 2017

- Schedule 4 of the Safeguarding Vulnerable Groups Act 2006 – for definitions of 'regulated activity'

- Child sexual abuse in the context of schools: Truth Project Thematic Report – IICSA Research Team – December 2020[355]

---

[355] https://www.iicsa.org.uk/document/truth-project-thematic-report-child-sexual-abuse-context-schools .

- Effective leadership of child protection – IICSA hearing materials [356]

Published serious case reviews can extend a reader's understanding of how adult/child safeguarding risks can manifest in institutions, such as:

- William Vahey: Wonnacott, J. and Carmi. E. (2016) Serious Case Review: Southbank International School, Hammersmith and Fulham, Kensington & Chelsea and Westminster LSCB.

- Jonathan Thomson-Glover: Jones, P. (2016) Investigation into Safeguarding Issues at Clifton College Arising from The Prosecution Of X, Bristol: Clifton College.

- Vanessa George: Plymouth Safeguarding Children Board (2010) Serious Case Review re Nursery Z. Plymouth, Plymouth Safeguarding Children Board.

- Nigel Leat: North Somerset Safeguarding Children Board (2012) Serious Case Review: The Sexual Abuse of Pupils in a First School Overview Report, Weston-Super-Mare, NSSCB.

- Jeremy Forrest: East Sussex Safeguarding Children Board (2013) Serious Case Review: Child G, Brighton, East Sussex Safeguarding Children Board.

---

[356] https://www.iicsa.org.uk/investigation/effective-leadership-child-protection?tab=hearing .

The Standard on Safeguarding Boarders

Introduction

The safeguarding standard discussed above covers all pupils, including boarders. There are, however, additional requirements for boarders. The Children Act 1989 covers the welfare of children in boarding schools at section 87.

> *87 Welfare of children in boarding schools and colleges*
>
> *(1) Where a school or college provides accommodation for any child, it shall be the duty of the relevant person to safeguard and promote the child's welfare.*

ISS paragraph 8 provides a statutory bridge between the Children Act 1989 and Education and Skills Act 2008 with the effect that a failure to meet the NMS for boarding can be enforced by the Secretary of State as a failure to meet the standards.[357]

The detail of the NMS, which are a comprehensive set of standards in themselves, is outside the scope of this book save for a few references where relevant to other issues. When advising boarding schools it is important always to consider whether the additional requirements of the NMS.

ISS paragraph 8

> *Where section 87(1) of the 1989 Act applies in relation to a school the standard in this paragraph is met if the proprietor ensures that—*
>
> *(a) arrangements are made to safeguard and promote the welfare of boarders while they are accommodated at the school; and*
>
> *(b) such arrangements have regard to the National Minimum Standards for Boarding Schools or, where applicable, the*

---

[357] The NMS also apply to boarding schools which are not independent schools and under some inspection frameworks are inspected separately hence they are not simply amalgamated into the standards.

National Minimum Standards for Residential Special Schools.[358]

<u>*Where Section 87(1) [Children Act] 1989 applies*</u>

ISS paragraph 8 applies when a school or college provides accommodation to any child.

> *87 (1A) For the purposes of this section and sections 87A to 87D, a school or college provides accommodation for a child if—*
>
> *(a) it provides accommodation for the child on its own premises, or*
>
> *(b) it arranges for accommodation for the child to be provided elsewhere (other than in connection with a residential trip away from the school).[359]*

It would not apply where a school is registered as a children's home as there are separate standards for those.[360]

NMS for boarding

The NMS for boarding are made by the Secretary of State under section 87C (1) of the Children Act 1989, as amended by the Care Standards Act 2000 and the Education Act 2011. A new version has come into force on 5 September 2022.

---

[358] The previous inclusion of the *National Minimum Standards for Accommodation of Students under Eighteen by Further Education Colleges* was removed by The Independent Educational Provision in England (Inspection Fees) and Independent School Standards (Amendment) Regulations 2018.

[359] Section 87 Children Act 1989.

[360] See section 1(6) of the Care Standards Act 2000 for when a school is a Children's Home. There is a threshold of providing accommodation for more than 295 days in a year (to the same child) for two consecutive years and further detail. See also the Children's Homes (England) Regulations 2015 as amended in 2018.

87C Boarding schools: national minimum standards.

(1) The Secretary of State may prepare and publish statements of national minimum standards for <u>safeguarding and promoting the welfare</u> of children for whom accommodation is provided in a school or college.

They are incorporated into the standards primarily by ISS 8 but other NMS also make direct reference to the NMS, such as the premises standards.

All the NMS are therefore safeguarding standards by definition and a failure to meet any one of them could impact compliance with ISS 8. Some of the NMS follow the same wording as corresponding provisions in the independent school standards so the alignment between the two sets of standards is streamlined. In particular, NMS 8 replicates ISS 7:

8.1 The school ensures that:

- *arrangements are made to safeguard and promote the welfare of pupils at the school; and*

- *such arrangements have regard to any guidance issued by the Secretary of State.[361]*

NMS 8.1 also footnotes KCSIE and WT as the relevant guidance. So, the standard for safeguarding boarders incorporates both the NMS and KCSIE/WT.

NMS for residential special schools

The NMS for residential special schools are also made under section 87C(1).

Inspection arrangements differ for boarding schools and residential special schools.[362] Given the lack of definition for independent special

---

[361] From the NMS 2022.

[362] Where the NMS for residential special schools are deemed to apply, all inspections of boarding care are by Ofsted, even when the educational provision in the school

schools, other than those registered under section 342 of the Education Act 1996, where there is any doubt, schools should liaise with the DfE or relevant inspectorate if necessary to clarify which standards apply before their first or next inspection. This will be particularly important where a school has formally changed its admissions criteria or the balance needs of the pupil cohort is changing significantly.

Interpretation of the NMS

The NMS for boarding use words such as 'suitable', 'adequate' and 'appropriate' from time to time to describe the required level of provision. The preface to the NMS for boarding explains that this is assessed by reference to:

> ... the adequacy or suitability for the specific needs of boarders residing at the school having regard to their ages, numbers and sex and any special requirements they may have.

'Special requirements' are defined:

> A student has 'special requirements' if the student has any needs arising from physical, medical, sensory, learning, emotional or behavioural difficulties which require provision which is additional to or different from that generally required by children of the same age in schools other than special schools.[363]

From 5 September 2022, quality terms have been introduced into the NMS to raise the bar to 'good' in several standards, in place of 'suitable' or 'adequate'. The preface explains :

> Where the term 'good' is used within the standards, the quality of provision should be such that a reasonable person would consider it to be good in relation to the specific needs of the boarders residing at the school, having regard to their ages, numbers, sex and any special

---

is inspected by an independent inspectorate. The inspection cycles also differ, for example.

[363] Footnote 6 of the NMS for boarding.

requirements they may have. It does not necessarily mirror the term 'good' within inspection quality judgements.

This change follows submissions to IICSA about confusion around the quality of provision required to meet the NMS. For schools which already interpreted 'suitability' and 'adequacy' in the context of high expectations, this will not be a substantive change. Others will need to raise the quality of their provision.

Particular safeguarding risks in boarding

Various safeguarding risks are recognised as peculiar to boarding schools:

- Excessive isolation from families, particularly those overseas

- Inappropriate child-on-child relationships, particularly where there is a gender imbalance among pupils

- Extra vulnerabilities of pupils with SEND

- Insufficient free time for pupils away from 'other school requirements such as prayer'[364]

In addition, for boarders from overseas:

- Language and cultural barriers

- Risks associated with unregulated educational guardians.

KCSIE para. 157 et seq. and *The Independent School Standards: Guidance for independent schools, April 2019* – para. 4.17. See also Part C of *The IICSA Residential Schools Investigation Report, March 2022.*

Conclusion

The NMS cover some of the same ground as the standards. In some places they replicate requirements, in others they enhance them for boarders and in yet others they cover ground not touched by the standards, such as food, activities and free time, quality of bedding, and independent listeners. Readers should always check the NMS for additional requirements.

Further reading:

- Child sexual abuse in residential schools: A literature review – IICSA, November 2018[365]

- Independent overview expert report on the subject of sexual abuse and/or harmful sexual behaviours involving children in residential and day school settings – Professor Simon Hackett, Durham University – IICSA – July 2019 – EWM000489[366]

- The IICSA Residential Schools Investigation Report, March 2022

- Safeguarding children from sexual abuse in residential schools – Independent Inquiry into Child Sexual Abuse, NatCen Social Research that works for society – April 2020[367]

---

[365] https://www.iicsa.org.uk/key-documents/7747/view/child-sexual-abuse-residential-schools%3A-a-literature-review-november-2018.pdf .

[366] https://www.iicsa.org.uk/key-documents/14669/view/EWM000469.pdf .

[367] https://www.iicsa.org.uk/reports-recommendations/publications/research/safeguarding-children-sexual-abuse-residential-schools .

CHAPTER TWELVE

OTHER WELFARE, HEALTH AND SAFETY STANDARDS – ISS PART 3 CONTINUED

The Behaviour Standard

ISS paragraph 9

> *9. The standard in this paragraph is met if the proprietor promotes good behaviour amongst pupils by ensuring that—*
>
> *(a) a written behaviour policy is drawn up that, amongst other matters, sets out the sanctions to be adopted in the event of pupil misbehaviour;*
>
> *(b) the policy is implemented effectively; and*
>
> *(c) a record is kept of the sanctions imposed upon pupils for serious misbehaviour.*[368]

Overarching requirements of the behaviour standard

The standard requires the school to

- have a written policy. In practice this is often combined with the anti-bullying strategy below as there is considerable overlap between the two standards. [369]

- implement the policy effectively

- keep a record of sanctions imposed for serious misconduct.

---

[368] For boarding schools, also see NMS 15 and Appendices A and B.

[369] See also NMS 15 of the NMS for boarding 2022.

The policy should cover both how the school promotes good behaviour and how it sanctions misbehaviour both on and offline. Effective implementation will entail all staff implementing the same suite of measures. 'Off-policy' idiosyncratic approaches by individual teachers or departments are to be avoided.

The record of sanctions must be kept even if it has no entries.

Details of records are not prescribed but should be sufficient to enable senior leaders to spot and address patterns such as that incidents are linked to a particular pupils, classes or year groups who need more support, staff members who need further training, support and guidance, particular locations, times of the day or activities where supervision may need strengthening.

An extended list of requirements for boarding schools is prescribed by NMS 15.1.

Guidance

A range of advice and resources is available from the DfE or signposted from their guidance. For independent schools these are non-statutory but they may be helpful in formulating a policy. The following is a small selection only:

- **New:** *Behaviour in schools: Advice for headteachers and school staff* – July 2022 for use from September 2022

- *Behaviour and discipline in schools:* Advice for headteachers and school staff – January 2016

- *Getting the simple things right: Charlie Taylor's behaviour checklists*

- *Creating a culture: a review of behaviour management in schools* – September 2020

- *Respectful School Communities: Self Review and Signposting Tool*

- *Use of reasonable force in schools*

- **New**: *Searching screening and confiscation at school* – July 2022 for use from 1 September 2022

'Well-managed schools create cultures where pupils and staff flourish in safety and dignity' explains *Behaviour in Schools: advice for headteachers and school staff* 2022. The advice steps schools through some of the key issues to consider in a rounded approach to the standard: codes of conduct, incentives, praise, staff training, development and support, staff behaviour code, acceptable forms of sanction, behaviour support for pupils, pastoral care, mentors, counselling, planning, building positive relationships with parents, communication, connection to SEN policy (seeking external assessment), searching and confiscation, connection to the safeguarding policy especially in relation to child-on-child abuse.

Equality and rights issues

Reasonable adjustments

A good policy will recognise the need for reasonable adjustments for pupils with disabilities which affect their behaviour. This will not simply be a case of adjusting a 'three strikes and you're out' policy to another number, but will entail recognising that some pupils will need a different approach, such as pastoral and educative interventions. See, for example, Ashdown House v JKL and MNP [2019]UK.

Behaviour in Schools – Advice for headteachers and school staff 2022[370] explains that a school should not assume that because a pupil has SEND it must have affected their behaviour on a particular occasion. It is important to try to understand the underlying causes of behaviour and whether additional support is needed.

See further discussion in Chapter Four on Equality and Chapter Twenty about SEND.

---

[370] Para.s 56 – 60.

Discriminatory behaviour

KCSIE requires schools to make a clear statement in their safeguarding policies that there should be a 'zero tolerance approach to abuse and it should never be passed off as "banter", "just having a laugh", "part of growing up" or "boys being boys" as this can lead to a culture of unacceptable behaviours and an unsafe environment for children'. To ensure implementation, that statement should be reflected in the behaviour and anti-bullying policies also. It should cover sexual harassment but may also be relevant to other types of protected characteristics. 'Zero tolerance' does not mean that pupils must be excluded for every error. As ever, the response of the school should be proportionate, and tailored to the pupil and situation.[371]

Use of force and isolation

Force can never be used as a sanction. The behaviour policy should state the school's position on reasonable force and, if it permits it to be used, signpost where more information can be found, such as in the safeguarding policy or a stand-alone policy. See Chapter Eleven on safeguarding and:

- KCSIE, paragraphs 162–164

- NMS 15

- *Use of reasonable force in schools, Reducing the need for restraint and restrictive intervention* – DfE

- *Positive environments where children can flourish* – Ofsted

As to isolation, the DfE advises:

> *Any use of isolation that prevents a child from leaving a room of their own free will should only be considered in exceptional circumstances. The school must also ensure the health and safety of pupils and any requirements in relation to safeguarding and pupil welfare.*[372]

---

[371] This has been confirmed in the DfE's response to the consultation on KCSIE *2022*.

[372] Para. 42 of *Behaviour and discipline in schools: Advice for headteachers and school staff*. See para.s 42 and 43 in full.

Also:

> *Locking pupils in rooms for any reason (including pupil or staff safety) is potentially illegal except in those few schools where a pupil is subject to a detention and training order issued by a court: it is not just a breach of the standards.*[373]

Arguably, pupils should never be confined in locked rooms in schools. There is clearly a litigation risk and inspection risk for schools which do so.[374]

Cross-over with other standards

Problematic pupil behaviour may give rise to questions about whether other standards are being fully met. For example, depending on the type of behaviour manifest, one or all of the following could be engaged: the teaching standard (which requires effective strategies for managing behaviour – ISS 3(h)); the SMSC standard (which requires schools to promote principles which encourage respect for other people, paying particular regard to the protected characteristics – ISS 5(b)(vi)); the RSE standard (which expects schools to teach pupils about acceptable behavioural boundaries in some contexts – ISS 2A); the bullying standard (which requires schools to have an effective anti-bullying strategy – ISS 10); the supervision standard (ISS 14); the safeguarding standard (which requires schools to make arrangements to safeguard and promote the welfare of pupils – ISS 7); the leadership and management standard (ISS 34).

---

[373] *The Independent School Standards: Guidance for independent schools, April 2019* at para. 4.8.

[374] See In the matter of D(A child) [2019]UKSC 42 for a thorough discussion of deprivation of liberty although the case did not concern a school. Behaviour In Schools: advice for headteachers and school staff 2022 explains that there may be exceptional situations In which It Is necessary to physically prevent a pupil from leaving a room In order to protect the safety of pupils or staff from immediate risk, but this Is a safety measure and not a disciplinary sanction – para. 86(c).

The Anti-bullying Standard

ISS paragraph 10

> *10. The standard in this paragraph is met if the proprietor ensures that bullying at the school is prevented in so far as reasonably practicable, by the drawing up and implementation of an effective anti-bullying strategy.*[375]

Overarching requirements:

- A written anti-bullying <u>strategy</u>

- Fully implemented

The standard is outcome focused: bullying is prevented in so far as reasonably practicable.

The policy should include *'measures to prevent bullying, including cyberbullying, prejudice-based and discriminatory bullying'.*[376] It should link to the safeguarding policy

> *...when there is 'reasonable cause to suspect that a child is suffering, or is likely to suffer, significant harm' a bullying incident should be addressed as a child protection concern under the Children Act 1989.*[377]

It should cover child-on-child abuse as described in KCSIE and other issues relevant to the school, such as sexual harassment and sexualised bullying, initiation ceremonies (where these may constitute bullying), or serious violence.

Boarding schools should also see the extensive requirements of NMS 15.4, 16 and 17.

---

[375] For boarding schools also see NMS 16 and Appendix A of the NMS.

[376] KCSIE 2022, para. 13 and 98.

[377] Preventing and Tackling Bullying, p. 6.

Guidance

There is a range of statutory and non-statutory DfE advice for schools about preventing bullying:

- *Preventing and tackling bullying: Advice for headteachers, staff and governing bodies* – July 2017[378]

- *Cyberbullying: Advice for headteachers and school staff*[379]

- *Tackling Race and Faith Targeted Bullying Face To Face and Online: A Guide For Schools 2017* (UK Council for Child Internet Safety (UKCCIS) and the Anti-Bullying Alliance (ABA))

- KCSIE – All sections on child-on-child abuse, such as paragraphs 32 – 35 and Part 5

- *The Ofsted review of sexual abuse in schools and colleges* – 2021 (which contains recommendations for how school leaders can better tackle sexualised bullying, also known harassment)

- *DfE Guidance on Sharing nudes and semi-nudes: advice for education settings working with children and young people* – 2020 (includes cases where there is coercion)[380]

---

[378] https://assets.publishing.service.gov.uk/government/uploads/system/uploads/attachment_data/file/623895/Preventing_and_tackling_bullying_advice.pdf .

[379] https://www.gov.uk/government/publications/preventing-and-tackling-bullying .

[380] https://www.gov.uk/government/publications/sharing-nudes-and-semi-nudes-advice-for-education-settings-working-with-children-and-young-people/sharing-nudes-and-semi-nudes-advice-for-education-settings-working-with-children-and-young-people .

Elements of a potentially effective strategy

The following is based on the materials above.

<u>A written policy</u> – covering the following ground, which is fully implemented.

<u>A working definition of bullying, including online bullying</u> – This should be flexible and open-ended.

<u>Types of bullying</u> – This assists the school community to recognise some behaviours or even traditions as bullying, for example, dangerous or humiliating initiation ceremonies, sexual harassment, sexualised banter, racist or derogatory language aimed at peers. The school's zero tolerance of sexualised bullying, sexual violence and harassment should be restated.

<u>The seriousness of bullying and its impact</u> – The potential impact should be explained. This should include particular seriousness of bullying in relation to protected characteristics.

<u>The school's preventative measures</u> – These should include cultural approaches, the school values, educative approaches through PSHE and RSE, assemblies, pastoral approaches, listening to pupils to understand their experience, parental engagement, IT measures, such as filters in school, partnership with other organisations.

<u>The school's procedures for reporting and managing incidents of bullying</u> – Pupils should know what to do if they are bullied, witness bullying, or become aware of bullying incidents. The school culture should support disclosure. Pupils should know that their concerns will be taken seriously and that they will be supported and kept safe. *A victim should never be given the impression that they are creating a problem by reporting abuse, sexual violence or sexual harassment. Nor should a victim ever be made to feel ashamed for making a report.*[381]

---

[381] KCSIE 2022, para.s 18, 468, pp. 123 etc.

How the bullying strategy fits with the safeguarding and behaviour policies (if separate)

How the school responds to bullying – Schools should have a continuum of measures available to respond to bullying, to provide support and challenge where appropriate (educative, sanctions, pastoral, as mentioned above).

The threshold for dealing with a matter as a safeguarding issue – See KCSIE for more. In principle, the threshold for dealing with bullying incidents under legal safeguarding procedures is when they put pupils at risk of significant harm. LAs publish threshold criteria for when to refer through those channels and NPCC provides guidance: *When to call the police*.

Staff training

Record keeping – Part of an effective strategy will include record keeping so that the school will have a clear picture of incidents throughout the school and can take consider how to develop its overarching strategy. It is good practice to distinguish in records any incidents which are connected to protected characteristics.

The Health and Safety Standard

ISS paragraph 11

> *11. The standard in this paragraph is met if the proprietor ensures that relevant health and safety laws are complied with by the drawing up and effective implementation of a written health and safety policy.*[382]

Introduction and overarching requirements

Health and safety (H&S) in schools could warrant a dedicated book, given that the standard imports all 'relevant health and safety laws'. This chapter gives an overview only.

The relevant laws are not defined but would include items such as:

- The Health and Safety at Work Act 1974

- Management of Safety at Work Regulations 1999[383]

- Workplace (Health, Safety and Welfare) Regulations 1992[384]

The Health and Safety at Work Act 1974 covers both 'persons at work' and 'others' against H&S risks 'arising out of or in connection with the

---

[382] See also NMS 9.1 and appendix 1, and EYFS 3.55 for a similar provisions for boarders and early years. The First Edition of this text suggested that the unqualified breadth of this standard meant that it could also extend to the H&S of staff and others. However, the relevant empowering legislation permits the Secretary of State to set standards relating to 'the health and safety of students' only – section 94(1)(c) Education and Skills Act. So, it is likely that 'relevant health and safety laws' are only imported into the standard insofar as they relate to pupils and, therefore, that only the H&S of pupils are properly within the remit of inspections under the Education and Skills Act 2008. However, where DfE guidance refers to the safety of both pupils and staff, this text echoes that approach which reflects the approach typically taken by schools.

[383] Concerns – risk assessments, principles of prevention to be applied, planning, organisation, control, training, record keeping etc.

[384] Concerns pragmatic issues such as lighting, cleanliness, warmth, toilet and washing facilities, drinking water etc.

activities of persons at work'. This brings pupils within the scope of the legislation.[385]

The primary regulator for H&S at work is the Health and Safety Executive (HSE). The HSE does not routinely inspect schools on a regular cycle but the inclusion of H&S in education inspections under the auspices of the schools regulator means that education inspectors can note any obvious H&S hazards which require attention and potentially alert other agencies such as the HSE or Fire and Rescue Service (FRS) where a higher level of expertise may be required. This standard allows the Secretary of State to take action if necessary in the event of adverse findings by inspectors but also courts and expert H&S agencies such as the HSE and FRS.

The H&S standard requires schools to have a strategic approach to all H&S issues connected to the school, both on and off site, including educational visits. It is closely linked to the standards on Fire, First Aid, Premises and Risk Assessment.[386]

An important case to be aware of is Woodland v Essex County Council [2012] UKSC 66. The Supreme Court confirmed that independent schools owe a non-delegable duty of care to pupils in relation to health and safety.[387]

Guidance

The key guidance is:

- *Health and safety: responsibilities and duties for schools, DfE April 2022*[388]

---

[385] Section 1(1)(b) Health and Safety at Work Act 1974.

[386] The Premises standard has direct parallels to several matters covered by *The Workplace (Health, Safety and Welfare) Regulations 1992*.

[387] Woodland v Essex County Council [2012] UKSC 66 at para. 25(5).

[388] https://www.gov.uk/government/publications/health-and-safety-advice-for-schools/responsibilities-and-duties-for-schools .

- *Health and safety on educational visits, DfE 2018[389]*

- *Sensible health and safety management in schools, HSE[390]*

- *Emergency planning and response for education, childcare, and children's social care settings, DfE June 2022[391]* – a non-statutory overview of processes including public health, severe weather and security

For further detail see:

- *Leading health and safety at work[392]*

- *Workplace health, safety and welfare. Workplace (Health, Safety and Welfare) Regulations 1992. Approved Code of Practice and guidance[393]* (and the helpful abbreviated version: *Workplace health, safety and welfare, a short guide for managers[394]*)

These signpost a series of other sources about important topics such as asbestos, onsite vehicle movement, ventilation, safety in science and PE lessons. The topic is very broad. For the purpose of compliance with education inspections, the primary focus is on the welfare of the pupils and the matters highlighted by the DfE guidance.

---

[389] https://www.gov.uk/government/publications/health-and-safety-on-educational-visits/health-and-safety-on-educational-visits .

[390] https://www.hse.gov.uk/services/education/sensible-leadership/index.htm .

[391] https://www.gov.uk/government/publications/emergency-planning-and-response-for-education-childcare-and-childrens-social-care-settings#full-publication-update-history

[392] https://www.hse.gov.uk/leadership/ .

[393] https://www.hse.gov.uk/pubns/priced/l24.pdf .

[394] https://www.hse.gov.uk/pubns/indg244.pdf .

Competent person

While legal accountability remains with the proprietors, day to day responsibility is usually delegated to the head and senior leadership team. Schools, like other employers, must appoint a competent person or people to help them meet their H&S legal duties.[395]

> *(5) A person shall be regarded as competent for the purposes of paragraphs (1) and (8) where he has sufficient training and experience or knowledge and other qualities to enable him properly to assist in undertaking the measures referred to in paragraph (1).*

They should have the skills, knowledge and experience to be able to recognise hazards in school and assist the school to put in sensible controls to protect pupil, employees and others. While formal qualifications can help, they are not a legal requirement. The HSE recommends: *If there's a competent person within your workforce, use them rather than a competent person from outside your business.*

Schools which are large, sometimes multi-sited, complex operations typically work with external consultants and may even appoint an external person as the competent person. This does not remove the legal responsibility to meet the standard or H&S legislation from the school proprietor(s).

Policy

The standard requires schools to have a written policy. The guidance explains the policy in 4 elements: Plan, Do, Check, Act and suggests the following non-exhaustive list of policy coverage. The policy should be proportionate to the school and it is important to tailor it to the risks relevant to the particular setting, adding more elements where necessary:

- *a general statement of the policy*

- *who is responsible for what (delegation of tasks)*

---

[395] The Management of Health and Safety at Work Regulations 1999: Regulation 7.

- *arrangements for risk assessments and the practical control measures to reduce risk*

- *how the school will establish, monitor and review its measures to meet satisfactory health and safety standards*

- *proportionate control measures for health infections* [**new** in 2022]

- *line management responsibilities*

- *arrangements for periodic site inspections*

- *arrangements for consulting and involving employees*

- *staff health and safety training, including assessment of risk*

- *recording and reporting accidents to staff, pupils and visitors – including Reporting of Injuries, Diseases and Dangerous Occurrences Regulations 2013 (RIDDOR)*

- *policy and procedures for off-site visits, including residential visits and any school-led adventure activities*

- *dealing with health and safety emergencies, including procedures and contacts*

- *first aid for staff and pupils*

- *occupational health services*

- *how you will investigate accidents and incidents to understand causes*

- *how you will monitor and report performance and effectiveness of the health and safety policy*

Other areas to consider:

- *workplace safety for teachers, pupils and visitors – checklist for classrooms*

- *work at height*

- *slips and trips in educational establishments*

- *on-site vehicle movements*

- *managing asbestos in your school*

- *control of hazardous substances*

- *selecting and managing contractors*

- *good estate management for schools*

- *school building design and maintenance (and where necessary examination and testing)*

- *manual handling*

- *managing work-related stress*

- *ventilation in the workplace* [**new** in 2022]

In the guidance, hyperlinks are provided to advice for each of these items and many others, which schools can adopt or modify to their circumstances.

Risk assessments

Schools are obliged to assess risks to which employees are exposed while at work and to non-employees arising out of or in connection with the conduct of the school, and to put in place proportionate control measures. The risk assessments should cover what is needed to protect the health and safety of people such as pupils, staff, visitors (such as parents), contractors. Significant findings of H&S risk assessments must be recorded along with measures to reduce the risks and expected outcomes.[396]

---

[396] The Management of Health and Safety at Work Regulations 1999: Regulation 3 and the guidance below

Records of the assessment should be simple and focused on controls. Outcomes should explain to others what they are required to do and help staff with planning and monitoring.[397]

COVID-19

The DfE's COVID-specific guidance for schools was withdrawn in May 2022. In its place, there are two important pieces of guidance:

- *Health protection in education and childcare settings: A practical guide for staff on managing cases of infectious diseases in education and childcare settings,* UK Health Security Agency, May 2022. This gives guidance aimed at reducing disruption to education as we learn to live safely with coronavirus (COVID-19). It covers a range of infections spread by the respiratory route and provides advice on issues such as: infection prevention and control; managing specific infections and exclusion advice; actions in the event of an outbreak or incident including when and how to seek help; immunisation; additional considerations such as educational visits.

- *Contingency framework: education and childcare settings,* February 2022. This describes principles of managing local outbreaks of coronavirus. All education and childcare settings should have contingency plans (sometimes called outbreak management plans) detailing how they would exceptionally and temporarily reintroduce any measures to manage risk and minimise disruption to face-to-face education and childcare.

See also: *Health and safety: responsibilities and duties for schools, DfE* April 2022, described above.

---

[397] Health and safety: responsibilities and duties for schools – April 2022.

School security and emergency preparation

School security is covered by the H&S standard, overlapping with the Premises standard and potentially the Safeguarding standard in relation to issues such as serious violence, child criminal exploitation, and Prevent. The relevant guidance (non-statutory) is: *School and college security 2019* which signposts a range of guidance. [398]

The main points are the need for arrangements for:

- Risk assessment – identifying internal and external security risks including cyber-security threats

- Building partnerships with the police, LA, the wider community and expert advisors to share security related information

- Managing risks, including through school culture and curriculum

- Emergency planning- and testing procedures: business continuity planning, evacuation, bomb alert or threat, evacuation, lockdown

- Staff training

- post incident support

- debrief and lessons learned

Sport

The case of <u>MM v Newlands School and another</u> [2007] EWCA Civ 21 provides an example of when there can be a need for risk assessment in the context of school sport. The Court of Appeal considered that when deviating from the Junior Rugby Guidelines as normally applied,

---

[398] https://www.gov.uk/government/publications/school-and-college-security/school-and-college-security .

albeit within the latitude permitted by the guidelines, there should have been an assessment of the need to do so and the possible risks to players which might arise. The court found that there was negligence which was causal of the injury which followed to a player.

> *If a wrongful act or omission results in an increased risk of injury to the plaintiff and that risk eventuates, the defendant's conduct has materially contributed to the injury that the plaintiff suffers, whether or not other factors also contributed to that injury occurring.* [399]

An independent school in this situation might also be considered not to have met the Health and Safety standard and Risk Assessment standard at the relevant time.

School trips

The H&S standard covers school trips. The advice dedicated to school trips is:

- *Health and safety on educational visits, 2018.* [400]

The guidance distinguishes routine trips from those which require risk assessment and extra planning. In summary:

Parental consent

Parental consent is always needed for trips for children in the EYFS[401] but otherwise is only necessary for trips which require a higher level of risk assessment or are outside normal school hours. Parents can provide a single consent for all routine school trips but should still be informed about trips, if they have done so.

---

[399] Chester v Afshar [2005] 1 A C 134

[400] https://www.gov.uk/government/publications/health-and-safety-on-educational-visits/health-and-safety-on-educational-visits .

[401] *Health and safety on educational visits, 2018* at para. 2.

Educational visits coordinators

Schools should appoint an educational visits coordinator. Otherwise, the responsibility remains with the head. LAs will have an outdoor education advisor. The coordinator works with the local outdoor education advisor to support colleagues. Advice is also available from the OEAP (Outdoor Education Advisor Panel) website.

External activity providers

Schools must ensure external activity providers meet appropriate safety standards and carry liability insurance. The Council for Learning Outside the Classroom (LOtC) awards the LOtC Badge to organisations who meet nationally recognised standards. Schools can check whether a provider holds the accreditation through an online database. Where an organisation does not hold the LOtC badge, schools must check for themselves:

- *their insurance*

- *that they meet legal requirements*

- *their health and safety and emergency policies*

- *their risk assessments*

- *control measures*

- *their use of vehicles*

- *staff competence*

- *safeguarding arrangements*

- *accommodation*

- *any sub-contracting arrangements they have*

- *that they have a licence where needed*

Schools should have an agreement with the activity provider that makes clear their respective responsibilities, especially where they will be supervising children.

Adventure activities and trips abroad

Organisations needs a licence to provide some activities Schools should ensure providers of activities hold the LOtC quality badge or similar local accreditation.

Emergency planning

Schools should have an emergency response plan for incidents away from school. They should also have a communications plan for both routine communications, (regular calls to check-in for reassurance) and emergencies.

Post-trip evaluation

Records should be kept of incidents, accidents and near misses. Trips should be evaluated after conclusion for whether planning worked and to learn any lessons.

In addition to matters mentioned in H&S guidance about trips, various serious case reviews concern safeguarding incidents on school trips. Trips should therefore be considered and risk assessed also from a safeguarding perspective. See the Safeguarding Standard in Chapter Eleven and the Risk Assessment Standard, below.

The Fire Safety Standard

ISS paragraph 12

12. The standard in this paragraph is met if the proprietor ensures compliance with the Regulatory Reform (Fire Safety) Order 2005.[402]

Introduction

The fire standard for schools reflects the law for other organisations and their premises. The central requirements are a fire risk assessment (rather than a policy) and fire precautions, such as equipment, training, drills and so on.

Non-statutory guidance:

- *Fire safety in new and existing school buildings* – 2014

- *Fire safety risk assessment – (non-residential) educational premises – 2006*

See also

- *A short guide to making your premises safe from fire*

Note, as with other chapters the overview which follows is no substitute for reading the various available guidance documents in full.

Outline guide

The responsible person must:

---

[402] For boarding schools, also see NMS 10 and NMS Appendix 2. At least one drill per year must be carried out overnight, unless the school has assessed that this would be detrimental to boarders' welfare. The needs of flexi-boarders should also be catered for.

- carry out a fire risk assessment of the premises and review it regularly

- provide staff with information about the risks identified

- inform pupils, contractors and other non-employees about the risks relevant to them

- put in place, and maintain, appropriate fire safety measures

- ensure that the premises and any equipment provided in connection with firefighting, fire detection and warning, emergency routes and exits are covered by a suitable system of maintenance, and are maintained by a competent person in an efficient state, in efficient working order and in good repair.

- plan for an emergency

- provide staff and others on the school site with information, fire safety instruction and training

- appoint one or more 'competent person(s)' to help, if the school does not have in-house expertise

Fire risk assessment

The following is taken from *Fire safety risk assessment – (non-residential) educational premises – 2006*

<u>Purpose</u>

The aims of the fire risk assessment are:

- To identify the fire hazards

- To reduce the risk of those hazards causing harm to as low as reasonably practicable

- To decide what physical fire precautions and management arrangements are necessary to ensure the safety of people in your premises if a fire does start

Outline 5 step methodology[403]

1. Identify fire hazards

    - Sources of ignition

    - Sources of fuel

    - Sources of oxygen

2. Identify people at risk

    - People in and around the premises

    - People especially at risk

3. Evaluate, remove, reduce and protect from risk

    - Evaluate the risk of a fire occurring

    - Evaluate the risk to people from fire

    - Remove or reduce fire hazards

    - Remove or reduce the risks to people

        o Detection and warning (smoke detectors, fire alarms)

        o Fire-fighting equipment and facilities (extinguishers, fire blankets)

        o Escape routes (with doors normally opening in the direction of escape)

        o Emergency lighting

---

[403] From *Fire safety risk assessment: educational premises.*

    o Signs and notices

    o Maintenance and testing

4. Record, plan, inform, instruct and train

- Record significant finding and action taken

- Prepare an emergency plan

- Inform and instruct relevant people; co-operate and co-ordinate with others

- Provide training

5. Review

- Keep assessment under review

- Revise where necessary

<u>Records</u>

The following are some of the records which should be kept for inspection.[404] They should be kept together in a specified place:

- the fire risk assessment, significant findings and action taken

- staff training

- fire evacuation drills

- testing and checking of escape routes, including final exit locking mechanisms, such as panic devices, emergency exit devices and any electromagnetic devices

- certificates of installation and testing of fire-warning systems, including weekly alarm tests, emergency lighting systems, fire

---

[404] Ibid.

extinguishers, hose reels and fire blankets etc and periodic maintenance by a competent person,

- recording of false alarms

- if appropriate, testing and maintenance of other fire safety equipment such as fire suppression and smoke control systems

- planning, organising, policy and implementation, monitoring, audit and review

- maintenance and audit of any systems that are provided to help the fire and rescue service

- the arrangements in a large multi-occupied building for a co-ordinated emergency plan or overall control of the actions you or your staff should take if there is a fire; and

- all alterations, tests, repairs and maintenance of fire safety systems, including passive systems such as fire doors.

The Fire and Rescue Service

Proprietors should advise the local FRS of proposed new schools and request that it inspects the premises. The FRS will assess whether this is necessary and, if so, when. The FRS also inspects schools periodically, as it does for other businesses, on a risk assessed basis. This is likely to mean more frequent FRS inspections, for instance, for boarding schools or those dealing with pupils who have special needs.[405]

A detailed inspection by the FRS or specialist external contractors can be useful evidence that the Fire standard is being met.

---

[405] See Registration of independent schools: Departmental guidance for proprietors and prospective proprietors of independent schools in England – 2019.

The First Aid Standard

ISS paragraph 13

> *13. The standard in this paragraph is met if the proprietor ensures that first aid is administered in a timely and competent manner by the drawing up and effective implementation of a written first aid policy.*[406]

Overarching requirements

This standard is outcome focused, the required outcome being that first aid is available and administered in a timely and competent manner when needed. The standard does not confine its remit to pupils.

There must be a written policy which is effectively implemented.

First-aid provision must be available at all times while people are on school premises, and also off the premises whilst on school visits. The DfE guidance adds:

> *Effective implementation of a policy will require adequate numbers of appropriately trained staff, and the provision of proper equipment, for off-site activities as well as in the school itself.*[407]

Guidance

For help, various non-statutory documents can be considered:

- *Guidance on first aid in schools: a good practice guide* – DfE[408]

- *First aid* – HSE[409]

---

[406] For boarding schools also see NMS 7 and NMS appendices A and B.

[407] Para. 4.23 – *The Independent School Standards: Guidance for independent schools, April 2019.*

[408] https://www.gov.uk/government/publications/first-aid-in-schools .

[409] https://www.hse.gov.uk/firstaid/index.htm .

In summary, the expectations entail:

- One or more suitably stocked recognisable first-aid containers (white cross on green background) – For how many, see risk assessment, below. *First aid in schools* provides a list of contents

- A first aid kit for travel, if relevant

- Sufficient first aiders with certificated training, renewed three-yearly

- Arrangements for hygiene control

- Arrangements for people with medical conditions

- An appointed person to take charge of first aid arrangements – including checking and re-stocking the first aid containers promptly

- Information to pupils and staff about first-aid arrangements (such as at induction and through notices)

- Information to parents after incidents

- A risk assessment to determine additional provision
  - Numbers of first aiders and appointed persons
  - Numbers and locations of first-aid containers
  - Arrangements for off-site and out of hours activities

- Record keeping
  - Records of any first aid given
  - Reportable injuries, diseases or dangerous occurrences
  - Accidents
  - RIDDOR record
  - Training records and certificates

- Insurance

The policy

The policy should outline how the school approaches the matters above, providing names of first aiders and the appointed person(s), locations of first aid kits, outlining training, record-keeping (by whom and where), include blank forms for informing parents, arrangements for risk assessment, guidance on when to call an ambulance and so on.

The Supervision Standard

ISS paragraph 14

> *14. The standard in this paragraph is met if the proprietor ensures that pupils are properly supervised through the appropriate deployment of school staff.*

This is an entirely outcome focused standard: the pupils are properly supervised. The supervision envisaged is by staff, rather than, say, CCTV. Adult:pupil ratios are not prescribed (except in the EYFS), allowing the provider discretion about the level of supervision required to ensure the safety and welfare of the pupils in view of variables such as their age, stage of development, needs and vulnerability, class size, activities, the experience and qualifications of the staff and proximity of colleagues and the physical characteristics of the school site.

While the standard does not require a written policy, schools will need to retain records of staffing rotas and guidance for staff about supervisory duties to evidence how the standard is usually met.

The standard is linked in practice to others such as H&S, behaviour or bullying, safeguarding and potentially risk assessment, as various types of incident may be traceable to a failure of supervision or risk mitigation.

The departmental guidance adds

> *This standard ... is intended to ensure that staffing levels devoted to supervision, including supervision during breaks from lessons and – in boarding schools – during pupils' leisure time, are sufficient to ensure that pupils are safe, that the school is reasonably orderly, and that emergencies can be dealt with promptly while still leaving adequate staffing to supervise unaffected children.*

> *In addition to the requirement in the standard, every school has a duty of care towards its pupils and this involves, amongst other things, staff with suitable training or experience supervising pupils, including those taking part in off-site activities.* [410]

---

[410] Para. 4.24 *The Independent School Standards: Guidance for independent schools, April 2019.*

The Registration Standard

ISS paragraph 15

> *15. The standard in this paragraph is met if the proprietor ensures that an admission and attendance register is maintained in accordance with the Education (Pupil Registration) (England) Regulations 2006.*

Introduction and overarching requirements

Monitoring attendance at school lays the foundation for ensuring children receive the efficient full-time education to which they are entitled and that action can be taken to safeguard their education and welfare if attendance is irregular or they go missing. Registration should therefore be seen as playing a part in safeguarding arrangements. Failure to comply with the registration regulations is a criminal offence under section 434(6) Education Act 1996.

The standard incorporates other regulations: the Education (Pupil Registration) (England) Regulations 2006 ('the registration regulations') as amended by the Education (Pupil Registration) (England) (Amendment) Regulations 2010, 2011, 2013 and 2016.[411]

Schools must keep two registers:

- Admissions (the school roll)

- Attendance

A pupil's name can only be deleted from the school roll when one of certain statutory grounds applies as set out in the registration regulations.

---

[411] Coronavirus amendments regulations concerning absence recording for reasons connected with the pandemic were withdrawn in the Spring of 2022.

The registers must be made in ink or, if by computer, must be backed up monthly, and either way must be preserved for three years from when entries are made. [412]

Guidance

The registration regulations are explained in:

- *Working together to improve school attendance* – September 2022 (at sections 7 and 8)

- *Children missing education – statutory guidance for local authorities* – 2016

Admissions register

Contents

The following must be recorded for each pupil:

- Name in full

- Sex

- Name and address of every parent known to the school

  - An indication of which parent the child normally lives with

  - At least one emergency contact telephone number for that parent (but see below)

  - If the child moves to live normally with the other parent, the date from which that will occur, where it is reasonably practicable for the school to ascertain this

---

[412] Regulations 13-15, Education (Pupil Registration) (England) (Amendment) Regulations 2006.

- Date of birth

- Date of admission/readmission to the school

- Name and address of last school attended, if any

- In boarding schools, whether the pupil is day/boarding – for each pupil of compulsory school age

- Name of other school if dual registered

- If the child is to leave or has left, name of destination school and the date they are due to start or started at their new school, where it is reasonably practicable to obtain this information[413]

Name and Sex

Where name and sex are referenced in the registration regulations, these mean legal name and legal sex. The admissions register is not a public document. Registration does not prevent a school from addressing or treating a pupil otherwise for other purposes.[414]

Emergency contacts

The registration standard requires at least one emergency telephone number for each child. KCSIE expects schools to hold more than one where reasonably possible.[415]

Regulation 5 of the Education (Pupil Registration) (England) (Amendment)Regulations as amended in 2016.

[414] Bellinger v Bellinger [2002] UKHL 21. R (on the application of Elan-Cane) v Sec of State for the Home Department_[2021] UKSC 56. See for example, Lord Reed at para.s 52 – 54.

[415] KCSIE 2022 para. 101.

Inclusion on register

A pupil should be included on the register from the beginning of first day agreed or notified for attendance.[416]

Deletions from the admissions register

A pupil can only be deleted from the admissions register where one of certain prescribed grounds are met. These are set out in Annex A of *Children missing education 2016*. The grounds differ depending on whether the pupil is of compulsory school age.[417]

A pupil's name can be deleted from the roll on grounds of absence (failing to return within ten days of authorised absence, or absence for twenty consecutive school days) but not until the school and LA have jointly made reasonable enquiries to establish the whereabouts of the child. This (the right to delete) also does not apply if the school has reasonable grounds to believe that the absence is on account of sickness or unavoidable cause unless a doctor has certified that they are too unwell to attend before they cease to be of compulsory school age and neither the pupil or their parent has indicated that they will wish to return for the sixth form.[418]

Returns to the LA

Schools must notify the LA of additions and removals of pupils to and from the admissions register at non-standard times, including where parents decide to home educate, and at other times on request. The details to be provided are set out in the 2016 registration regulations and *Working together to improve school attendance* . Notification must be within 5 days of an admission or, in the case of a deletion, as soon as the grounds for deletion are made out.

---

[416] The Education (Pupil Registration) (England) Regulations 2006, regulation 5(3).

[417] See regulation 8(1) and 8(3) of the registration regulations.

[418] Regulation 8(1)(f) and (g) Education (Pupil Registration) (England) Regulations 2006.

Attendance register

Contents

For contents see regulation 6 of the registration regulations and *Working together to improve school attendance* (applies from September 2022), at section 8.

Attendance codes

The attendance codes which are statutory for the state sector are optional for independent schools although they are often followed on a voluntary basis, with any adaptations needed.

Boarding

A school where all pupils are boarders is not required to keep an attendance register.[419] Daily registration provisions do not apply to boarders in schools with both day and boarding provision.[420] However, all boarding schools are required to know the whereabouts of the pupils in their charge at all times, or how to find their whereabouts.[421]

---

[419] Regulation 4(b) Education (Pupil Registration) (England) Regulations 2006.

[420] Ibid. at Regulation 6(1) (last line).

[421] NMS 20.5.

The Risk Assessment standard

ISS paragraph 16

16. The standard in this paragraph is met if the proprietor ensures that

(a) the welfare of pupils at the school is <u>safeguarded and promoted</u> by the drawing up and effective implementation of a written risk assessment policy; and

(b) appropriate action is taken to reduce risks that are identified.[422]

Introduction

Effective risk management is essential in any school, state-funded or fully independent, but the added emphasis on risk assessment in the independent school standards could be seen as a *quid pro quo* of the additional freedom of independent schools and the greater variety in the independent sector. Risk assessment was an integral part of the H&S and fire standards from 2003 but the introduction of the dedicated risk assessment standard in 2015 takes the duty wider and specifically includes all pupil welfare and safeguarding issues.

The DfE guidance explains:

4.28 The aim of this standard is not to make schools totally risk-averse. Learning about risk, meeting challenges and having new experiences are an important part of growing up. However, it is important that schools take an active approach to managing risk, and thereby reduce the likelihood that pupils will be harmed through negligence and a lack of foresight or proper planning.

---

[422] For boarding schools also see NMS 4.1, 9.3, 18.2 and appendices A and B .

Overarching requirements

The standard requires schools to take a systematic comprehensive approach to management of all risks to pupils across the school and all its operations, on and off-site including online. It requires

- a written risk assessment policy with a focus on proactive safeguarding of pupil welfare

- the policy to be put into practice effectively – that is, risks are assessed as prescribed by the policy

- appropriate action to be taken to reduce the risks noted.

Scope

Examples of how the strategic risk assessment policy should go wider than H&S are provided by the HSE's list of matters not covered by H&S law.

- Promoting the welfare and wellbeing of pupils

- Communicable diseases

- Behaviour and discipline of pupils

- Criminal record checks

- Food hygiene

- Driving/ licensing of school minibus drivers

- Use of seat belts on buses

- Waste and pollution control[423]

The DfE has also provided examples of risk which schools have sometimes failed to plan for and mitigate adequately:

---

[423] https://www.hse.gov.uk/services/education/sensible-leadership/is-it-really.htm.

a. public access to the school and its pupils when the school occupies shared premises, including premises which incorporate places of worship

b. safeguarding risks posed during educational visits, either from staff or from members of the public

c. safeguarding risks arising from the presence of non-staff adults (e.g. adult children of boarding staff) in boarding premises

d. risks arising from pupil access to roofs, poorly secured windows and so on

e. safeguarding risks posed by inadequate staffing cover at weekends in boarding schools

f. failure to consider dangers from traffic when large numbers of pupils leave a school building immediately adjacent to a road, e.g. between lessons and at the end of the school day

g. failure to consider dangers posed by other pupils and the risk of pupil-on-pupil abuse, including 'sexting[424]

Risk assessments, other than H&S and those above, which are mentioned by the standards, KCSIE and/or other guidance include:

- The Prevent risk assessments – overarching and for individuals where indicated

- Risk assessments when a person starts work before the DBS has processed their check and returned the certificate

- Risk assessments relating to pupils with disabilities, mental health issues or medical conditions such as eating disorders

- Assessments of risks pupils may pose to each other and themselves

---

[424] Para. 4.26 *The Independent School Standards: Guidance for independent schools, April 2019.*

- Assessments around welfare risks (such as bullying or harassment) presented by different parts of the site

- Assessments of site security

- Risk assessments around use of reasonable force

- Risk assessments to support creation of the first aid policy

Risk assessment is also helpful when making decisions where guidance is unclear, as it provides a structure for thinking through issues, options, who might be affected, controls, and ensuring they are implemented.

The policy should set out the school's strategic approach to risk assessment areas relevant to the school and cover questions such as who is responsible for assessing and implementing controls, processes for review, the requirements the school is setting for internal record-keeping, whereabouts records are kept, and when external advisors should be used.

Who

Risk assessments have often been the preserve of the school bursar because of the historic connection with H&S and premises. While a senior person should have oversight of the risk management strategy, risk assessments need to be carried out by persons competent in the particular area, such as the DSL for safeguarding risks and the school nurse or counsellor for health-related or mental health-related risks. In some instances it will be appropriate to use specialist external advisors for particular complex or high risks.

When and how

From the DfE guidance:

Risk assessment should be a constant process, with input encouraged from all staff and pupils.[425]

The extent to which risk assessments underlying the overarching policy should be recorded in writing is largely a matter for the discretion of the school, subject to any specific guidance to the contrary. However, the person(s) responsible for the particular area should still be noted in the policy along with any checks and balances. Significant risks should be in writing and risk assessments should be suitable and efficient. The need for 'dynamic risk assessment' should not be an excuse not to have a rigorous approach. The HSE has publicly available materials concerning risk management, although a noted these would need to be adapted for use in relation to non-H&S risks to pupils.

---

[425] Ibid. at para. 4.28.

CHAPTER THIRTEEN

THE SUITABILITY STANDARDS – ISS PART 4

Introduction

The standards in ISS Part 4 set standards for checking the suitability of people who work in schools or govern them. These provide legal underpinning for the duties described in part three of KCSIE (Safer Recruitment) in terms of steps schools 'must' take.[426] KCSIE also expands on the legal duties with broader guidance about recruitment and selection procedures.

There is a level on which the suitability standards are the most prescriptive and technically complicated of them all. But on another, they boil down to a requirement to put in place a rigorous, methodical vetting system, which ensures that the relevant checks are carried out every time and to keep a comprehensive record of checks.

This works best when the school is driven by a commitment to keeping children safe and an understanding of the important part vetting checks play in screening out people with the wrong intentions towards pupils. Otherwise, there may be a temptation to cut corners and mistakes can creep in over time. Those responsible for recruitment and vetting procedures are providing one of the school's crucial front-line defences against people who seek to access children for the wrong reasons – that is not to diminish the importance of a culture of vigilance post-recruitment. When checking does go awry, often it is because there is little understanding of the task, lack of ownership and therefore suitability checks are accorded low priority. A school may provide a

---

[426] Duties expressed as 'must' are underpinned by law. Schools must also 'have regard' to those expressed as 'should' and only depart from that guidance for good reason. See section 'KCSIE and WT' in Chapter Eleven.

wonderful education but fail an inspection on account of poor attention to recruitment processes.

There are a number of problems with the suitability standards:

- the internal cross-referencing is slightly defective

- there are issues of construction and in some places updating is needed to reflect changes resulting from other legislation

- KCSIE provides an account of the suitability requirements in terms accessible to lay people. This is not always entirely aligned with the detail of the standards.

- the list of checks which must be recorded on the SCR is less extensive than the list of checks which must be carried out (a potential source of confusion if schools seek to work backwards from one list to another)

- KCSIE adds requirements to those in the standards (albeit with 'shoulds' rather than 'musts') which again can lead to confusion.[427]

For all these reasons, those who struggle with the detail of Part four are not alone. This chapter will try to shine some light on the dark corners and address some common misconceptions, but is an overview only. All information about suitability checks has been gathered into this chapter, although some are requirements are rightly part of the safeguarding standard rather than ISS Part 4. This is to try to avoid adding to confusion by dividing information which naturally sits together across more than one chapter.

Much of the suitability standard is based on an understanding of 'regulated activity', as defined by the Safeguarding Vulnerable Groups Act 2006. The concepts of regulated activity and regulated activity providers are explained in Chapter Five, above.

---

[427] These are strong 'shoulds', with which it would be difficult to find a 'good reason' not to comply in practice.

Overview – in a nutshell

The basic premise underlying suitability requirements is that somebody somewhere must have carried out all the relevant checks on a person before they engage in regulated activity. Each employer is responsible for ensuring the suitability of their own staff.

The checks and recruitment processes to be done by schools on their own staff and proprietors, and by supply agencies on people they supply to work in schools, are tightly regulated under the standards as supplemented by KCSIE.

The checking requirements for others largely flow from KCSIE and allow more latitude (within parameters) for discretion depending on what is appropriate to the situation and all the facts. Much confusion flows from the assumption that there is a prescribed 'right' answer to every vetting question whereas there are often judgment calls to be made at the margins.

Where the staff of others will have contact with a school's pupils, schools should seek written confirmation from the other employer that they have appropriately vetted their employee for work with children and should also check the person's identity on arrival at school. Schools should take the lead in specifying and explaining to the third-party organisation what the school expects and requires by way of vetting and set this out in their contract with the other organisation.[428]

The checks for staff, supply staff and proprietors must be recorded on the Single Central Register (SCR). Schools are not required to record the staff of others on the SCR, but see later for more.

Structure of this chapter

- Roles, with corresponding vetting and SCR requirements

- List and outline of each of the suitability checks

- The Single Central Register (SCR)

---

[428] KCSIE 2022 para. 289.

Roles, with corresponding vetting and SCR requirements

The suitability standards are found in Part 4 of the standards. They are not reproduced here due to their length and complexity. They cover the checks which schools must run on the people in the following groups:

- Staff – ISS paragraph 18

- Supply staff – ISS paragraph 19

- Proprietors – ISS paragraph 20

KCSIE prescribes vetting checks for additional people who are not in these categories. Some workers could fall under more than one definition in which case the school may use their professional judgement about how to classify them. Some criteria for this are suggested later.

Staff

Definition

> *"Staff" means any person working at the school whether*
>
> - *under a contract of employment,*
>
> - *under a contract for services or*
>
> - *otherwise than under a contract,*
>
> *but does not include supply staff or a volunteer.*[429]

Working 'under a contract of employment' refers to employees.

Working 'under a contract for services' is understood to mean a contract between the individual and the school. This would cover self-employed people who provide services to the school, for example. (A person working at the school as an employee/under a contract with

---

[429] Reg 2 (Interpretation) of the Education (Independent School Standards) Regulations 2014.

another organisation, would be the staff of the other organisation rather than of the school. That company would be a contractor. See 'Vetting checks for contractors/contractor staff', later.)

'Working at the school … otherwise than under a contract' would cover staff such as visiting music teachers (instrumentalists) who are recruited and provided by the school but who contract directly with parents for their tuition services.

Staff – Who checks and what they check

The school must carry out the suitability checks prescribed by the standards and KCSIE which apply to each individual. More detail is given about the checks and when they are applicable in the next section. It is acceptable and indeed normal to include information in the SCR which goes beyond minimum legal requirements.

Staff: Checking and SCR recording requirements

Checks required	SCR recording requirements ISS 21

From ISS 18 and KCSIE
• Identity
• Barred list
• Prohibition from teaching (where applicable)
• Prohibition from management (where applicable)
• Qualifications (where appropriate)
• Enhanced DBS
• Overseas information (inc letter of prof.standing)
• Right to work
• Medical fitness
• Agreements: NMS19 (see later)
	• [Name
	• Role
	• Date person starts work[430]]
	Whether the following checks have been carried out and if so the date completed or certificate seen:
	  • Identity
	  • Barred list
	  • Prohib'teaching
	  • Prohib' management
	  • Qualifications
	  • Enhanced DBS
	  • Overseas
	  • Right to work

---

[430] In addition to the legal requirements, these are essential.

From KCSIE and the Childcare Act 2006 • Disqualification under the Childcare Act 2006 **From KCSIE** • Employment history/application form etc • References • Online search	

Suggested additional information for the SCR

Schools commonly include all the required checks on the SCR, whether or not their inclusion is mandated by ISS 21, for the benefit of having a complete ready overview:

- medical fitness*[431]

- employment history (application form)

- references

- online search

- disqualification from childcare (where applicable)*

- NMS agreements (where applicable)*

- Notes column

---

[431] * Indicates that the check is legally required ('must' rather than 'should').

Supply staff

<u>Definition</u>

In common parlance in the education sector, 'supply' is often understood to mean *ad hoc* teachers. But 'supply staff' is a legally defined term in the standards. It is not limited to teaching staff and does not encompass staff, *ad hoc* or otherwise, who are not from an agency:

> *"Supply staff" means any person working at the school supplied by an employment business*
>
> *"Employment business" has the meaning given in section 13(3) of the Employment Agencies Act 1973[432]*

Section 13(3) of the Employment Agencies Act 1973 provides:

> *13(3) For the purposes of this Act "employment business" means the business (whether or not carried on with a view to profit and whether or not carried on in conjunction with any other business) of supplying persons in the employment of the person carrying on the business, to act for, and under the control of, other persons in any capacity.*

Essentially these are temping agencies. Workers under these arrangements are paid by the agency to work under the supervision of someone else and have a modified form of employment rights in relation to the agency. The individual substitutes for school staff and works under direction of the school.

---

[432] Reg 2 (Interpretation) of the Education (Independent School Standards) Regulations 2014.

Supply staff – Who checks and what they check

The agency must do all the vetting checks which a direct employer would otherwise be obliged to do, including references.[433] Ideally this would also include not just vetting checks but also safer recruitment processes although this does not come through strongly in KCSIE.

The school must not allow an agency person to start work until

- they have evidence (written confirmation from the agency) that the employment business has undertaken the necessary checks on each named individual. The evidence must be specific to each individual, not simply a general statement that checks are carried out on staff supplied by the employment business

- they have checked the identity of the person (in addition to the identity check by the agency). This is usually done on arrival at the school

- they have had sight of the DBS certificate. This is usually satisfied by the person producing the original to the school the first time they attend the premises. [434]

---

[433] https://www.gov.uk/employment-agencies-and-businesses – for vetting requirements see also the Conduct of Employment Agencies and Employment Businesses Regulations 2003, reg 22 which requires agencies to take up two references.

[434] *The Independent School Standards: Guidance for independent schools, April 2019*, para. 5.5, explaining ISS 19. ISS para.19(2)(a)(ii) requires schools always to see the enhanced DBS certificate before supply staff start. KCSIE 2022, para. 286. appears to limit the requirement to view DBS certificates to where the certificate discloses information. Limiting the duty in this way would only be appropriate where the information about whether or not the certificate contains information comes from a reliable third-party source such as an automated secure online checking service.

Supply staff: Checking and SCR recording requirements

Checks required ISS 19/KCSIE	SCR recording requirements ISS 21

• As for staff
 	
Plus
 	
• On-arrival identity check by school
• Sight of Enhanced DBS certificate – usually on arrival
	• [Name, role, dates worked]
	• Date written notification received from the supply agency that it has made checks of
	   ○ Identity
	   ○ Barred list
	   ○ Qualifications
	   ○ Enhanced DBS (or DBS Status Check)
	   ○ Overseas information (where applicable)
	   ○ Right to work in the UK
	   ○ Prohibition from teaching check (where applicable)
	   ○ Prohibition from management check (where applicable).
	• Dates of each of the underlying checks in the case of boarding staff
	• Whether the school has seen a copy of the DBS certificate (usually recorded as another date)

Suggested additional information for the SCR

As with staff, schools commonly include additional information such as dates worked.

Proprietors

Definitions

ISS 20 divides proprietors into three types:

- individual proprietors

- the chair of a 'body of persons' (whether or not incorporated)

- other members of a 'body of persons'. This would include people such as trustees, charity trustees and/or company directors of the proprietorial body.

Proprietors – Who checks whom and how

'Individual' proprietors refers not only to 'sole' proprietors. Individual proprietors, including members of a small group of individual proprietors, must each be vetted by the DfE, on behalf of the Secretary of State. Once a group appoints a chair, the DfE carries out the vetting checks on the chair only and the chair (through the school) is responsible for ensuring the other (non-chair) members of the proprietorial body are subject to the required checks.

Schools must contact registration.enquiries@education.gov.uk to inform the DfE when there is a change of chair and follow instructions received. Likewise, where there is a group of individuals and no chair, schools must alert the DfE to the introduction of new individuals so that they can be vetted.

Complex cases

The DfE can advise who should be regarded as proprietor or chair in difficult cases. See Chapter Two (Who is the proprietor?) for the legal definition from the Education Act 1996. Where there are layers of companies under a holding company, the proximate company is usually treated as the proprietor. Where there is central ownership of a group of schools under a single company with advisory boards performing the role of governors for individual schools in the group, the proprietorial body is usually the company and the directors/trustees would be vetted as proprietors. The advisory boards are unlikely to have any legal status so the members of those boards would normally be vetted as for volunteers. Enhanced DBS checks are appropriate. Barring information would be required if, for example, members will have the opportunity for regular unsupervised access to children.

These are issues to explore on first registration. Advisors coming in later should start by considering the information on GIAS, which should show which entity/person has been deemed the proprietor and correspond with the DfE if there are issues or updating may be needed.

Proprietors: Checking and SCR recording requirements

Checks required	SCR recording requirements ISS 21
From ISS 20 and KCSIE • Identity • Enhanced DBS (countersigned by the Secretary of State if sole proprietor / chair) • Right to work • Overseas information (where relevant) • Barred list (if will engage in RA) • Prohibition from teaching (where applicable) • Prohibition from management **From KCSIE and the Childcare Act 2006** • Disqualification under the Childcare Act 2006 (if relevant)[435]	• [Name, role, dates in role] • Individuals who have been checked by the DfE (eg sole/chair) – not required on register Non-chair members of the proprietorial body • Enhanced DBS • Identity • Right to work in the UK • Overseas checks, where applicable

---

[435] Disqualification from childcare is not covered by the DfE's checks and would have to be done by the school where relevant.

Suggested additional information for the SCR

The standards do not require sole proprietors, individual proprietors (where there is no chair) or the chair to be included on the register. These are vetted by the DfE, when informed by the school, and the DfE confirms this to the school in due course. A school would not be in a position to know the dates on which the DfE had performed the relevant checks although schools commonly note the names and roles of all proprietors on the SCR, with the date appointed, date DfE informed and date of response from DfE.

Being a proprietor of a school is not regulated activity *per se* but barring information will be available as part of an enhanced DBS check for members of the proprietorial body who will visit their school regularly and have opportunity for unsupervised access to pupils.

Other roles covered in KCSIE and the NMS for boarding

KCSIE provides extensive guidance about how to ensure the suitability of a range of people in addition to those expressly addressed in the standards. Schools must have regard to that guidance but inevitably there are judgment calls to be made in some situations as the guidance cannot cover every situation. See later for more.

- Volunteers

- Visitors

- Contractors and third-party staff

- Trainee/student teachers

- Adults who supervise children on work experience

- Host families and private fostering

- Educational guardians[436]

Of these probably only three require additional definition:

<u>Volunteers</u>

A volunteer is defined as

> *'Any person engaged in an activity which involves spending time, unpaid (except for travel and other approved out-of-pocket expenses), doing something which aims to benefit some third party and not a close relative.'*[437]

Where there is difficulty distinguishing volunteers from visitors or staff, it can help to think about whether they are being remunerated and whether the 'activity' could be considered 'work'.

Example: parents who watch sports matches and then mingle with pupils over the post-match tea are visitors. Parents who, in addition, help run the match and supervise pupils are volunteers.

A supervised volunteer is not in regulated activity – unless they carry out personal care, healthcare or an overnight activity with pupils. Schools are 'required' to undertake a written risk assessment and use their professional judgment to decide which checks, if any, should be used. KCSIE prescribes minimum criteria for the risk assessment to consider. The risk assessment should be recorded.[438]

<u>Visitors</u>

Vetting requirements generally apply to workers. A visitor who is not working does not require vetting checks. (There are exceptions in the NMS and EYFS for people who live on premises where regulated

---

[436] NMS 22.1 These should be subject to the same recruitment procedures as staff, here appointed by the school.

[437] KCSIE 2022 footnote 161.

[438] KCSIE 2022 para. 305-307.

activity occurs.) The need to escort and supervise visitors is a matter of discretion for the head.[439]

Working visitors could include people such as educational psychologists and therapists. Where they are supplied by an external organisation, as for supply staff, the other organisation should be asked to confirm that the appropriate checks have been done. Identity should be checked on arrival. It Is not necessary for the school to view the DBS certificate. [440]

Contractors

This is the category which causes most confusion due to factors such as the wide ill-defined range of workers it covers and the scope for overlap with the defined categories above. Sometimes it is assumed erroneously to encompass only builders and caterers. In addition, third parties can have difficulty accessing the necessary formal checks. For example, parents and self-employed people are not able to make an application to the DBS direct about someone they have employed or about themselves, and only schools, LAs and teacher supply agencies can access teacher status checks through Teacher Services. Schools may therefore sometimes need to assist to carry out checks for contractors.

How to distinguish supply staff from other third-party staff

	Supply staff	Third party staff
The third-party/contractor is an employment agency	Yes	No
The staff work under the direction of the school	Yes	No, usually
The agency/third party organisation does the checks	Yes	Yes – except where they need help from the school
The school must obtain confirmation that the relevant checks have been done	Yes	Yes

---

[439] KCSIE 2022 para. 298 – 303.

[440] KCSIE 2022 para. 301.

The checks are prescribed in the ISS	Yes	No
The school is required to see the DBS check	Yes	No
The DBS must be less than 3 months old at the start date, unless the 3-month rule applies	Yes	No
School must obtain written confirmation that relevant checks have been carried out	Yes	Yes – more flexibility about level of detail appropriate to the situation
School must check identity on arrival at school	Yes	Yes

<u>Vetting checks for contractors/contractor staff</u>

Contractors/contractor staff could be regular or occasional, permanent or temporary. They may or may not work directly with or have access to children or have been vetted on entry to their profession or professional association. This makes for a complex assessment when it comes to vetting requirements.

The suitability checks expected in relation to contractor staff are arrived at through a combination of analysis and professional judgment. There may be more than one 'compliant' approach available. Checks may not always need to be done afresh; pre-existing checks by a third-party employer or professional body could suffice. The various forms of the three-month rule for DBS checks, discussed below, only apply to staff and supply staff. It does not apply by law to contractors.

Whatever the school decides, schools should set out their safeguarding requirements in the contract with the third-party organisation.[441]

Questions to consider:

- Will the person be working in regulated activity? If so an enhanced DBS check with barred list information is required –

---

[441] KCSIE 2022 – para. 289.

which also entails the employer checking identity by means prescribed by the DBS.

- Will they have opportunity for regular contact with children, while not being in regulated activity (eg a regular tradesperson)? If so an enhanced DBS check without barring information is appropriate.

- Will they have occasional opportunity for contact with children? If so consider (risk assess) whether a DBS check at the basic level would be appropriate and/or supervision.

- Will they be carrying out work for which task-specific checks are prescribed (childcare, teaching work, management)? If so each relevant check is required (disqualification from childcare, prohibition from teaching, prohibition from management).

- As a matter of assessment and management of risks to children, should the school require any additional measures or assurances from the contractor such as in relation to their recruitment processes and other checks which may be relevant to the role or person such as references, medical fitness or overseas information?

Where a self-employed person could be either staff or a contractor, as a rule of thumb, the greater the length of contract, the vulnerability of children and opportunity for contact with children, then the higher the risk. Where there is higher risk, this would indicate that more stringent vetting would be appropriate and that the self-employed person should, therefore, be vetted as for staff and included on the SCR.

Where contractor staff are intrinsic to the school's operations, such as catering staff, this would indicate that the school should take a stringent approach to recruitment in line with the requirements on agencies.

Schools do not have a right to see personal data about the employees of other organisations and other organisations are unlikely to be able to share it on account of rules relating to privacy and data protection. In respect of contractor staff, schools should therefore ask for written confirmation from the other organisation of the checks which have been done (where checks ae needed) but are not required to ask for sight of a DBS certificate. (This differs from the requirements in the case of agency staff where the school must see the DBS certificate.) The school should also check that the person who presents at school is the same person on whom checks have been made.

Where there are complex facts, schools should make a reasonable decision about how to proceed. There may be a range of reasonable approaches which could all assure the safety of pupils. Risk assessment can be used to support that process.

List and outline of suitability checks and how they apply

The various types of vetting checks and how to do them are described in KCSIE. In addition, schools would be well-advised to run internet checks for completeness particularly when formal checks are not available. The following is an outline only.

<u>Employment history/application form</u>

- Employment history should be taken from job applicants by application form and interview, rather than C.V. alone

- KCSIE 2022 sets out extensive details to be required by application forms – paragraph 211 – 214

- Required for staff and supply staff (a 'have regard' duty)

<u>References</u>

- Extensive guidance is provided in KCSIE 2022 – paragraphs 221 – 223

- Required for staff and supply staff (a 'have regard' duty)

<u>Interview and pre-interview declarations</u>

- Candidates who are short-listed should be asked to provide and declare various information for discussion at interview if necessary – contents are prescribed in KCSIE 2022 paragraph 215 – 218

- Guidance about interviews is in KCSIE 2022 – paragraphs 224–228

- Required for staff and supply staff (a 'have regard' duty)

Barred list check

- Normally accessed as part of an enhanced DBS check. A standalone check can be accessed by employers from the Teaching Regulation Agency but this must only be done in specified circumstances.[442] See: *Teaching Regulation Agency Employer Access, Schools web service: A guide for users*[443]

- Required for

   o anyone working in regulated activity

   o persons aged 16 and over, including members of staff households, who live on same premises as boarders (NMS19.2)

Enhanced DBS checks

- Accessed by new application to the DBS, through the DBS Update Service (for subscribers) or by adoption of a check under the three-month rule. See DBS website and KCSIE for details.

- Required for

---

[442] KCSIE 2022 para. 247. For non-staff and members of staff households living on site, a barred list check must be done as part of an enhanced DBS check.

[443] User Guide Teacher Services – Employers (education.gov.uk).

○ Anyone working in regulated activity – subject to 'the three-month rule' – even if they say they have not worked in the UK[444]

○ Persons who are not engaging in regulated activity relating to children, but whose work provides them with an opportunity for regular contact with children[445] (barring information not required here)

○ Persons aged 16 and over, including members of staff households who live on the same premises as boarders but are not employed by the school (NMS 19.2)[446]

○ Persons aged 16 and over resident in external boarding lodgings arranged by the school whilst pupils are staying, with satisfactory outcomes known before any pupil is placed (NMS 23.4)

○ Persons 16 and over who live on same premises where childcare is delivered (EYFS 3.10)

• DBS three-month rule – Schools are not required to obtain a new DBS certificate or carry out new checks for events overseas if during a period which ended not more than three months before the person's appointment, the applicant has worked in a school in England in:

○ A post which brought the person regularly into contact with children; or

○ if appointed after 12th May 2006 any post in a school; or

---

[444] KCSIE 2022 para. 479.

[445] KCSIE 2022 para. 291 and ISS 18(2)(d) and reg 2(5)(b) of the Education (Independent School Standards) Regulations 2014.

[446] The same premises are now defined to include, for example, an abbey or teacher housing on the same grounds as a school, requiring the use of the same entry and exit points. NMS 19.2.

o in the further education sector in England, or in a 16-19 academy, in a post which involved the provision of education which brought the person regularly into contact with children or young persons.[447]

If a school accepts a pre-existing DBS under the three-month rule it must make a separate check of the barred list.

Supply staff – In the case of supply staff, the DBS check must be no more than three months old unless the three-month rule applies.[448]

New for 2022, even when the three-month rule is available, schools should 'carefully consider' whether to request a DBS check anyway. [449]

- <u>DBS checks not required</u> – DBS checks are not required for people such as visitors, trades people, supervised volunteers (who do not carry out personal care etc), under-16s on work experience, people onsite when pupils are not present, pupils from other schools. It is not a legal requirement to renew DBS checks at regular intervals or for those who take a break but maintain continuity of employment (e.g. maternity leave or furlough).

<u>Standard DBS checks</u>

- Offered by some contractors whose staff are not in regulated activity (not 'required' by the standards or KCSIE but may be information to take into account in assessing level of supervision needed to mitigate any risks)

---

[447] Para. 232 KCSIE 2022.

[448] ISS 19(3) and (4) and also *The Independent School Standards: Guidance for independent schools, April 2019*, para. 5.5.

[449] KCSIE 2022 para. 234.

Basic DBS checks

- These are not currently a requirement but, when a DBS check is not mandated, some schools sometimes ask for them as a matter of policy from contractors who are not in regulated activity. Some such contractors also volunteer them. They can be taken into account when assessing issues of risk and supervision.

- KCSIE advises: *where the contractor does not have opportunity for regular contact with children, schools and colleges should decide on whether a basic DBS disclosure would be appropriate- paragraph 291.*

Prohibition from teaching[450]

- Prohibition information is accessed through the TRA's Employer Access Service.[451] Pre-2012 sanctions by the former GTCE may also still be in force. This should also be checked via the TRA's Secure Access system.

- Required for

  o appointments from April 2012 which will involve 'teaching work'

  o includes those 'teaching' in the early years from age 3, where children are registered as 'pupils' of the school

- 'Teaching work' is defined in the Teachers' Disciplinary (England) Regulations 2012 to encompass:

  o planning and preparing lessons and courses for pupils

  o delivering lessons to pupils (including remotely)

---

[450] The standards reference directions under section 142 of the Education Act 2002. KCSIE relies on section 141B of the Education Act 2002.

[451] https://teacherservices.education.gov.uk .

- o assessing the development, progress and attainment of pupils

  - o reporting on the development, progress and attainment of pupils.

- Not required for teaching assistants who work under 'supervision and direction' of a teacher. Teaching assistants, sports coaches, invigilators, nursery nurses for example, may need individual consideration case by case, as to whether they are carrying out teaching work or working under supervision[452]

- It is irrelevant whether the 'teacher' has QTS or is peripatetic.

Section 128 direction (prohibition from management of independent school)[453]

- Applies to appointments from 12th August 2015

- Information is accessible via the TRA's Employer Access Service, and also (for those who will work in regulated activity) as part of an enhanced DBS check with barring information[454]

- Required for:

  - o Proprietors, governors and trustees

  - o Head and members of senior leadership team (whether or not teachers)

---

[452] IICSA has recommended that all teaching assistants, learning support staff and cover supervisors should be brought within the misconduct jurisdiction of the Teaching Regulation Agency. The Secretary of State's response to this is not yet known.

[453] See section 128 Education and Skills Act 2008 and the Independent Educational Provision in England (Prohibition on Participation in Management) Regulations 2014.

[454] See the DfE's letter to all schools dated May 2018: https://www.isi.net/support/publications/dfe-letter-all-schools-may-2018 and KCSIE 2022 para. 255 – 261.

- ○ Teaching heads of departments

- ○ Internal promotions to these positions

Identity

- Required for everyone within reason (such as staff, supply staff, proprietors, contractors, visiting speakers – not the postman)

- ID checks to support DBS checks are tightly regulated by the DBS. See *DBS ID checking guidelines*[455]

- Birth certificates – a best practice recommendation[456]

- ID checks in other situations, such as when a contractor arrives at school, must be simply sensible and sufficient to satisfy the school.

Mental and physical fitness for responsibilities of the post

- There is no prescription about how this is checked. Self-declaration forms are often used for junior staff and medicals for the most senior roles

- Required for staff and supply staff

Right to work

- This check applies to schools as it does to all employers

- Guidance is available about how to check a person's right to work in the U.K.: *Checking a job applicant's right to work*[457]

- Required for: staff, supply staff and proprietors. Third parties are responsible for checking their own staff

---

[455] https://www.gov.uk/government/publications/dbs-identity-checking-guidelines .

[456] Para. 231 KCSIE 2022.

[457] https://www.gov.uk/check-job-applicant-right-to-work .

Qualifications, where relevant

- The standards require this for staff and supply staff. Qualifications are not prescribed by government for independent schools (except for those who work in the EYFS)

- Schools should check that applicants have any qualifications which the school takes into account when making the appointment

Overseas information

- Required where an enhanced DBS certificate is 'unlikely to be sufficient to establish suitability to work in a school on account of applicants living or having lived outside the UK'

- Schools must make 'such further checks as they consider appropriate having regard to any guidance' from the DfE. Since Brexit this applies also to applicants from EEA countries.

- Required for staff, supply staff and proprietors

- The guidance is KCSIE. See also the directory of what is available at: Guidance on the application process for criminal records checks overseas[458]

- For teacher applicants – KCSIE recommends obtaining a letter of professional standing from the regulatory body for the country (or countries) where the applicant has worked.[459] Applicants can find contact details of regulatory bodies in the EU/EEA and Switzerland on the Regulated Professions database.[460] Applicants can also contact the UK Centre for

---

[458] The Independent School Standards: Guidance for independent schools, April 2019 at para. 5.5. For the directory see:
https://www.gov.uk/government/publications/criminal-records-checks-for-overseas-applicants

[459] KCSIE 2022 para. 279.

[460] https://ec.europa.eu/growth/tools-databases/regprof/ .

Professional Qualifications[461] who will signpost them to the appropriate EEA regulatory body

Disqualification under the Childcare Act

- Schools have discretion about how to approach this. People must be informed and reminded from time to time of their duty to declare if they are disqualified from childcare. This is often approached by annual written reminder which is signed and returned by way of self-declaration that the individual is not disqualified. See the statutory guidance: Disqualification under the Childcare Act 2006.[462]

- Required for staff working in 'childcare', that is, with children in the early years including reception, and wraparound childcare (such as breakfast clubs and after school care) for children up to age 8.

- Includes volunteers and agency staff and those with direct management of early years/later years provision (the head and those with day-to-day management, but not governors)

Internet search

- Visiting speakers (recommended as part of a clear protocol to ensure suitability)[463]

- This text recommends that internet searches should be widely used to support formal suitability checks.

- **New** from September 2022, KCSIE recommends schools 'consider' carrying out an online search pre-interview as part of their due diligence on short-listed candidates

---

[461] https://cpq.ecctis.com/ .

[462] https://www.gov.uk/government/publications/disqualification-under-the-childcare-act-2006/disqualification-under-the-childcare-act-2006 and KCSIE 2022 para. 262 et seq.

[463] See the statutory guidance for the Prevent duty.

Agreements

- Adult non-employees (aged 16 and over) in boarding schools living on same premises as children (see NMS 19.2 for 'on the same premises' and NMS 19.3 for required content)

- Adults (aged 16 and over) providing long term lodgings to boarding pupils (see NMS 23.1 and 23.6 for more)

- Educational guardians and homestay hosts (NMS 24.6)

- Can be used more widely as a management tool, for example, with contractors.

Risk assessment and supervision

- Risk assessment is a tool to support decision-making in tricky cases

- 'Required' by KCSIE for:

  o Volunteers – a written risk assessment covering prescribed ground should be undertaken and retained[464]

  o People who have lived overseas when information is not available for the period overseas[465]

  o Contractors who are not in regulated activity but who have opportunity for contact with children[466]

  o Staff who start work in regulated activity before their enhanced DBS certificate is available. A separate barred list check is required. The person must be under 'appropriate supervision'[467]

---

[464] KCSIE 2022 para. 305 – 307.

[465] KCSIE 2022 para. 281.

[466] KCSIE 2022 para. 291/2.

[467] KCSIE 2022 para. 246/7 – What is 'appropriate' is a risk-based decision.

o Deciding whether to employ a person with information on their DBS check[468]

o Visiting speakers[469]

Timing of checks

All checks must be completed 'pre-appointment'. They may also be repeated where concerns arise but it is not usually a requirement to do this routinely.

<u>Exceptions</u>

There are the following exceptions:

- Enhanced DBS – Applications for DBS certificates should be made before a person starts work. If the resultant certificate is not received before they start work, subject to risk assessment, they may start work under supervision if all other checks have been completed. See KCSIE.

- Disqualification under the Childcare Act – Disclosure should be sought pre-appointment and those to whom it applies should be reminded intermittently (such as annually) that they are under a continuing duty to disclose.

- References – Should be taken up pre-interview 'where possible', see KCSIE. The refusal of applicants to provide referees at that early stage is a 'good reason' schools may not always be able to follow the guidance before an offer has been made. Certainly references must be taken up before an unconditional offer is made and the person starts work in regulated activity.

- Internet searches – Should be carried out pre-Interview.

---

[468] KCSIE 2021 para. 243 – 244.

[469] KCSIE 2022 para. 302/3.

The Single Central Register (SCR)

<u>What/why</u>

The SCR is a management tool which should enable senior leaders and proprietors to see readily whether key suitability checks are being undertaken on relevant people. The SCR is also a vital tool for demonstrating compliance to inspectors.

<u>Who</u>

The SCR must cover

- staff

- supply staff

- proprietors

Volunteers are also usually included as a matter of good practice but it is not a requirement. It is not a requirement to include the employees of other organisations unless they come within the definition of supply staff, above. However, schools should know who is on site and will need a record somewhere of regular workers who could have access to children, hence contractor staff and volunteers are typically included on the SCR under separate tabs.

<u>Form</u>

The content of the SCR is regulated but not the form. Schools commonly use an electronic tabulation with tabs for different categories of people. Paper formats are also acceptable if they work in terms of achieving a central record and providing an accurate overview.

<u>Practical tips about the SCR</u>

The SCR must be printable for inspection purposes if required. [470]

It is helpful to include a notes column for additional information, for example, to explain why a check was not applicable or about a delay

---

[470] ISS paragraph 21(2).

('not in regulated activity', 'not in a teaching role', 'DBS delayed – Under constant supervision by [name/initials of relevant colleague]').

The statutory requirements of the register are quite limited in that the requirements to record on the SCR are narrower than the requirements to undertake checks. The SCR can become onerous because schools commonly use it as a central record not only of the other suitability checks they have undertaken but also of the safeguarding training attended and wider employment information such as dates of birth, addresses, contact numbers for next of kin, and numbers for passports, pension registration, professional registrations etc.

Legal advisors should be alert to the data protection implications of this practice, particularly for when individuals leave the school or the school has to share the register with inspectors. Although KCSIE advises removing people once they leave, inspectorates ask that the statutory part of the records is not cleansed until the end of the academic year and then archived on a separate tab until after the next inspection.

As regards the checks which are required to be done but not required to be included on the SCR, schools are well-advised either to include all or none of each type on the SCR. Partial inclusion, or keeping records about certain checks in several different ways, can create confusion or the impression that the checks in question are not carried out consistently and that the school does not have a robust system. Misunderstandings can be time-consuming to unpick.

CHAPTER FOURTEEN

THE PREMISES AND ACCOMMODATION STANDARD – ISS PART 5

Introduction and overview

Due to its length, this standard is examined in parts below. The Premises standard replicates the School Premises (England) Regulations 2012 which apply to state schools. It overlaps with the Health and Safety Standard and also with the duty to create an accessibility plan, see Chapter Four.

The relevant guidance is:

- *Advice on standards for school premises: For local authorities, proprietors, school leaders, school staff and governing bodies (non-statutory) – March 2015*[471]

- *The Independent School Standards: Guidance for independent schools – April 2019* at Part 5

The Premises standard covers the headline issues of the Workplace (Health, Safety and Welfare) Regulations 1992. While the guidance above is adequate in nearly every case, where another layer of detail is required, the workplace regulations and the supporting code of practice may provide a further source of advice.

<u>'Suitable'</u>

In the premises standard:

> *31 (b) any requirement that anything provided under this Part must be 'suitable' means that it must be suitable for the pupils in respect of*

---

[471] https://www.gov.uk/government/publications/standards-for-school-premises .

whom it is provided, having regard to their ages, numbers and sex and any special requirements they may have; and

(c) a pupil has 'special requirements' if the pupil has any needs arising from physical, medical, sensory, learning, emotional or behavioural difficulties which require provision which is additional to or different from that generally required by children of the same age in schools other than special schools.[472]

Accessibility plans

Accessibility plans should also cover premises. The DfE advises:

Accessibility plans should include intentions for improving the physical environment of the school for the purpose of increasing the extent to which disabled pupils are able to take advantage of education, benefits, facilities and services provided or offered by a school.[473]

ISS paragraph 23 – Toilets and changing accommodation

23 (1) Subject to sub-paragraph (2), the standard in this paragraph is met if the proprietor ensures that—

(a) suitable toilet and washing facilities are provided for the sole use of pupils;

(b) separate toilet facilities for boys and girls aged 8 years or over are provided except where the toilet facility is provided in a room that can be secured from the inside and that is intended for use by one pupil at a time;[474] *and*

---

[472] See a similar explanation of 'adequate and suitable' on p.5 of the NMS for boarding 2015.

[473] *The Independent School Standards: Guidance for independent schools, April 2019* at para.6.1.d.

[474] See NMS 4.3 and NMS footnote 10. The position is similar in boarding.

(c) suitable changing accommodation and showers are provided for pupils aged 11 years or over at the start of the school year who receive physical education.

(2) Where separate facilities are provided under sub-paragraph (1)(a) for pupils who are disabled, they may also be used by other pupils, staff, supply staff, volunteers and visitors, whether or not they are disabled.

Number of fittings

Numbers of fittings are not prescribed in the standard. The non-statutory advice[475] suggests:

- Children aged under 5 years: one toilet and washbasin per ten pupils

- Ages 5-11: one toilet and washbasin per 20 pupils

- Ages over 11: one toilet per 20 pupils with few washbasins (than above) where facilities are shared.

Planning and design

Pupils should be able to wash their hands within or in the immediate facility of every toilet. Rooms should be well-lit and adequately ventilated. There should be easy access to the facilities in terms of their location and to allow for informal supervision without compromising pupil privacy.

Unisex

Unisex toilet facilities are permissible where the privacy of occupants is ensured. The legal standard requires a lockable 'room' for one person.[476] The non-statutory advice is not quite as clear, giving an

---

[475] *Advice on standards for school premises: For local authorities, proprietors, school leaders, school staff and governing bodies (non-statutory)* – March 2015 at p. 5.

[476] See NMS 4.3 for the position for boarders – a lockable 'room' and reg 20(1)(c) of the Workplace (Health, Safety and Welfare) Regulations 1992 which also requires *'separate rooms containing conveniences are provided for men and women except where*

example of an 'adequate enclosure and a full-height door'. This is an issue which is known to give rise to problems occasionally in practice, linked with the Behaviour and Supervision standards.

Disabled

The guidance spells out what 'suitable' will look like for facilities for disabled pupils:

> *Each toilet for disabled pupils needs to contain one toilet and one washbasin (and possibly a shower or other wash down fitting) and have a door opening directly onto a circulation space that is not a staircase and which can be secured from the inside. Where possible, the number and location of accessible toilets will be sufficient to ensure a reasonable travel distance for users that does not involve changing floor levels.*[477]

Disabled toilets may be used also by staff and visitors.

Changing and showers

Showers should provide adequate privacy and ideally be in areas separated from toilets. [478]

ISS paragraph 24 – Medical accommodation

> *24 (1) The standard in this paragraph is met if the proprietor ensures that suitable accommodation is provided in order to cater for the medical and therapy needs of pupils, including—*

---

and so far as each convenience is in a separate room the door of which is capable of being secured from inside'.

[477] *Advice on standards for school premises: For local authorities, proprietors, school leaders, school staff and governing bodies (non-statutory)* – March 2015 at p.6.

[478] See reg 24(2) of the Workplace (Health, Safety and Welfare) Regulations 1992 for the workplace parallel which references separation of changing rooms for men and women 'for reasons of propriety' but limits its application to persons at work and in various other ways. NMS 4.1: *'Accommodation gives boarders appropriate privacy, taking into account sex, age and any special requirements. Where children share a bedroom, they are able to express a preference about whom they share with.'*

(a) accommodation for the medical examination and treatment of pupils;

(b) accommodation for the short term care of sick and injured pupils, which includes a washing facility and is near to a toilet facility; and

(c) where a school caters for pupils with complex needs, additional medical accommodation which caters for those needs.

(2) The accommodation provided under sub-paragraphs (1)(a) and (b) may be used for other purposes (apart from teaching) provided it is always readily available to be used for the purposes set out in sub-paragraphs (1)(a) and (b).

(3) For the purposes of sub-paragraph (1)(c), a pupil has "complex needs" if the pupil has profound and multiple learning difficulties in addition to other significant difficulties, such as a physical disability or sensory impairment, which require provision which is additional to or different from that generally required by children of the same age in schools other than special schools or by children with special requirements.

This standard is self-explanatory. The spaces in (a), (b) and (c) need not all be the same space. There is a range of provision in schools from elaborate to spartan. The adequacy of the provision should be considered through the eyes of the potential sick pupil in the context of the cohort of pupils and school. Therapy spaces will require suitable privacy and quiet but, depending on the type of provision and facilities needed to support that, may not need to be a dedicated room. The most common question concerns the proximity of the accommodation to the toilet facility. In practical terms, it needs to be near enough for a sick child to be able to get there quickly without a loss of dignity.

ISS paragraph 25 – Maintenance, health and safety

25. The standard in this paragraph is met if the proprietor ensures that the school premises and the accommodation and facilities provided therein are maintained to a standard such that, so far as is reasonably practicable, the health, safety and welfare of pupils are ensured.

The focus of this standard is maintenance. It is outcome focused, the required outcome being that the premises are in a good state of repair to ensure the health safety and welfare of pupils. This will extend to matters already addressed above, such as fire equipment, but also covers the premises aspects of security issues which could impact the welfare of pupils. The DfE's advice is:

- *Schools and college security*[479]

- *Site security guidance*[480]

This standard would also cover building work, where relevant. See: the Building Regulations 2010.

The DfE guidance advises:

> *If a school is unsafe for reasons not specifically covered by other paragraphs in Part 5 (for example, unsafe wiring or an unsafe roof) then this standard could potentially be breached.*

ISS paragraph 26 and 27 – Acoustics and lighting

> *26. The standard in this paragraph is met if the proprietor ensures that the acoustic conditions and sound insulation of each room or other space are suitable, having regard to the nature of the activities which normally take place therein.*
>
> *27. The standard in this paragraph is met if the proprietor ensures that—*

---

[479] https://www.gov.uk/government/publications/school-and-college-security/school-and-college-security .

[480] https://www.gov.uk/government/publications/school-and-college-security/site-security-guidance .

(a) the lighting in each room or other internal space is suitable, having regard to the nature of the activities which normally take place therein; and

(b) external lighting is provided in order to ensure that people can safely enter and leave the school premises.

These standards are outcome focused and provide the DfE with regulatory tools if necessary. People should be able to see and hear each other clearly so that they can understand and concentrate with minimal disturbance from unwanted sources of noise such as traffic, fans, motors, adjoining areas or light such as glare from sunlight.

The acoustics should be suitable for the function of the room, so they may need to vary from a mainstream classroom to a special needs resource, music practice room and so forth. Normal lighting should be by natural light so far as reasonably practical, subject to the use to which the room is put and any necessary reasonable adjustments (below).

See:

- *Advice on standards for school premises For local authorities, proprietors, school leaders, school staff and governing bodies March 2015*

The guidance gives suggestions around reasonable adjustments which may be needed for pupils with disabilities and visual impairments. Specialist advice may be required in some instances.

ISS paragraph 28 – Water

28 (1) The standard in this paragraph is met if the proprietor ensures that—

(a) suitable drinking water facilities are provided;

(b) toilets and urinals have an adequate supply of cold water and washing facilities have an adequate supply of hot and cold water;

(c) cold water supplies that are suitable for drinking are clearly marked as such; and

(d) the temperature of hot water at the point of use does not pose a scalding risk to users.

(2) The facilities provided under sub-paragraph (1)(a) will be suitable only if—

(a) they are readily accessible at all times when the premises are in use; and

(b) they are in a separate area from the toilet facilities.

Pupils should have ready access to drinking water. Sources should be clearly marked 'drinking water'. Extremes of interpretation are not required as regards the labelling duty, as long as it is clear to pupils where they can access a drink of water. Supplies must be clean and in good working order. It is preferable for drinking water to come from the cold water main, to avoid the issues which can arise from tanked supplies.[481]

Hot water should generally not exceed 43°C to avoid the risk of scalding. But see also:

- *Managing legionella in hot and cold water systems* (HSE)[482]

ISS paragraph 29 – Outdoor space

29 (1) The standard in this paragraph is met if the proprietor ensures that suitable outdoor space is provided in order to enable—

(a) physical education to be provided to pupils in accordance with the school curriculum; and

(b) pupils to play outside.[483]

---

[481] See also NMS 6.3.

[482] https://www.hse.gov.uk/healthservices/legionella.htm .

[483] See also NMS 18.

31 For the purposes of this Part—

(a) "physical education" includes the playing of games;

The outdoor space should be suitable for both sport as part of the curriculum and free play. The standard does not specify the proximity of the outdoor space to the school but it should be accessible within a reasonable distance in the context of the purpose for which it will be used. Children need informal play every day and therefore some outdoor space should be adjacent to the school. See the EYFS for particular requirements for young children. Where older children have to travel, or cross a road, access arrangements should be properly risk assessed and any risk managed through appropriate measures such as supervision, to ensure the safety of pupils.

ISS paragraph 30 – Boarding premises and accommodation

30 The standard in this paragraph is met if the proprietor ensures that, where the school provides accommodation, regard is had to Standard 5 of the National Minimum Standards for Boarding Schools or, where applicable, Standard 5 of the National Minimum Standards for Residential Special Schools.

NMS 4 covers matters such as: accommodation for sleeping, studying and social purposes, toilet and washing facilities, heating, lighting, ventilation, reasonable adjustments for disabled pupils, security and surveillance.

CHAPTER FIFTEEN

THE PROVISION OF INFORMATION STANDARD – ISS PART 6

Introduction

Independent schools are not subject to the Freedom of Information Act 2000 (FOIA). FOIA provides a statutory right of access to a wide range of information from public bodies. Instead the standards provide the Secretary of State, the inspectorates and parents of pupils/prospective pupils with access to defined information. Varying degrees of proactive sharing are required from independent schools depending on the type of information. Some is to be posted on the website (if there is one), some proactively 'provided' and some merely 'made available' on request. Some must be published in several ways. Information can also be accessible under data protection law.

Many schools avoid these distinctions by putting all or most of the following information on their website.

Part 6, ISS paragraph 32

The standard is not reproduced here due to its length and complexity but should be read in full for the detail. The following summarises what it means in practice.

For further guidance see the DfE's: *The Independent School Standards: Guidance for independent schools, April 2019*

Definitions

'Made available' and 'provided' are defined in Regulation 2(3) and (4) respectively, of the Education (Independent School Standards) Regulations 2014.

<u>Made available</u>

Information is 'made available' if:

- It is published accessibly on the school website and available for inspection in school during the school day by parents of pupils and prospective pupils, and parents have been alerted to this[484]

- If it is not on the website or there is no website, a free copy is sent or given to parents of pupils and prospective pupils on request, and parents are alerted to the fact that they can ask for it.

<u>Provided</u>

Information is 'provided' if:

- The information, a copy of the document or a link to it, is emailed to the person and they are also allowed to see it in school during the school day, or

- It is sent or given to the person in hard copy.

Note it must be automatically provided without request.

Information which must be on the school website

The following must be on the school website if it has one:

- The safeguarding policy[485]

---

[484] 'Reasonable steps' are taken to ensure parents know – Reg 2(3)(a)(ii) and 2(3)(b)(i).

[485] ISS 32(1)(c).

- The RSE policy[486]

- Inspection reports since 2015, except pre-registration and material change reports. New reports must be published by a date specified by the inspectorate[487]

- Particulars of certain regulatory actions by the DfE or a Justice of the Peace[488]

Information which must be 'made available'

The following must be made available to parents of pupils and prospective pupils:

- The policy and arrangements for admissions, misbehaviour and exclusions[489]

- Particulars of education and welfare provision for pupils with EHC plans and English as an additional language[490]

- The curriculum policy[491]

- The behaviour policy[492]

- The anti-bullying strategy

---

[486] This arises under ISS 2A(1)(g) rather than Part 6.

[487] ISS 32(1)(d). This standard refers to inspections under section 108 and 109 of the Education and Skills Act 2008. Material change and pre-registration inspections are under other legislation or sections.

[488] This includes: decision by the Secretary of State or a JP to remove the school from the register, a restriction imposed by the Secretary of State – ISS 32(1)(i), 34(4) and (5).

[489] ISS 32(3)(a).

[490] ISS 32(3)(b).

[491] ISS 32(3)(c).

[492] ISS 32(3)d) covers behaviour, bullying, health and safety and first aid.

- The health and safety policy

- The first aid policy

- Details of the academic performance of the school in the preceding academic year, including results of any public exams[493]

- Complaints procedure and number of formal complaints during the preceding school year[494]

- Inspection reports as they occur[495]

Information which must be 'provided'

The following must be 'provided' automatically to parents of pupils and prospective pupils

- The school address and telephone number, name of the head[496]

- the proprietor, either

  o individual proprietor – full name, address for correspondence both in and out of term time, telephone number on which they can be contacted

  o body of persons – address of registered principal office, phone number of registered or principal office[497]

- name and correspondence details of the chair, where there is a governing body[498]

---

[493] ISS 32(3)(e).

[494] ISS 32(3)(f).

[495] ISS 32(3)(g) – same definition as in ISS 32(1)(d) above.

[496] ISS 32(2)(a).

[497] ISS 32(2)(b). The identity of the proprietor should match the registration information on GIAS.

- a statement of the school's ethos and aims, including any religious ethos[499]

- the safeguarding policy where there is no website (provided to parents on request)[500]

- inspection reports as they occur – to parents of current registered pupils only. Boarding reports (if separate) need go only to the parents of boarders, including flexi-boarders[501]

- annual report on progress and attainment for a pupil – to their parents, except that no report need be provided to a parent who has agreed otherwise[502]

- an annual statement of income and expenditure for publicly funded pupils (unless it is only EY funding), including pupils with publicly funded EHC plans – to the relevant LA[503]

- information reasonably required to support the annual review of EHC plans – to the relevant LA[504]

A common question concerns the right of a parent who is not paying the fees to receive the pupil's annual school report, particularly if the parents are estranged. Both parents are entitled to receive the annual report unless they agree otherwise or a court directs otherwise.

---

[498] ISS 32(2)(c).

[499] ISS 32(2)(d).

[500] ISS 32(1)(c).

[501] ISS 32(1)(d) and (e).

[502] ISS 32(1)(f).

[503] ISS 32(1)(h) and (i).

[504] ISS 32(1)(i).

Information to the Secretary of State and inspectorates

- Any or all of the above, on request[505]

- Any information reasonably requested in connection with an inspection which is required for the purpose of the inspection, and access to the school's admission and attendance registers[506]

This standard is interpreted to include not only school records but access to wider information which inspectors rely on schools to facilitate for inspection purposes, such as pupil interviews, responses to parent, pupil or staff questionnaires, information held at the head office of a group of schools, access to governors. Where schools fail to co-operate with the inspection process they may not be able to demonstrate compliance with the provision of information standard. This includes where late production of information compromises the inspection.

---

[505] ISS 32(1)(a) and (b).

[506] ISS 32(1)(g).

CHAPTER SIXTEEN

THE COMPLAINTS-HANDLING STANDARD – ISS PART 7

Introduction and overview

The complaints standard is detailed and prescriptive. As such it should be one of the easiest to meet because it tells schools exactly what is required. Essentially it requires a transparent three-stage dispute resolution process: informal, formal and panel.

ISS paragraph 33

33. The standard about the manner in which complaints are handled is met if the proprietor ensures that a complaints procedure is drawn up and effectively implemented which deals with the handling of complaints from parents of pupils and which—

(a) is in writing;

(b) is made available to parents of pupils;

(c) sets out clear time scales for the management of a complaint;

*(d) allows for a complaint to be made and considered initially on an **informal** basis;*

*(e) where the parent is not satisfied with the response to the complaint made in accordance with sub-paragraph (d), establishes a **formal** procedure for the complaint to be made in writing;*

*(f) where the parent is not satisfied with the response to the complaint made in accordance with sub-paragraph (e), makes provision for a hearing before a **panel** appointed by or on behalf of the proprietor and consisting of at least three people who were not directly involved in the matters detailed in the complaint;*

(g) ensures that, where there is a panel hearing of a complaint, one panel member is independent of the management and running of the school;

(h) allows for a parent to attend and be accompanied at a panel hearing if they wish;

(i) provides for the panel to make findings and recommendations and stipulates that a copy of those findings and recommendations is—

(i) provided to the complainant and, where relevant, the person complained about; and

(ii) available for inspection on the school premises by the proprietor and the head teacher

The policy

The policy should largely follow the wording of the standard, with the addition of details such as time limits. It may also cover matters such as those below and in particular the school's approach to persistent or vexatious complaints.

Scope and definitions

'Handling of complaints'

In drafting their process, schools should keep its application broad but need not use the process for resolution of matters where the standard permits or requires other procedures or for parts of complaints for which external organisations (such as exam bodies) prescribe another resolution process. Parents may be directed to the most appropriate policy. A complaint which amounts to a disclosure of abuse, for example, would be processed through safeguarding procedures and there is unlikely to be a role for the complaints process.

'Parents of pupils'

The process must be available to parents of current pupils. It need not be offered to parents of prospective or former pupils except in the latter case where the dispute was on-going before the pupil was withdrawn. It need not, therefore, be used for

- admission appeals from parents of prospective pupils unless the school wishes to do so (and indeed the standards do not require schools to offer a process for admission appeals)[507]

- complaints from current or former pupils. The NMS for boarding require a process for securing boarders' views, including complaints, but that stands separately from the complaints standard in the ISS[508]

- complaints from parents of current pupils where the complaint relates to a sibling who has left.

There is nothing to stop a school from allowing more generous access to the statutory complaints process than the standards require but that Is a matter for their discretion.

Exclusions

The standard does not require this process to be available for exclusion processes; that is a matter for the discretion of the school. Exclusions will be covered in the process made available to parents under ISS 32(3)(a), other relevant policies such as behaviour and sanctions and also the parent/school contract.

'Clear time scales'

These should cover every stage, for example, the time within which the parent can bring or escalate a complaint at each stage (usually counted from the date of the trigger event) and the time within which the school will acknowledge receipt, investigate and provide a substantive response. Some schools, for example, limit complaints they will deal with under the policy to those brought within three months of the matter complained of, on the basis that this is similar to the period allowed for

---

[507] Para. 8.2 *The Independent School Standards: Guidance for independent schools, April 2019.*

[508] NMS 13.1

bringing a judicial review, usually. Flexibility should be allowed to accept complaints later where there are extenuating circumstances (such as parental sickness).

As regards the duties of the school, words like 'normally' can be used and it should be clear whether time runs during times when the school is closed, but an outside time limit should be specified.

Complaint against the head

Complaints are commonly responded to by the head at the formal stage. Where the complaint is against the head, there is likely to be a conflict of interest if the matter were to be investigated by the head. While this is not addressed in the standards, governing bodies often specify a different process for a complaint against the head to ensure it will be investigated objectively.

The panel stage

Independent of the management and running of the school

The DfE advises that the requirement for a panel member who is independent of the management and running of the school means that the independent member

- should be outside the school's workforce

- should not be a member of governing body/proprietorial body

- should not be otherwise involved with the management of the school. The example is given of a solicitor who regularly acts for a school.[509]

---

[509] Para. 8.2(d) of *The Independent School Standards: Guidance for independent schools, April 2019.*

Legal representation

The right of parents to be accompanied to a panel hearing does not confer a right to legal representation at the hearing. It is a matter for the discretion of the school whether they allow this at the hearing. For fairness, it is usual for either both sides or neither to be legally represented.

The parental right to use the complaints process is not forfeit if they involve lawyers in correspondence, even if litigation has been threatened.

School insurers and lawyers

Where schools wish to involve their insurers in a dispute, it may be necessary to draw the attention of the insurers to the requirements of the independent school standards. Insurers may wish to take control of a serious dispute and instruct their own lawyers but experience indicates that they are not always aware of the requirements of the standards.

A term in a contract (including an insurance policy) requiring another to break the law is likely to be void for illegality so schools and their representatives should push back against insurers who would prevent the school from meeting the Complaints-handling standard, for example by prohibiting a panel hearing. Schools will not be excused from meeting the standard on inspection because they have been wrongly advised.

The hearing

Where the parent is not satisfied with the school's response to their complaint at stage two and indicates a wish to continue to stage three, a panel hearing should take place unless the parent later indicates that they are now satisfied and do not wish to proceed further. If a parent does not exercise the right to attend a panel hearing, this does not remove the school's obligation to hold the hearing in conformity with its complaints policy.

The school's arrangements for the panel hearing should be reasonable in order to facilitate the parents exercising their right of attendance.

Interestingly, it is not clear that the parental right to attend before a panel gives parents the right also to make oral representations.

Stage three should be a full consideration of the merits of the complaint, not merely a review of the process followed.

When instructing panels, schools need to provide clear terms of reference which include the timeframe for providing a final decision in accordance with the policy.

The decision

Inspectors are alert to complaints which may indicate an area where the standards are not always being met, such as provision for pupils with SEND or the effectiveness of the anti-bullying strategy. Such complaints could give rise to a line of enquiry on inspection. Any reporting, however, is at a strategic level although it could lead to regulatory action by the DfE in an appropriate case.

Neither inspectorates nor the Secretary of State can adjudicate on whether decisions made through the complaints process are 'correct' or compel school to alter its decision or take particular action for a specific pupil.

Record keeping and retention – ISS paragraph 33(j) and (k)

> 34 ..... *a complaints procedure is drawn up and effectively implemented which deals with the handling of complaints from parents of pupils and which—*
>
> ...
>
> > *(j) provides for a written record to be kept of all complaints that are made in accordance with sub-paragraph (e) and—*
> >
> > *(i) whether they are resolved following a formal procedure, or proceed to a panel hearing; and*
> >
> > *(ii) action taken by the school as a result of those complaints (regardless of whether they are upheld); and*

(k) provides that correspondence, statements and records relating to individual complaints are to be kept confidential except where the Secretary of State or a body conducting an inspection under section 109 of the 2008 Act requests access to them.

Records must be kept of formal complaints and panels. Retention of records of informal complaints can assist senior leaders to identify systemic issues which need to be addressed before they escalate.

The period of retention can be determined by schools in accordance with normal data protection principles. On a six-year inspection cycle, a retention period of seven years for documents relevant to inspection would allow for inspections and progress-monitoring inspections. Where complaints relate to safeguarding, KCSIE 2022 advises:

416. Schools and colleges have an obligation to preserve records which contain information about allegations of sexual abuse for the Independent Inquiry into Child Sexual Abuse (IICSA), for the term of the inquiry (further information can be found on the IICSA website). All other records should be retained at least until the accused has reached normal pension age or for a period of 10 years from the date of the allegation if that is longer.

Persistent correspondence

Once the complaints process has been exhausted, the standards do not require schools to continue to correspond with the parent about that matter.

Additional requirements for EYFS and boarding

EYFS

Where a complaint relates to early years provision, there is an additional requirement that providers must investigate written complaints relating to their fulfilment of the EYFS requirements and notify complainants of the outcome of the investigation within 28 days of having received the complaint. See paragraphs 3.75 of the statutory framework for the

EYFS for more information. For complaints about other parts of their provision, schools may set their own time limits.

<u>Boarding schools</u>

In addition to the requirements of the standards about parental complaints, boarding schools are required to have clear and easily accessible systems for boarders to provide their views about the operation of boarding provision, raise concerns and make complaints. Boarders must not be penalised for raising a concern or making a complaint in good faith. The complaints process for boarding pupils need not be a three-stage process as prescribed by the standards for parents but the procedures should be clear about how the school will respond to complaints from boarders. Schools can be creative about finding effective ways to hear the concerns of pupils informally and formally.

The boarding school's record of complaints must identify those relating to boarding provision and action taken as a result, whether or not the complaints were upheld. The record should include complaints made but later withdrawn. The schools should keep under review any emerging patterns arising from complaints.[510]

---

[510] NMS 13.1 and NMS 14

CHAPTER SEVENTEEN

THE LEADERSHIP AND MANAGEMENT STANDARD – ISS PART 8

ISS paragraph 34

(1) The standard about the quality of leadership and management is met if the proprietor ensures that persons with leadership and management responsibilities at the school—

(a) demonstrate good skills and knowledge appropriate to their role so that the independent school standards are met consistently;

(b) fulfil their responsibilities effectively so that the independent school standards are met consistently; and

(c) actively promote the well-being of pupils.

(2) For the purposes of paragraph (1)(c) "well-being" means well-being within the meaning of section 10(2) of the Children Act 2004.

Overview

The DfE's guidance about this standard is in *The Independent School Standard: Guidance for independent schools, April 2019.*

In line with the principles underlying independent education, discussed in Part One of this book, the Secretary of State does not prescribe qualifications for leaders, managers, proprietors or governors or set requirements around the structures or processes they use for management or governance. This allows schools freedom to continue the traditions of their heritage or faith on condition only that their approach prioritises the well-being of pupils and ensures the standards are met consistently.

Looking ahead to 2023, this could be a space to watch as IICSA has recommended that the standards should be amended to include requirements for an effective system of governance based on

- openness to external scrutiny,

- transparency and honesty within the governance arrangements

- ability of governors to have difficult conversations both internally and with those providing external scrutiny.

These changes have not yet occurred.[511]

Key points from the guidance

The leadership and management standard is capable of encompassing governance, as well as leadership and management.[512]

It does not prescribe structures and processes for how independent schools should be governed although a few points are contained in other standards such as the NMS and KCSIE.

It is an outcome focused standard. The required outcome is that, whatever structures and systems the school chooses to use, all the other standards are met and the well-being of pupils is actively promoted. Proactive governance and leadership will entail ensuring there is effective training, performance management and monitoring in place to ensure compliance.

There is a focus also on consistency. This potentially enables the Secretary of State to take action not only in relation to schools which are not meeting the standards at one particular time but in respect of those which do not sustain a consistent record of compliance across successive inspections and between inspections.

---

[511] For more see: Recommendation 3 (page 186) of : *The IICSA Residential Schools Investigation Report, March 2022.*

[512] NMS 2.1 and 2.2 are explicit about this for boarding schools from September 2022.

Domino standards

ISS paragraphs 34(1)(a) and (b) are only usually engaged when one or more of the underlying standards are unmet. However, whenever any other standard is not met *'this is evidence pointing to the leadership and management standard not being met'.*[513]

When a school does not consistently meet the other standards, ISS 34(1)(a) and (b) can assist the DfE to locate the causes of the problem in terms of whether the issues stem from (a) insufficient skill and knowledge among leaders, managers or proprietors, or (b) lack of diligence or an ineffectual approach at that level.

Well-being

The DfE guidance explains:

> *The last limb of the leadership and management standard is intended to ensure that the underlying ethos of any independent school should be to develop and nurture the well-being of its pupils, and that therefore, the well-being of pupils should be actively promoted by those who are leading or managing it.*

For the purpose of the duty to 'actively promote the well-being of pupils' in ISS paragraph 34(1)(c), well-being is defined in section 10(2) of the Children Act 2004. It means:

> *(a) physical and mental health and emotional well-being*
>
> *(b) protection from harm and neglect*
>
> *(c) education, training and recreation*
>
> *(d) the contribution made by them to society*
>
> *(e) social and economic well-being.*

---

[513] *The Independent School Standards: Guidance for independent schools, April 2019* – para. 9.1

This is perhaps the broadest and most flexible standard. It is possible for a school to fail this last limb of the leadership and management standard even though other standards are being met. It encompasses the culture and ethos of the school and a holistic view of the school's provision. The DfE advises that it may not be sufficient for a school to be able to meet a standard only with the help of external advisors; arrangements need to be in place *to sustain that improvement through the work of the school leadership itself.*

New for 2022

Values

KCSIE requires ('should') schools to have a *clear set of values and standards upheld and demonstrated throughout all aspects of school life.* These will underpin many of the required policies and be reinforced throughout the curriculum, including RSE.[514]

Governor training

KCSIE also introduces a requirement ('should') for governors to undertake safeguarding training.[515] This is echoed in the NMS for boarding 2022, which introduce a requirement for the leaders, managers and governors for boarding to 'undertake appropriate training as required'.[516] The training requirement for governors of boarding schools goes wider than safeguarding.

These duties arise under ISS 7 and are mentioned here because they are relevant to leaders and governors.

---

[514] KCSIE 2022, para. 130.

[515] See Chapter Eleven. These changes may flow from the discussions and recommendations in the *IICSA Residential Schools Investigation Report, March 2022* at p 186.

[516] NMS 2.2.

PART THREE

APPLYING THE STANDARDS TO COMMON ISSUES

CHAPTER EIGHTEEN

WHAT THE STANDARDS SAY ABOUT PASTORAL CARE

Introduction and overview

The independent school standards break down behaviours and situations into artificially separate components for the purpose of analysis and accountability, as explained in Chapter Three. Applying the standards to the real-life scenarios about which parents seek legal advice typically entails drawing on aspects of a range of standards. Due to overlap between standards, there may be more than one possible analysis. This part aims to give readers examples of how to work with the standards.

There is no standalone standard dedicated to 'pastoral care' although it can be one of the ways, alongside other strategies, for schools to meet several of the standards. For example, it is implicit in KCSIE, the NMS for boarding schools, and the statutory guidance on RSE, that schools will have some system of pastoral support available for pupils. Pastoral support may be a form of 'early help' for children in need or at risk, within KCSIE and ISS paragraph 7. It may also be a reasonable adjustment for some pupils with disabilities where it would help to alleviate disadvantage by supporting them to engage with the curriculum or manage other aspects of school life, within ISS paragraph 3(j).[517] It can be a means for a school to ensure it meets the SMSC standard, promoting principles which enable pupils to develop self-esteem and self-confidence (ISS paragraph 5(b)(i)), or to respond to bullying and child-on-child abuse (ISS 10 and 7).

---

[517] See Chapter Four for the definition of disability. The weakness in disability provisions may lie in the definitional requirement for the disability to have lasted or be likely to last at least a year which is likely to be an inappropriate threshold for many pupils in need of pastoral care.

There is very little prescription as to what pastoral care should look like, leaving schools considerable discretion in how they address the needs of their pupil cohort. The sections below signpost the places where the most obvious references to pastoral care can be found.

KCSIE – ISS paragraph 7

Pastoral support is one of the ways staff may respond to concerns about the welfare of a child[518] alongside undertaking an early help assessment and/or making a referral to statutory services. It is a means of 'promoting welfare' of children who need a social worker.[519] Schools are advised to consider providing extra pastoral support and attention to pupils with SEN/D in recognition of the additional challenges they face, along with ensuring that any appropriate support for communication is in place.[520] LGBT pupils should be provided a safe space to speak out and share concerns with members of staff.[521] Some cases of sexual harassment, such as one-off incidents, can be handled internally through the school behaviour policy and pastoral support.[522] It is part of the role of the DSL to liaise with pastoral support colleagues and support them in their work.[523]

The statutory guidance on RSE – ISS paragraph 2A

The DfE's guidance takes a broad approach to relationships and sex education: *'All of these subjects should be set in the context of a wider whole-school approach to supporting pupils to be safe, happy and prepared for life beyond school'.*[524] The subjects encompassed within RSE *'can*

---

[518] KCSIE 2022 para. 54.

[519] KCSIE 2022 para. 172.

[520] KCSIE 2022 para. 198 – 200.

[521] KCSIE 2022 para. 203.

[522] KCSIE 2022 para. 486, 501

[523] KCSIE 2022 pp. 162 and 16.

[524] RSE para. 113

support young people to develop resilience, to know how and when to ask for help, and to know where to access support'.[525]

Schools are advised to consider the makeup of their own student body, including the gender and age range of their pupils, *'and consider whether it is appropriate or necessary to put in place additional support for pupils with particular protected characteristics (which mean that they are potentially at greater risk)'.*[526]

> *31. Schools should be alive to issues such as everyday sexism, misogyny, homophobia and gender stereotypes and take positive action to build a culture where these are not tolerated, and any occurrences are identified and tackled. Staff have an important role to play in modelling positive behaviours. **School pastoral and behaviour policies should support all pupils.***

See also paragraphs 112 and 113:

> *112. ... the curriculum on relationships and on sex should complement, and be supported by, the school's wider policies on behaviour, inclusion, respect for equality and diversity, bullying and safeguarding (including handling of any reports pupils may make as a result of the subject content). The subjects will sit within the context of a school's broader ethos and approach to developing pupils socially, morally, spiritually and culturally; **and its pastoral care system.** This is also the case for teaching about mental health within health education. The curriculum on health education should similarly complement, and be supported by, the school's wider education on healthy lifestyles through physical education, food technology, science, sport, extra-curricular activity and school food.*

---

[525] RSE para. 1.

[526] RSE – para. 30.

The behaviour standard – ISS paragraph 9

The non-statutory guidance: *Behaviour in schools* 2022, provides advice about the role of pastoral care, mentoring and coaching in supporting the behaviour of some pupils.

The anti-bullying standard – ISS paragraph 10

The non-statutory guidance: *Preventing and tackling bullying* provides extensive advice for schools about supporting children who have been bullied and also those who bully.

The NMS for boarding 2022 – ISS paragraph 8

NMS 7 and 11 set standards for boarders' health and wellbeing. Boarders must be able to contact any member of staff with personal, academic or welfare concerns. All staff should know what to do if a boarder approaches them with a concern. Boarding schools must identify at least one person other than a parent, outside the staff and those responsible for the leadership and governance of the school, who boarders may contact directly about personal problems or concerns at school ('the independent person'). Boarders must be informed who this person is and feel comfortable talking to them. Boarders must know how to contact them and they must be easily accessible. Boarders must also be provided with one or more appropriate child specific helpline(s) or outside telephone numbers, including the Office of the Children's Commissioner, to contact in case of problems or distress. Boarding schools must also have and implement effectively appropriate policies to ensure the mental health and emotional wellbeing of boarders is promoted.

Leadership and management – ISS paragraph 34(1)(c)

At times pastoral care may be what is needed to 'actively promote the well-being of pupils'.

Conclusion

Although there is no standard dedicated to pastoral care, failure to provide it can lead to a school not meeting a range of standards.

CHAPTER NINETEEN

WHAT THE STANDARDS SAY ABOUT CHILD-ON-CHILD SEXUAL ABUSE

Overview

In 2021, many pupils started to speak out publicly, often on social media, about their experiences of gender-based harassment, sexual assault and violence, in and out of school, naming other pupils among the perpetrators of abuse and expressing concern about the difficulty in accessing support. Often concerns are also expressed about the attitudes and organisational cultures in school which allow abusive behaviours to develop and become normalised.

The DfE commissioned a rapid review by Ofsted which was published in June 2021: *Review of sexual abuse in schools and colleges*.[527] The report found that sexual harassment and online sexual abuse of children and young people are widespread, indeed so commonplace that some see no point in reporting them. The findings concerning prevalence corroborated those of earlier reports such as that of the Women and Equalities Select Committee in 2016.[528] At the same time, in response to other events, HM Inspectorate of Constabulary, Fire and Rescue Service reported an 'epidemic of violence against women and girls (VAWG)' and called for a cross-system approach to responding.[529]

Schools have a role to play in teaching about healthy relationships, inculcating values of respect, challenging misogyny and other

---

[527] https://www.gov.uk/government/publications/review-of-sexual-abuse-in-schools-and-colleges/review-of-sexual-abuse-in-schools-and-colleges

[528] *Sexual violence and sexual harassment in schools: Women and Equalities Committee Report*, September 2016. A wide range of further evidence is cited in the Ofsted review.

[529] HMICFRS: *Police response to VAWG: final inspection report*, 17 September 2021

prejudices, providing support and ensuring the school itself is a safe place to be while also playing a part in preparing children for life in modern Britain. The issue of child-on-child abuse engages a wide range of the standards such as: safeguarding and online safety, RSE, SMSC, curriculum, behaviour, supervision, bullying, risk assessment, leadership and management. This chapter highlights a few of these.

Relationships and sex education (RSE) – ISS paragraphs 2A

The statutory RSE curriculum provides a framework for expressly teaching pupils how to interact with others safely, in and out of school and including online. Preventative education is viewed as key to tackling child-on-child abuse. The RSE curriculum should be properly planned, lessons should be timetabled and reinforced throughout the whole curriculum, and pupils' learning should be assessed.[530]

The extensive statutory guidance covers recognising caring friendships and respectful, healthy relationships, online relationships and being safe. Senior school pupils must also be informed about issues such as consent (including the legal age of consent), sexuality, gender identity and sexual exploitation. The guidance emphasises *the importance of making clear that sexual violence and sexual harassment are not acceptable, will never be tolerated and are not an inevitable part of growing up*.[531]

RSE should be set in the context of the school's ethos and pastoral care system and a wider whole-school approach to supporting pupils to be safe and happy. It should dovetail with and complement the school's SMSC curriculum[532] (respect for diversity) and policies on behaviour, bullying and safeguarding (including the handling of any disclosures made by pupils in response to subject content). Schools should consider

---

[530] KCSIE 2022, para. 130. RSE guidance, page 43, also para 11

[531] RSE guidance, para. 32.

[532] Spiritual, moral, social and cultural development of pupils – para. 5 of the standards.

how their teaching can help support the development of important attributes in pupils such as honesty, kindness, tolerance and courtesy.[533]

The NMS for boarding set additional requirements for boarding settings. Pupils are to be supported to develop good relationships with fellow pupils and staff. Staff should understand and help boarders to understand what makes a healthy, nurturing relationship. Staff should be trained to think curiously about and recognise signs of children at risk or involved in damaging relationships, including teenage relationships abuse and child-on-child, and to take appropriate action when they have a concern. [534]The school's anti-bullying strategy should reflect that unlike at day schools, boarders who are being bullied (offline) cannot escape their bullies for long periods of time as they are not going home as often.[535]

Safeguarding- ISS paragraph 7

Safeguarding policy

The school safeguarding policy outlines the school's approach to safeguarding and promoting the welfare of pupils, including online. The Ofsted review found that child-on-child abuse was so prevalent that schools should assume it is an issue in their school even if they are not aware of it. The policy should therefore cover child-on-child abuse in detail,[536] including the forms it can take and recognition of the gendered nature of child-on-child abuse[537] while being clear that all peer abuse is unacceptable. It must set out processes for preventing and responding to it. Part five of KCSIE 2022 provides extensive statutory guidance about how to manage reports and allegations of child-on-child sexual violence and sexual harassment.

---

[533] RSE guidance, para. 113.

[534] NMS 17.

[535] NMS 16.3.

[536] KCSIE 2022 155-6.

[537] KCSIE advises that it is '*more likely that girls will be victims of sexual violence and sexual harassment and more likely that it will be perpetrated by boys*'.

KCSIE explains that sexual violence and harassment exist on a continuum and may overlap. Schools should therefore make a statement of 'zero tolerance' of sexual violence and sexual harassment. They should consistently challenge and address disrespectful, problematic behaviours which can lead to an unsafe environment '*and in worst case scenarios to a culture which normalises abuse*'. They should not downplay it as only 'banter' or 'just having a laugh'.

Listening to pupils

Listening to the pupil voice is central to turning policy into effective safeguarding practice. KCSIE and *WT* set an expectation for a 'culture of listening to children'.

> *Systems should be in place, and they should be well promoted, easily understood and easily accessible for children to confidently report abuse, knowing their concerns will be treated seriously, and knowing they can safely express their views and give feedback.*[538]

These systems should be effective for all pupils, including those who are less confident such as those with additional needs.

Responding and referring

Pupils who speak up about child-on-child abuse should always be reassured and supported to feel safe. They should never be made to feel ashamed for making a report or given the impression that they are creating a problem by making a report.[539]

All members of the school community should know how to refer concerns (whether relating to matters arising in or outside school) to the DSL who must report on to other agencies as usual in accordance with local procedures and thresholds. Referrals might be needed for both alleged victims and alleged perpetrators, in appropriate cases. The NPCC guidance '*When to call the police*' provides guidance about reporting to the police.

---

[538] KCSIE 2022 para. 96, 156 and 459.

[539] KCSIE 2022 para. 18, 468

The DfE advice: *Sharing nudes and semi-nudes: advice for education settings working with children and young people* will inform schools' responses to incidents involving images.

Staff training

Staff should receive appropriate training in all these matters, regularly updated, including recognising signs of abuse, understanding how children communicate (including behaviour and presentation), understanding the added vulnerabilities of some pupils, the school behaviour policy and anti-bullying strategy.

School culture

The organisational culture in the school should enable issues of safeguarding and promoting the welfare of pupils to be addressed. See Chapter Eleven for more about safeguarding culture.

Behaviour and bullying – ISS paragraphs 9, 10 and others

Ofsted reported that some pupils expressed frustration that there was not explicit teaching in their schools of what was acceptable and unacceptable behaviour.

Such schools could be failing to meet the standards which require the proprietor to:

- promote good behaviour – ISS paragraph 9

- implement an effective anti-bullying strategy which prevents bullying as far as reasonably practicable – ISS paragraph 10

- ensure pupils are taught how to stay safe – ISS paragraph 7 and ISS paragraph 2A

- ensure that *'principles are promoted which*

  o *encourage respect for other people, paying particular regard to the protected characteristics* – ISS paragraph 5(b)(vi)

> ○ *enable pupils to distinguish right from wrong and to respect the civil and criminal law of England'* – ISS paragraph 5(b)(ii)

It may be difficult for pupils to respect what they do not know about; meeting the latter standard therefore necessitates schools providing pupils with information about the protected characteristics and how the law views sexual harassment and sexual assault, and consent. These are requirements of the RSE and PSHE standards.

Risk assessment – ISS paragraph 16

KCSIE describes the need for a risk assessed approach to the handling of child-on-child abuse.[540] The school risk assessment policy should have processes in place for this, specifying who would carry out those assessments, such as the DSL/DDSL or it could be an external expert in complex cases.

Leadership and management – ISS paragraph 34

The overarching expectation of the standards of leaders is that they should 'actively promote the wellbeing of children'. In view of the findings of the Ofsted review of safeguarding, the urgency with which issues of child-on-child abuse need to be addressed and the priority being accorded to it by inspectorates cannot be underestimated. The biggest challenge for leaders and governors may lie in creating avenues for young people to seek help when they need it and a culture that enables this to happen.

---

[540] KCSIE 2022 Part 5 and para. 479.

What the standards say about child-on-child abuse

Curriculum	
The PSHE curriculum must encourage respect for others paying particular regard to the protected characteristics.	ISS 2(2)(d)(ii) and ISS 5(b)(vi)
Principles must be promoted which enable pupils to develop self-knowledge, self-esteem and self-confidence.	ISS 5(b)(i)
The curriculum must provide for effective preparation of pupils for the opportunities, responsibilities and experiences of life in British society.	ISS 2(2)(i)
The proprietor/school must actively promote principles which enable pupils to distinguish right from wrong and to respect the civil and criminal law of England.	ISS 5(b)(ii)
The proprietor/school must promote principles which encourage pupils to accept responsibility for their behaviour.	ISS 5(b)(iii)
RSE	
RSE entails teaching respect for others and the facts and law about important issues such as consent and acceptable behaviour.	ISS 2A See RSE guidance
RSE should be a planned programme.	RSE para. 5 and others
RSE should be taught in regular timetabled lessons.	KCSIE 2022 para. 130
Progress in RSE should be assessed. For example, tests, written assignments or self-evaluations, to capture progress.	ISS 2A RSE para.s 123-125 ISS 4
Teaching	
Lessons (including RSE) must be planned on the basis of a good understanding of the needs of pupils.	ISS 3(d)

Safeguarding	
Schools must have regard to KCSIE.	ISS 7 and 8 NMS 8
Schools must implement a written risk assessment policy and ensure appropriate action is taken to reduce risks that are identified.	NMS 9.3 ISS 16 NMS 8.4
Staff should understand and should help boarders understand what makes a healthy, nurturing relationship.	NMS 17.3
RSE is considered to be preventative education. Schools should create a culture of zero tolerance for sexism, misogyny/misandry, homophobia, biphobia and sexual violence/harassment.	KCSIE 2022, para. 130, 446, 494, 502 and others
Elements of RSE which clearly cross-over with the safeguarding standard and should be tackled at age-appropriate stages: Health and respectful relationships, boundaries and consent, stereotyping, prejudice and equality, body confidence and self-esteem, how to recognise an abusive relationship, including coercive and controlling behaviour, the concepts of, and laws relating to- sexual consent, sexual exploitation, abuse, grooming, coercion, harassment, rape, domestic abuse, so called honour-based violence such as forced marriage and Female Genital Mutilation (FGM), and how to access support, and what constitutes sexual harassment and sexual violence and why these are always unacceptable.	KCSIE 2022, para. 130, 556 and others
KCSIE 2022 – What all staff should know Staff should be aware that pupils may not feel able to speak about abuse and therefore it is important for staff to exhibit appropriate professional curiosity, build trusted relationships to facilitate communication and report concerns.	KCSIE 2022, para. 19.
All staff should be able to recognise child on child abuse. Details of forms it can take are provided. Abuse should never be passed off as 'banter' or 'having a laugh'.	KCSIE 2022, para.s 32-35

Staff should be trained to think curiously about and recognise the signs of children at risk or involved in damaging relationships, including teenage relationship abuse, and child-on-child abuse, and to take appropriate action when they have concerns.	NMS 17.3
KCSIE 2022 – Management of safeguarding Governors should be aware of abuse is a breach of human rights and failure to tackle it where it affects pupils with protected characteristics may be a breach of equalities duties.	KCSIE 2022, para.s 83 – 90
Leaders should ensure the school has a culture of listening to children. Pupils should be able to report abuse and give feedback confidently.	WT page 59. KCSIE 2022, para. 96.
Governors should ensure they facilitate a whole schools approach to safeguarding, underpinned by a suite of policies (behaviour codes, anti-bullying etc). Then safeguarding policy should cover the school's response to child-on-child abuse in detail.	KCSIE 2022, para.s 94 – 99, 155-156
KCSIE 2022 – Part five – Child-on-child sexual harassment Schools should have regard to the extensive guidance on how to respond to child-on-child abuse.	KCSIE 2022, Part five
Behaviour, bullying	
Schools must promote good behaviour and ensure bullying is prevented as far as reasonably possible through an effective anti-bullying strategy. Pupils should be protected from prejudice-bullying relating to protected characteristics.	ISS 9, ISS 10, ISS 3(j) and 3(h) NMS 15 and 16
Pupils should be supported to develop good relationships with fellow pupils and staff that are based on mutual trust and respect.	NMS 17
Supervision	
Adequate supervision is likely to be key to prevention of bullying.	ISS 14

Risk assessment	
Provision for particular pupils may require risk assessment to keep them safe, with appropriate action being taken to reduce any risks identified – for example, when a pupil might pose a risk to themselves or others, or may be at risk of being bullied or exploited by other pupils.	ISS 16
School premises may also need to be risk assessed to identify locations where there is a higher risk of child-on-child abuse and means to reduce or eliminate the risk.	ISS 16
Leadership and management	
Leaders must actively promote the well-being of pupils	ISS 34(1)(c)

CHAPTER TWENTY

WHAT THE STANDARDS SAY ABOUT SPECIAL EDUCATIONAL NEEDS AND DISABILITIES (SEND)

Overview

In the independent school standards, pupils are not defined by groups. This does not mean that they have nothing to say about provision for pupils with SEND. All standards apply to all pupils, unless the standards indicate otherwise. Some standards expressly indicate 'all pupils'. This is best understood as emphasis rather than an indication that the other references to 'pupils' apply only to some, although there is no judicial authority on this point.

Quality of education – ISS paragraphs 2-4

In summary, the standards say that the teaching the pupils receive, including those with SEND, should be based on a good understanding of their needs, informed by regular thorough assessment of their work which feeds into lesson planning. Through well-planned lessons, effective teaching and effective use of a good range of good quality resources, the teaching should deliver a curriculum suitable to the needs of the pupils, including those with SEND. Pupils with SEND should be enabled to make good progress according to their ability, like any other pupils. The detail is provided in the table below.

Reasonable adjustments – ISS paragraph 3(j)

The teaching must not discriminate unlawfully against pupils with disabilities (or other protected characteristics). This can be read as incorporating into the standards the duty to make reasonable adjustments for pupils with disabilities, as required by the Equality Act 2010. See Chapter Three for more detail and sources.

Non-statutory advice from the DfE about how schools could approach various issues can be a source of ideas about what might be considered reasonable, although they are not expressed in terms of reasonable adjustments.

For example, while *Supporting pupils at school with medical conditions* is not statutory for independent schools, the suggestions it makes could be relevant and reasonable for individual pupils with disabilities, such as

- an individual healthcare plan

- a responsible person

- suitably trained staff

- arrangements to cover absence of support staff

- briefing for supply teachers

- risk assessments for school visits, holidays and other activities.

The duty to make reasonable adjustments is also relevant to how the behaviour policy is applied – ISS paragraph 9. See Ashdown House-v-JKL and MNP [2019] UKUT 259(AAC)

In boarding, reasonable adjustments must be made to provide adequate accessible accommodation for any boarders with disabilities – NMS 4.4.

Funding of reasonable adjustments

A particular issue for independent schools is the funding of reasonable adjustments. It is clearly unlawful to charge for reasonable adjustments, but there is a confusing element of circularity in the definitions in so far as reasonable adjustments are defined in part by what it would be reasonable for the particular school to have to provide for the particular pupil without making an additional charge. There can therefore be no national edict that, for example, the provision of laptops to pupils with disabilities is or is not a reasonable adjustment; reasonable adjustments are a pupil and context specific judgment. Funding issues do not fall squarely within the remit of the standards, although the connected outcome does (whether pupil needs are being met).

The SEN Code of Practice

The SEN Code of Practice is not statutory for independent schools except in relation to state-funded provision. This would include pupils with LA-funded EHC plans and in receipt of LA-funded early years provision. As the SEN Code sets out a systemic approach, it can be hard to apply it to individual pupils and it may make sense for schools to adopt the code's processes more widely.

Exam access arrangements for pupils with disabilities

The Equality Act 2010 requires qualification bodies to make reasonable adjustments for disabled candidates where they would be put at a substantial disadvantage in undertaking an exam. When making adjustments (known as 'access arrangements') for public examinations, schools as exam centres must comply with detailed requirements set by the exam boards which are themselves regulated by Ofqual. The requirements are updated annually and are available to view on the website of the Joint Council for Qualifications (JCQ), a membership body for exam boards.

This area is outside the remit of this book save to say that, in principle, a school which does not have systems and processes in place for applying the permitted access arrangements in a reasonable way could potentially be viewed as not meeting standards such as those on discrimination (ISS 3(j)) and/or assessment (ISS 4).

Other

The standards relating to RSE, respect for others, self-esteem, safeguarding, behaviour, bullying, premises and provision of information are all relevant to provision for pupils with SEND. See the table below and Chapter Eighteen concerning pastoral care.

Example

The mechanisms for enforcing EHC plans sit outside the ISS and there is no standard in the ISS specifically requiring schools to make the provision in EHC plans.[541] However, failure to provide could be grounds for a complaint and could put the school in breach of some of the standards.

E.g.: An EHC plan for a pupil with autism specifies the need for small group tuition, using certain programmes and a particular approach to behaviour management. Failure to make this provision could put the school in breach of standards such as:

- ISS 3(a) – if the pupil is not enabled to make good progress

- ISS 2(1)(b)(i) – if the alternative schemes of work are not appropriate

- ISS 3(d) – if the approach taken does not show a good understanding of this needs

- ISS 3(f) – if teaching resources are not of good range and quality

- ISS 3(h) – if the school's approach to behaviour management is not effective (meaning effective from the pupil's perspective also, not simply that they are contained)

- ISS 3(j) – if the small group tuition, resources and approach to behaviour could be considered reasonable adjustments, or other reasonable adjustments are not being made

- ISS 9 – if the school behaviour policy is not sufficiently comprehensive.

---

[541] The primary obligation to secure the provision in an EHC plan sits with the local authority. It is relatively rare for independent schools to be named in EHC plans and to receive public funding to make the provision. See the Children and Families Act 2014.

What the standards say about provision for pupils with Special Educational Needs and Disabilities (SEND)

Curriculum	
The school curriculum, plans and schemes of work must take into account the aptitudes and needs of pupils with SEND ('all pupils'). Pupils with an EHC plan are expressly mentioned.	ISS 2(a) and 2(1)(b)(i)
The curriculum, plans and schemes of work should ensure that pupils with SEND ('all pupils') have the opportunity to learn and make progress.	ISS 2(2)(h)
Pupils with SEND have a right to access the breadth of curriculum set out in ISS 2(2), including academic subjects, skills, etc.	ISS 3(j)
The PSHE curriculum must encourage respect for others including for people with disabilities.	ISS 2(2)(ii) and 5(b)(vi)
Principles must be promoted which enable pupils to develop self-knowledge, self-esteem and self-confidence.	ISS 5(b)(i)
There must be appropriate up-to-date careers advice which helps to encourage pupils, including those with SEND, to fulfil their potential.	ISS 2(2)(e)
Pupils, including those with SEND, must receive effective preparation for the opportunities, responsibilities and experiences of life in British society.	ISS 2(2)(i)
There must be a programme of activities appropriate to the needs of any sixth form pupils, including those with SEND.	ISS 2(2)(g)
Curriculum for children in the early years	
There must be a programme of activities appropriate to the educational needs of EY pupils with SEND, including personal, emotional, physical development, communication and language skills NB – This is usually met through delivery of the statutory framework for the EYFS.14	ISS 2(2)(f)

The school must deliver the EYFS framework (53 pages) for all the children in the provision, including early learning and welfare requirements[542]. *Providers must have arrangements in place to support children with SEN or disabilities. … all providers who are funded by the local authority to deliver early education places must have regard to the Special Educational Needs Code of Practice.*	*EYFS 3.67*
RSE	
Pupils with SEND must be provided with RSE except where they have been lawfully withdrawn by their parents.	ISS 2A
The RSE statutory guidance is clear that RSE must be accessible for all pupils and has a section specifically about pupils with SEND – see paragraphs 33-35 [543] *High quality teaching that is differentiated and personalised will be the starting point to ensure accessibility* – paragraph 33. *Schools should be aware that some pupils are more vulnerable to exploitation, bullying and other issues due to the nature of their SEND* – paragraph 34. In designing and teaching RSE, schools should consider the additional vulnerabilities of pupils with SEND – paragraph 34. Content may need to be tailored to meet specific needs – paragraph 35. Reasonable adjustments must be made for pupils with disabilities, when providing RSE – paragraph 28.	"
Teaching	
All parts of the teaching standard have a bearing on SEND. Some examples follow:	ISS 3
Lessons must be planned on the basis of a good understanding of the needs, aptitudes and prior attainments of pupils, including those with SEND.	ISS 3(d)

---

[542] Independent schools can claim exemptions from EY academic goals but there are no exemptions form welfare requirements. See section above about ISS 2(2)(f) in Chapter Seven.

[543] Paragraph numbers here refer to paragraphs of the statutory guidance n RE/RSE.

Pupils, including those with SEND should be enabled to make good progress, increasing their knowledge, skills and understanding, according to their ability.	ISS 3(a)
There should be a good range of good quality 'resources' which should be used effectively.	ISS3(f)
Where SEND give rise to behavioural issues, there should be effective strategies to make these.	ISS 3(h)
The teaching must not discriminate unlawfully. In other words, reasonable adjustments must be made for pupils with disabilities to ensure they are included in the life of the school.	ISS3(j)
Assessment	
There should be a system for regularly assessing the work of pupils, including those with SEND, and using the information to plan teaching so that they can progress.	ISS 3(g)
Safeguarding	
The guidance and systems described in *KCSIE*[544] apply to all pupils, including those with SEND.[545] In addition, *KCSIE* expects schools to be alert and cater for the particular vulnerabilities of pupils with SEND. A few examples from *KCSIE* are below. All fall under ISS 7.	ISS 7
Early help – staff should be alert to the potential need for help by pupils with SEND, whether or not they have a EHC plan – paragraph 20 *KCSIE*.	"
Governors – should ensure children are taught how to stay safe including online, recognising children with SEND may need an individualised approach – paragraph 128 *KCSIE*.	
Requirements for the safeguarding policy – the policy should recognise the additional challenges for pupils with SEND which may need to be covered, as appropriate – paragraphs 198 – 201 KCSIE.	"
Sharing safeguarding/welfare information with a pupil's new school – paragraph 121 *KCSIE*.	"

---

[544] Paragraph numbers in the Safeguarding section refer to KCSIE 2022.

[545] See also: *Safeguarding disabled children: practice guidance*, from the DCSF.

Reasonable force – there are particular considerations in relation to pupils with SEND: careful risk assessment, reasonable adjustments, positive support and preventative strategies to reduce the need for force – paragraph 164 *KCSIE*.	"
Child-on-child abuse and sexual violence between children – staff to be aware that pupils with SEND are among those at greater risk. They are up to three times more likely to be abused than their peers – para. 448 *KCSIE*.	"
Role of the DSL – includes working with the SENCO – p. 162 *KCSIE*.	"
Training of the DSL – The DSL should be trained in identifying and responding to specific needs such as SEND and certain health conditions which can increase vulnerability to risks and supporting pupils with SEN to stay safe online– pp. 164.	"
Residential special schools – see further considerations – paragraphs 157 – 161. See also the National Minimum Standards for Residential Special Schools – or for Boarding Schools, as appropriate.	"
Behaviour	
Schools must promote good behaviour. Schools must make reasonable adjustments to their policies to cater for pupils with SEND.	ISS 3(j), ISS 9
Longer term plans (non pupil-specific) to make the curriculum accessible to pupils with disabilities which give rise to behavioural barriers to learning can be approached through the accessibility plan.	Accessibility plan EqA 2010, Schedule 10
Bullying	
Bullying of (or by) pupils with SEND must be prevented as far as reasonably practicable.	ISS 10. (See also ISS 7, above.)

See the DfE's non-statutory advice, *Preventing and tackling bullying*, which contains influential advice about matters such as staff training, particular vulnerabilities of pupils with SEND (such as additional hurdles those with social communication difficulties might face when seeking help), pastoral support for pupils with SEND, considering whether the child engaging in bullying has SEND, bullying outside of school and online.	"
Health and safety **Supervision** **Fire** **First aid**	
The policies and processes must be suitable to cover the needs of all pupils, including on school trips. There is nothing specific to SEND in the guidance but all policies, processes, risk assessments would be expected to cover the health and safety of all relevant pupils, including those with SEND: - In the case of fire, for example, procedures must ensure the safety of all pupils – including those with disabilities - Supervision – all pupils must be '*properly supervised through appropriate deployment of staff*' – ISS 14 – what is 'appropriate' may vary with the needs of a particular pupil or cohort - Trips – not permitting a pupil to participate in an educational trip or activity might be discrimination (ISS 3(j)) unless a lawful exception applies - First aid/health &safety – the arrangements must cater for all pupils. See the DfE guidance: *First aid in schools* and *Supporting pupils at school with medical conditions*.	– ISS 11, 12, 13, 14 and ISS 16
Risk assessment	
Provision for particular pupils may require risk assessment to keep them safe, with appropriate action being taken to reduce any risks identified – for example, when a pupil might pose a risk to themselves or others, or may be at risk of being bullied or exploited by other pupils.	ISS 16

Medical and therapy accommodation	
The school must have suitable accommodation, always readily available to cater for the medical and therapy needs of pupils.	ISS 24(1)(2) and (3)
Definitions of 'suitable'.	ISS 31 (b) and (c)
Information	
Parents are entitled to access the policies setting out the above arrangements.	ISS 32
For pupil with EHC plans, schools must provide the LA with and a statement of income and expenditure of public monies and information to support the annual review of plan	ISS 32 (h) and (i)
Leadership and management (including governance)	
Leaders must actively promote the well-being of pupils	ISS 34(1)(c)

CHAPTER TWENTY-ONE

WHAT THE STANDARDS SAY ABOUT MENTAL HEALTH ISSUES

Introduction

Pupil well-being should be at the centre of school culture and ethos. While there are no direct references to 'mental health' in the standards, failure to support pupils with mental health difficulties could call into question whether several standards are fully met. For example, KCSIE and the NMS for boarding both touch on mental health and well-being and the over-arching duty on schools to 'active promoting the well-being of pupils' in the Leadership and Management standard is also highly relevant to pupils with mental health issues.[546] Other standards potentially engaged are those relating to bullying, discrimination and supervision. The list is very similar for those for pupils with SEND and relating to pastoral care in the previous chapters.

NB. Guidance is clear that while school staff are well placed to identify *children whose behaviour may suggest that they are experiencing a mental health problem,*[547] they *are not expected to, and should not, diagnose mental health conditions or perform mental health interventions.*[548]

---

[546] ISS 34(1)(c).

[547] KCSIE 2022 para. 46.

[548] See Promoting and supporting mental health and wellbeing in schools, September 2021: https://www.gov.uk/guidance/mental-health-and-wellbeing-support-in-schools-and-colleges

Promoting children and young people's mental health and wellbeing – A whole school or college approach – September 2021 (43 pages)[549]

This non-statutory guidance has been produced jointly by Public Health England, DfE and the Children and Young People's Mental Health Coalition. It describes eight principles which if promoted consistently and comprehensively, would help contribute towards protecting and promoting pupil mental health and wellbeing:

- Leadership and management

- Ethos and environment

- Curriculum, teaching and learning

- Student voice

- Staff development and wellbeing

- Identifying need and monitoring impact

- Working with parents, families and carers

- Targeted support and appropriate referrals

Together these present a coherent framework for approaching mental health in school. While this structure is not replicated in the independent school standards in this format, many of the principles find echoes in the standards. Ethos and environment, pupil voice, identifying need, working with parents, targeted support and appropriate referrals fall within the guidance in *KCSIE* and WT – ISS paragraph 7. The advice around curriculum, teaching and learning references PSHE and relies on the RSHE guidance. There is no requirement for independent schools to 'have regard to' the health section of the latter although following it is likely to be a 'safe harbour' for the purpose of meeting the 'health' element of the PSHE curriculum.

---

[549] https://www.gov.uk/government/publications/promoting-children-and-young-peoples-emotional-health-and-wellbeing

Schools are encouraged in the guidance and KCSIE to identify a senior mental health lead to take leadership for implementing the school's approach to mental health and wellbeing in the setting, but this is not a requirement. That said, a school which does not teach about mental health and take effective steps to promote the wellbeing of pupils, within the role of an education provider, would be at risk of not meeting the PHSE and leadership and management standards and possibly others.

Reasonable adjustments – ISS paragraph 3(j)

Teaching must not discriminate unlawfully against pupils with disabilities including those related to mental health. Where pupils are disabled by poor mental health, reasonable adjustments are likely to be called for across a range of policies and practices such as behaviour, bullying, safeguarding. However, the anti-discrimination standard will not always be engaged because to be 'disabled' within the EqA there is a definitional threshold that the impairment must have lasted or be likely to last at least a year. Clearly intervention and support will often be needed much sooner. In other cases, it is unlikely to be appropriate for schools to gatekeep access to help and support by reference to the definition of disability as this might put them at risk of not meeting other standards (such as safeguarding, pupil well-being and quality of education).

Boarders' mental health and wellbeing – ISS paragraph 8 and NMS 7

The NMS for boarding contain express provisions concerning boarders' mental health and wellbeing.[550] All parts of NMS 7 are relevant starting with NMS 7.1:

> *The school has, and implements effectively, appropriate policies for the care of boarders who have medical conditions and/or are unwell,*

---

[550] See Chapter Eleven above for how the NMS for boarding are incorporated into the standards.

ensures that the physical and mental health, and emotional wellbeing of boarders is promoted and prompt action is taken when health concerns are identified. These include first aid, care of those with chronic conditions and disabilities, ….

'Wellbeing' here means wellbeing within the meaning of section 10(2) of the Children Act 2004.

Subsequent parts of NMS 7 cover such as: counselling, accommodation for pupils who are unwell and staffing for the accommodation; access to local specialist services, storage and use of medication, including self-medication; confidentiality and Gillick competence.

Safeguarding – ISS paragraph 7

Mental health needs are recognised in KCSIE as a potential safeguarding issue. Familiar safeguarding arrangements (many of them referenced in the guidance above) may be appropriate to pupils with mental health issues, such as:

- Ensuring children know who they can talk to

- Developing avenues for listening to children (both the 'pupil voice' generally and individual pupils) and providing in-school support (pastoral care system, counselling, a mental health lead in school)

- Basic training for staff to recognise signs of cause for concern, know to how to respond and the school's systems for recording and sharing concerns

- Developing communication channels with other agencies and professionals

- Working with and sharing information with parents, unless to do so may cause greater harm and taking the wishes of pupils into account (especially where Gillick competent)

- Developing risk assessment capability for mental health risks with particular attention to managing school-related issues such as attendance, exam pressure, pressure of parental expectations, bullying and behaviour

- Seeking external support, whether through local processes or privately-funded channels

- Requesting statutory assessment under the SEN Code where appropriate

- Record keeping

PSHE – ISS paragraph 2(2)(d)

Health education, including mental health, is statutory as part of the PSHE curriculum. The health section of the RSE guidance is not statutory for independent schools but provides helpful structure and advice for this part of the curriculum.

Other guidance

In addition to KCSIE, there is a wealth of advice available for schools such as:

- *Promoting children and young people's mental health and wellbeing – A whole school or college approach* – September 2021 (above)[551]

- *Preventing and tackling bullying*[552]

- *Mental health and behaviour in schools*[553]

- *Supporting mental health in schools and colleges*[554]

---

[551] https://www.gov.uk/government/publications/promoting-children-and-young-peoples-emotional-health-and-wellbeing

[552] https://www.gov.uk/government/publications/preventing-and-tackling-bullying .

[553] https://www.gov.uk/government/publications/mental-health-and-behaviour-in-schools--2

- *Medical conditions: supporting pupils at school*[555]

- *SEND code of Practice*

- *Counselling in schools: a blueprint for the future*[556]

What the standards say about provision for pupils with mental health issues

Curriculum	
Health education is statutory for independent schools as part of PSHE. Health education includes mental health.	ISS 2(2)(d)
The PSHE curriculum must encourage respect for others including for people with disabilities.	ISS 2(2)(ii) and ISS 5(b)(vi)
The curriculum, plans and schemes of work should ensure that pupils with SEND ('all pupils') have the opportunity to learn and make progress.	ISS 2(2)(h)
Principles must be promoted which enable pupils to develop self-knowledge, self-esteem and self-confidence.	ISS 5(b)(i)
Teaching	
Lessons must be planned on the basis of a good understanding of the needs of pupils.	ISS 3(d)
The teaching must not discriminate unlawfully. In other words, reasonable adjustments must be made for pupils with disabilities, including mental health issues, and all must be included in the life of the school.	ISS 3(j)
Safeguarding	
Schools must have regard to KCSIE.	ISS 7

---

[554] https://www.gov.uk/government/publications/supporting-mental-health-in-schools-and-colleges

[555] https://www.gov.uk/government/publications/supporting-pupils-at-school-with-medical-conditions--3

[556] https://www.gov.uk/government/publications/counselling-in-schools

KCSIE 2022 – Safeguarding information for all staff	
Schools should be particularly alert to the potential need for early help for a child who has a mental health need – KCSIE 2022 paragraph 20.	"
Mental health is listed as a potential safeguarding issue – KCSIE 2022 paragraphs 45 – 47 contain information and sources for schools.	"
All staff should be aware that mental health problems can in some cases be an indicator of safeguarding issues – KCSIE 2022 paragraph 45.	"
If staff have a mental health concern about a child that is also a safeguarding concern, immediate action should be taken, following their child protection policy and speaking to the DSL/DDSL – KCSIE 2022 paragraph 47.	"
KCSIE 2022 – Management of safeguarding	
Reasonable force – there are particular considerations in relation to pupils with mental health conditions. Careful consideration of risks, reasonable adjustments, positive support and preventative strategies should be used to reduce the need for force – paragraph 164 KCSIE which also sign-posts resources.	"
'Children requiring mental health support' are listed as a group potentially at greater risk of harm – paragraphs 179 – 185.	"
Schools are 'expected' [not a directive 'should'] to have a senior mental health lead who is a member of (or supported by) the SLT, such as the SENCO, pastoral lead or DSL. Resources and the availability of grants for training are signposted – paragraph 182/3 KCSIE.	"
Role of the DSL	
The role of the DSL – includes working with the senior mental health lead – p. 162 KCSIE.	"

Safeguarding of boarders	
ISS 8 incorporates the NMS for boarding, all of which relate to safeguarding and promoting the welfare of children. The following are particularly relevant: - NMS 7 – emotional wellbeing - NMS 9.3 – risk assessment – reducing risks to welfare - NMS 18.4 – demands on boarders should not affect their welfare unacceptably - NMS 8 – safeguarding and promoting welfare - NMS 2.1 and 2.5 – the governing body has a welfare role	ISS 8
Behaviour, bullying	
Schools must promote good behaviour. Schools must make reasonable adjustments to their policies to cater for pupils with disabilities.	ISS 3(j), ISS 9, and the accessibility plan.
Bullying of (or by) pupils with mental health difficulties must be prevented as far as reasonably practicable.	ISS 10. See also ISS 7, above.
Health and safety, first aid, supervision and risk assessment	
Health and safety arrangements must extend to pupils with mental health issues.	ISS 11
Adequate supervision is likely to be key.	ISS 14
Provision for particular pupils may require risk assessment to keep them safe, with appropriate action being taken to reduce any risks identified (such as self-harm, eating disorders) – for example, when a pupil might pose a risk to themselves or others, or may be at risk of being bullied or exploited by other pupils.	ISS 16
If a pupil were to self-harm, the first aid standard would be relevant.	ISS 13

Premises	
Suitable accommodation must be available for therapy needs	ISS 24(1)
Toilets and washing facilities must be 'suitable'. If there is a risk that pupils will use that accommodation as a space to self-harm, the suitability of provision for the needs of the pupils may need to be reconsidered and changes made.	ISS 23(1)(a)
Leadership and management	
Leaders must actively promote the well-being of pupils	ISS 34(1)(c)

CHAPTER TWENTY-TWO

WHAT THE STANDARDS SAY ABOUT ADMISSIONS AND EXCLUSIONS

Introduction

Admissions to and exclusions from independent schools are largely contractual matters and unregulated by the state except through the Equality Act 2010. The admissions code and guidance on exclusions which are statutory for the state sector do not apply to independent schools. Instead, independent schools may design their own approach, subject to the following.

Admissions

Schools are required to make their policy on and arrangements for admissions available to parents of pupils and prospective pupils – ISS paragraph 32(3)(a).

The standards do not require schools to provide a process to appeal admission decisions. If a school in its discretion formally provides such a process, it should be described in its admissions policy. Schools are not required by the standards to make the school complaints process available for admission appeals as this need only be available to parents of pupils.[557]

Parents may be able to challenge an admissions decision under the EqA 2010 via the first-tier tribunal in the case of disability discrimination or county court action for other forms of discrimination. These are outside of the scope of the standards and this text.

---

[557] For the definition of 'pupil' see section 138(1) Education and Skills Act 2008, and the Education Act 1996, section 3.

All pupils once admitted must be registered in accordance with the requirements of the Education (Pupil Registration) (England) Regulations 2006, as amended.[558] See Chapter Two for registration details and the DfE guidance: *Working together to improve school attendance,* May 2022 applies from September 2022 .

Schools must inform the local authority for where the school is situated[559] within five days of admitting a pupil at a non-standard transition point[560] as explained in *Working together to improve school attendance* (above) and also the DfE guidance: *Children missing education: statutory guidance for local authoritie*s. The notification must include all the details contained in the admission register for the new pupil.

Exclusions

When advising in relation to an exclusion from an independent school, there are (at least) three types of law to consider:

- contract

- the EqA 2010

- the standards

These give rise to differing legal risks or remedies from a school or a parental perspective. This text is concerned primarily with the standards as the strand of the law which opens the gateway to regulatory action by the DfE. For fuller discussion of exclusion from independent schools see other texts in this series such as: *A Practical Guide to The Law in Relation to School* Exclusions by Charlotte Hadfield and Alice de Coverley.

---

[558] See the Admissions standard at ISS paragraph 15

[559] The Education (Pupil Registration) (England) Regulations 2006 – reg 2

[560] The Education (Pupil Registration) (England)(Amendment) Regulations 2016 – reg 5, amending regulation 12 of the 2006 regulations.

<u>Contract</u>

An exclusion from an independent school entails bringing to an end the parent/school contract. The terms of parent/school contracts vary widely between schools but commonly provide grounds for termination on the basis of pupil misbehaviour. Other grounds may be included relating to considerations of the best interests of the pupil, the pupil's ability to benefit from the school's provision or the school's capacity to provide for the pupil's needs. Yet others may be unconnected with the pupil such as unpaid fees, parent behaviour or breakdown of relationship between the parents and the school.

A school itself may view terminations which are unrelated to pupil discipline as contractual matters, rather than 'exclusions'. A court or tribunal would, of course, make its own determination on the evidence and some such cases have been found to be unlawful discrimination.

<u>The EqA 2010</u>

Independent schools must comply with the EqA 2010 and failure to do so may be actionable by parents and/or pupils through the county court or first tier tribunal as described in Chapter Twenty-Four. Such actions are outside the scope of this book.

Regarding exclusions, the *Technical Guidance for Schools in England,* from the EHRC explains:

> *The Act does not prohibit schools from excluding pupils with particular protected characteristics, but does prohibit schools from excluding pupils <u>because of</u> their protected characteristics or from discriminating during the exclusions process. Schools also have a duty to make reasonable adjustments to the exclusions process for disabled pupils.*[561]

For example

> *A school excludes a pupil because he has declared his intention to undergo gender reassignment and is beginning to present in the style*

---

[561] Para. 4.3 Technical guidance for schools in England

of the opposite sex. This would be direct gender reassignment discrimination.[562]

The *Technical Guidance for Schools* in England provides a range of further instructive examples of discriminatory exclusions covering sex, racial, pregnancy and disability discrimination, direct, indirect and by association.

The Standards

Information

Under the standards, schools are required to make their policy on and arrangements for misbehaviour and exclusions available to parents of pupils and prospective pupils – ISS paragraph 32(3)(a). This implies a requirement to have a properly formulated policy and process in anticipation of exclusions, although this is not clearly stipulated and has not been confirmed judicially. This is the only express reference in the standards to exclusion.

Behaviour

The behaviour policy must set out, among other matters, the sanctions to be adopted in event of pupil misbehaviour. This should expressly mention exclusion (in whatever terms the school uses) if the school uses it as a sanction. A record must be kept of sanctions imposed for serious misbehaviour – ISS 9.

To be compatible with equality legislation and the anti-discrimination standard, ISS 3(j), the behaviour policy should provide for reasonable adjustments to avoid putting pupils with disabilities at a disadvantage. This principle should be clear to readers of the policy. Where the behaviour of a pupil with a disability may put the pupil at risk of exclusion, reasonable adjustments are particularly important to ensure that for the well-being of the pupil, every step is taken to avoid the exclusion so that it is only used where it would be a proportionate means of achieving a legitimate aim. See Chapter Four. When a pupil is

---

[562] Para. 4.7 Technical Guidance for Schools in England, EHRC.

excluded, this could call into question whether the teaching utilises 'effective strategies for managing behaviour', discriminates against pupils contrary to Part 6 EqA' and whether the leadership and management actively promote the wellbeing of pupils. – ISS paragraph 3(h), 3(j) and 34(1)(c).

Bullying

While there is no statutory content for the anti-bullying strategy required by ISS 10, the non-statutory guidance, *Preventing and Tackling Bullying* describes the sort of ground which an effective strategy would cover. This includes disciplinary sanctions which reflect the seriousness of an incident and convey a deterrent effect. The guidance advises that strong sanctions such as exclusion may be necessary in cases of severe and persistent bullying. As with other policies, it may be helpful to note in the policy that bullying because of a protected characteristic is taken seriously but equally,[563] the need to make reasonable adjustments to this policy for pupils with disabilities before applying strong sanctions.

Neither the 'zero tolerance' approach required by KCSIE for sexualised bullying nor the advice to treat prejudice-based bullying seriously means that schools are required to exclude pupils in these circumstances. The appropriate response (educational, pastoral, sanctions etc) will be a matter for the discretion of leaders, depending on variables such as the age and needs of the child and the seriousness of the misdemeanour.

Reasonable adjustments for pupils with disabilities

The case of Proprietor of Ashdown House School v (1) JKL (2) MNP [2019] UKUT 259 (AAC) is essential reading about the need for reasonable adjustments before deciding to exclude a pupil with a disability.

The various advice and guidance documents for state schools, although non-statutory for independent schools, may also give schools and parents ideas about what bespoke adjustments may be relevant and reasonable for a particular child. See for example, *Mental health and behaviour in schools*, and *Charlie Taylor's Behaviour Checklist*.

---

[563] See the Technical guidance at para 3.7.

Various approaches which might be considered reasonable adjustments, with a view to avoiding an exclusion of a pupil with disabilities which impact their behaviour, might also be considered good teaching, risk management and leadership and management within ISS 3 and ISS 16, ISS 34(1)(c) such as:

- formally assessing risks (of all types) to the pupil, other pupils and staff and taking steps to mitigate these

- informing parents of the risk of exclusion so that they can, for example, seek medical advice about a change of prescription, or seek a statutory assessment by the local authority or an early review of their child's EHC plan (if any)

- contacting the local authority to seek a statutory assessment or reassessment, or early review of an existing EHC plan

- setting up systems for regular communication with parents so that the school and parents can work together

- seeking assessment and advice from relevant independent external specialists

- providing additional pastoral support for the pupil

- providing additional relevant training and support for staff

- proactively seeking and gathering all information in school and using it for planning of provision

- creating a behaviour support plan

- sharing information appropriately with those who need to know it, in accordance with data protection principles

- assessing whether classroom resources are adequate and refreshing as necessary

- regularly reviewing and updating internal plans.

This is a non-exhaustive list of generic suggestions. The information and advice received through taking such steps are likely to disclose further or alternative adjustments suitable for the particular pupil.

For guidance on factors to take into account when considering what adjustments might be reasonable, see the *Technical Guidance for Schools in England* at paragraph 6.26.

Failure to make reasonable adjustments in the provision for pupils with disabilities could put a school in breach of ISS 3(j) at that time. Whether this leads to a finding of non-compliance in a subsequent inspection report would depend on whether the issue has been rectified or whether systemic issues remain in that connection at the time of the inspection.

Fixed term exclusions and exclusion from trips and events

The use of fixed term exclusions and the circumstances in which pupils may be excluded from trips or events should be covered at a high level in the school behaviour policy. Policies commonly leave such matters to the discretion of the head or another member of the senior leadership team.

Decisions made in applying school policies or exercising operational discretion, are likely to be deemed part of day-to-day behaviour management and therefore to come within scope of the teaching standard. The way the school models respect for inclusion could also be considered to engage the duty to actively promote principles which encourage respect for other people, paying particular regard to the protected characteristics, ISS 5(b)(vi). Fixed term exclusions are therefore permissible, but care should be taken that their use does not discriminate against pupils with protected characteristics. So doing could potentially both give rise to litigation under the EqA 2010 and provide grounds for regulatory action under the standards.

While pupils are excluded but still on the school roll, the school continues to have a duty to educate them.

Exclusion for events outside school

There is nothing within the standards preventing schools from excluding pupils for behaviour outside of school, including online. Schools which may wish to take advantage of this should be clear in their relevant policies, such as the behaviour policy and the safeguarding policy, for example, where it covers the school's response to sexual harassment or bullying.

Remedies

Under the scheme in the standards, the process for an exclusion will be set out in the school's exclusion policy. Parents and pupils will only be entitled to an appeal hearing, for example, if this is provided for by either the parent/school contract or the school policy.

Schools may make the school complaints process available for hearing exclusion appeals but this is not a requirement.

See Gray v Marlborough College [2006] EWCA Civ 1262 for an example of litigation concerning an exclusion unrelated to discrimination. The court recognised a contractually implied duty of fairness. As to the content of that duty, the nature of the contract was relevant:

> Parents have a choice whether to commit their children to the particular regime and ethos of an independent school. They do so in the light of their expectations of what the school will provide and their understanding of what it requires from its pupils and their parents. That is what they pay for and the commitment they give. These are circumstances for which allowance may have to be made in applying notions of fairness ... [para 56].

Ultimately, fairness in the contractual context related to whether '*the parent "has had a fair deal of the kind that he bargained for"*' [para 57].

Informing the local authority

Schools must inform the local authority where the school is situated when they remove a pupil's name from the admissions register at a non-standard transition time – ISS 15.

The grounds for deleting a name from the admissions register are found in regulation 8 of the Education (Pupil Registration)(England) Regulations 2006, as amended by the Education (Pupil Registration)(England)(Amendment) Regulations 2016. Regulation 8(1)(m) covers exclusions of pupils of compulsory school age and regulation 8(3)(e) covers pupils not of compulsory school age.

The duty to inform the local authority arises as soon as the grounds for deletion are met and no later than the time when the pupil's name is deleted.

The information to be provided to the local authority is set out in regulation 12(7), as amended, regulation 5(1)(ca) if applicable and regulation 5(1)(g) if applicable, and also explained in both *Working together to improve school attendance 2022* and *Children missing education 2016*. The information must include parental contact details and name of the child's next school and the first date they are expected to attend, where it is reasonably practicable for the school to obtain those details.

The duty to provide the local authority with details of excluded pupils is referenced in *KCSIE* 2022 at paragraph 174, and as such is also part of a school's safeguarding duties under ISS 7.

<u>Ongoing duty to provide work or help find a new school</u>

Independent schools do not have a duty to continue to provide work for former pupils or to assist parents to find a new school. Although many provide advice, this is not a requirement of the standards. Once a pupil is out of school, their parents remain under a duty to ensure they receive suitable full-time education in school or otherwise. The pupil continues to have a right to free state education.

CHAPTER TWENTY-THREE

WHEN THINGS
GO WRONG

Overarching

This chapter gives practical tips about what to do when there are concerns that a school may not be meeting the standards, or indeed when a school has already been judged on inspection not to be meeting the standards.

Initial client instructions should be triaged for the nature of the concern (safeguarding, inspection, other), which standards apply (ISS, EYFS, NMS for boarding, NMS for residential special schools or a combination of these) and the most appropriate process or processes to follow.

Concerns about a school

Safeguarding concerns

For processes relating to safeguarding concerns (current pupils at risk or in need, allegations against adults), see Chapter Eleven about the Safeguarding standard.

Ideally the place to start will be the school's own Safeguarding Policy, although a poor policy may sometimes be part of the problem. The Safeguarding Policy must be readily accessible on the school website if it has one. It should explain clear processes through which the school applies the national guidance, KCSIE and WT, to its own setting and provide relevant contact details within school and at the local authority where the school is situated.

For a fuller picture, also see

- KCSIE – the statutory safeguarding guidance for schools

- WT – the statutory guidance on how the mosaic of agencies involved in safeguarding children should work together

- the local authority threshold document setting out the local criteria for action[564]

- the guidance for schools and colleges from the National Police Chiefs' Council on 'When to call the police'

<u>Children at risk</u>

In short, where a child (or children) is or might be at risk of significant harm, the following should be informed immediately (and no later than one working day):

- school's head or Designated Safeguarding Lead

- the LA children's social care

- the LADO, where there are safeguarding allegations against an adult at the school

- the police where a crime may have been committed.

The school, once informed, should take the lead in informing other agencies but this in-school protocol does not prevent others from contacting relevant agencies directly if they prefer and there may be good reasons to do so in some cases. More information about the processes which should follow after referrals have been made are set out in the statutory guidance. Schools should work co-operatively with parents in accordance with the principles described in WT, except where this is not in the child's best interest.

Safeguarding allegations from former pupils about former staff can be reported through the same channels. It is important that such

---

[564] WT, chapter one, para. 16. In short, the local authority where the school is situated would deal with investigations about the safety of children while at school. LA children's social care for the area where a pupil lives is responsible for providing support for the child.

allegations are followed up in case those alleged to have harmed children continue to have opportunity to cause harm.

Children in need

Where a child may be in need of help, again the school's Designated Safeguarding Lead is usually the first port of call. The DSL should follow-up the concern in-line with the school policy and with local processes and thresholds, which may entail providing early help in schools and/or making referrals to external agencies. Equally, anyone can make a referral direct to the LA where necessary. See Chapter Eleven on the Safeguarding standard.

Whether to inform the regulator of schools or inspectorate of safeguarding concerns between inspections

There is no legal obligation on schools or others (such as parents or LAs) to inform inspectorates or the DfE of safeguarding concerns between inspections, subject to a few exceptions for registered early years providers.[565] Usually there should be no need to do so because the relevant legal powers and duties sit with the LAs. However, it can sometimes be helpful to do so on a voluntary basis where there is doubt about issues such as whether a school is following statutory guidance, whether it is co-operating with other agencies or whether the LA is responding appropriately.

Sharing information between inspections can, for example:

- inform the risk assessments which determine the scheduling of routine inspections

- inform the focus of and planning for the next inspection

- assist inspectors to test evidence they are provided by the school at the next inspection

- trigger a non-routine inspection, in exceptional cases.

---

[565] See the statutory framework for the EYFS para.s 3.8. 3.16, 3.17, 3.50 and 3.52.

Decisions about whether the information should trigger an un-scheduled inspection and, if so when it should take place, are made by the DfE and/or potentially by Ofsted in the case of boarding care in schools which it inspects.[566] Decision makers can take into account any recommendations from the relevant inspectorate and local authority about the usefulness and timing of inspection activity.

If parent/pupil clients wish to share information with the DfE and/or inspectorate, it may be necessary to manage expectations about what will happen next. The DfE and relevant inspectorate are unlikely to be able to provide substantive feedback about next steps because of the risk that this could compromise section 47 enquiries, criminal investigations and prosecutions, or the 'notice' element of inspection activity. It should also not be assumed that an immediate inspection would always be in the best interests of pupils or that a lack of visible action indicates inaction behind the scenes. Further, if the information does trigger an inspection, any published report will as usual be at a strategic level in terms of whether the minimum standards are being met. Inspectors do not duplicate the work of the LA or police by further investigating the same matters. Their role is to report whether the statutory processes are being/have been followed appropriately, for example, by reporting matters externally as required and co-operating with any enquiries, so that the Secretary of State can take action where necessary.

School clients may also wish to consider proactively sharing their perspective with the DfE or inspectorate between inspections when there are issues. Although this is not a requirement or necessary, in a situation where a parent indicates that they are in communication with the DfE or inspectorate a school may take some comfort in ensuring the latter receive a balanced presentation of views while also demonstrating transparency. But that opportunity will in any event arise at the next inspection.

---

[566] Section 87- 87C of the Children Act 1989.

Other concerns

For parents the first step when things go wrong should usually be to contact the relevant member of staff or head of the relevant section of the school. In this way, most issues can be resolved quickly and informally. Thereafter, there can be escalation through the school complaints policy, if necessary. See Chapter Sixteen above.

<u>Advising parents</u>

School complaints processes are intended to provide a dispute resolution mechanism between the parties without the need for lawyers and legal proceedings. However, some parents bringing a complaint against a school need support to understand the regulatory context and the respective duties and responsibilities of the parties and external agencies. There can also be an important role for legal advisors in helping parents to structure their thoughts succinctly, focus on resolution and be clear about what they are seeking from the process, such as: information, practical changes to arrangements, reasonable adjustments, better implementation by the school of their policies, policy changes, an apology, an assurance that a matter is in hand or has been dealt with. It can also be easier for schools to resolve a matter quickly when it is presented clearly and succinctly.

Where litigation is an option, for example, where there the complaint is about discrimination, safeguarding, safety or other negligence, a preliminary question is whether to use the school complaints process at all. The First-tier tribunal is available for disability discrimination claims; the county court for others. Key considerations will be: the best interests of the child, the benefits of possible early resolution, the greater scope of remedies available through in-school processes, whether the family wish their child/children to remain in the school, the impact of litigation on relationships between the family and school (even recognising that litigation under the EqA 2010 is a protected act), whether trust between the parents and school has already broken down, cost, time limits.

Schools usually take complaints extremely seriously and the complaints process can therefore be an effective mechanism for dispute resolution. They are likely to recognise those complaints where litigation is a possibility and appreciate the opportunity to resolve issues without recourse to law. For governors, complaints are an important means of hearing direct from parents about the pupil experience.

If parents wish to proceed through the complaints process, an early consideration may be whether to represent the parents directly to the school or whether to simply support and advise parents to write on their own behalf. The involvement of lawyers may oblige a school to refer the matter to their insurers and thereafter to lawyers instructed by the insurers, potentially taking it out of the hands of the school. This can inhibit open discussions, information sharing and satisfactory resolution, particularly by way of apology, on account of confusion about how this could impact insurance cover. Section 2 of the Compensation Act 2006 provides that

> *An apology, an offer of treatment or other redress, shall not of itself amount to an admission of negligence or breach of statutory duty.*

For a fuller discussion of apologies, explanations and assurances, see the IICSA investigation report: Accountability and Reparations, 2019, at part C.

Tone will be important at all stages of the complaints process, including the informal stage, where the parent/family wishes to continue to have a good working relationship with the school for the sake of their child and any siblings in the school. The school/parent contract should be considered for terms about termination for breakdown of relationship between the school and parents. At the formal and panel stages, where the matter complained of falls within the standards, it can assist to map the events which occurred against any school policies which apply and the standards, including the NMS for boarding or EYFS where relevant, and any other relevant law such as the EqA 2010.

It may be advisable to manage expectations of parents. For example,

- schools are unlikely to be able to provide information (personal data) about members of staff, other pupils or parents of other pupils for reasons of data protection compliance

- schools must act within the regulatory framework provided by the DfE so some matters are outside their control

- the Complaints standard may in practice be met at the formal stage and panel stage by a single substantive written response at each stage. Schools are not obliged to enter into protracted, discursive correspondence at each stage

- schools are not required to permit parents to be legally represented at a panel hearing, but if they do so parents are likely to find that the school is also legally represented.

Advising schools

Much of the advice for parents applies also when advising schools. It is sometimes mistakenly assumed that there is some kudos in an inspection context for having no complaints or no upheld complaints. On the contrary, having no complaints may give the appearance of a school where members of the community are afraid to speak up or are not heard when they do. A better culture recognises the important role of complaints, is open with parents and inspectors and does not shy away from addressing issues when they inevitably arise and making improvements where warranted.

When relationships break down it is not uncommon for parents to complain not only about the original substantive issue but also about the way their complaint was handled. It is therefore important for schools to adhere closely to the written process, keeping it clean and simple. To state the obvious, it can help to be explicit in correspondence about actions under the policy, for example, 'This matter is being dealt with as an informal/formal complaint under stage xx of our complaints process. We will respond to you within xx days.' This can help avoid arguments later about whether the process was properly followed.

While there is no prescribed format for providing a substantive response to a complaint, it can help to summarise and address each point made by the complainant, being clear with reasons about whether that part of the complaint has been upheld, before moving to the next point. Finally, sum up and set out any next steps. In closing, be clear 'This concludes the informal/formal stage... If you wish to take the matter further...' or, in an appropriate case, 'This completes the school's complaints procedure and the matter is now closed'.

In composing responses, it can help to be alert to legal vocabulary from parents which may indicate the possibility of subsequent litigation, such as 'discrimination' or 'negligence'.

A clear process, firmly adhered to can help to manage the expectations of would-be persistent or vexatious correspondents.

Whether to inform the DfE/inspectorate between inspections

As with safeguarding matters discussed above, the DfE and/or the relevant inspectorate may be interested to receive information about complaints or concerns relating to the standards, but there is no obligation to provide it between inspections. Many of the same considerations apply to that decision as discussed above in relation to safeguarding complaints. Depending on the facts, it may be best if a complainant wishes to inform the DfE/inspectorate, to wait until after the school's internal complaints process has been exhausted as otherwise the correspondent will almost certainly be signposted back to that procedure. Neither the DfE nor inspectors investigate or adjudicate on individual complaints.[567] However, complaints, particularly clusters of complaints about similar issues, can flag areas to inspectors which require their attention and inform inspection trails.

The report of an inspection, even if triggered by a complaint, will not narrate events and draw conclusions about particular incidents, for example, that a certain child was bullied and a teacher failed to intervene appropriately, or that a certain child should receive specified SEN provision. It will report whether at the time of the inspection (as opposed to the time of the complaint) the school is meeting the relevant standards, for example, processing complaints in accordance with requirements, meeting the educational needs of pupils and implementing an effective anti-bullying strategy. Schools may be reported to meet the standards at the time of inspection even where they have not done so throughout the period since the last inspection if any deficiencies have been rectified, a subsequent track record of compliance has been established and no further action is needed to

---

[567] See the Old Co-operative Day Nursery v Ofsted [2016] EWHC 1126(Admin) at para. 78, where that occurred.

meet the standard. So sharing information about complaints with the DfE/inspectorate may drive school improvement behind the scenes but is of limited usefulness to parents if their goal is public vindication of a particular position.

Concerns about an inspection

Inspection is an independent school's opportunity to demonstrate to the DfE as regulator of schools that it continues to meet the standards and it should be permitted to remain on the register of schools. The onus to show compliance is on the school[568] and an inspection presents a very small window of time in which to do so. It is important to ensure that all relevant evidence is produced during the inspection. Good preparation is therefore essential, where possible. At the first sign that inspectors are doubtful whether one or more standards are met, it may be helpful for a school to be proactive in asking whether they need to produce more evidence on a point. After an inspection, schools are provided with a draft report for factual accuracy checking prior to publication.

Next steps when a school does not meet the standards

When a school is found not to be meeting one or more of the standards, the DfE contacts the school to let them know what will happen next. In short, schools are required, at the option of the Secretary of State, to produce an action plan to rectify the deficiencies. After a reasonable period, a progress monitoring inspection may be commissioned by the DfE to check how the school is progressing against its plan. Once compliance is achieved, the school can be returned to the routine inspection cycle.

The statutory provisions underpinning these processes are set out in the Education and Skills Act 2008, sections 109 – 118. The DfE has also produced guides:

---

[568] <u>Marshall v Commission for Social Care Inspection</u> [2009] EWHC 1286 (Admin).

- *Independent school action plans: Guidance on producing an action plan to meet independent school standards*

- *Independent schools: regulatory enforcement action policy statement*

The latter provides crucial advice and is clear that, although responsibility for drafting action plans rests with the proprietor, the DfE is happy to assist and discuss specific points in advance of submission of an action plan.

Practical tips for action plans

The steps needed to achieve compliance with most standards are usually self-evident from any relevant inspection report. However, the breadth of the leadership and management standard (ISS 34) sometimes leaves schools confused about how to address a finding of non-compliance. The following are generic suggestions could be worth considering in appropriate cases:

- updating policies and processes where weaknesses have been identified, disseminating them to the school community and training staff (and others where necessary, such as pupils) on the new expectations

- ensuring arrangements for 'hearing the pupil voice' remain adequate and effective for all pupils, and using the pupil perspective to strengthen arrangements

- reviewing and updating risk assessments relevant to area of deficiency

- addressing leadership culture to ensure the school always prioritises the best interests of pupils over the interests of the institution

- introducing or updating the performance management system for staff and/or leaders

- providing training and/or mentoring for leaders in relation to relevant matters

- bringing in external experts to provide support and advice on relevant matters to secure rapid improvement

- restructuring arrangements to strengthen leadership and management for the longer term

- governor training

- refreshing the governing body.

How to challenge an inspection

Each of the inspectorates of independent schools provides processes for challenging inspection findings. The website for the relevant inspectorate should be consulted for the most up to date information.

The processes for challenging inspection include:

- on-inspection dialogue

- immediate correspondence

- the factual accuracy check process, by whatever name

- the inspectorate's complaints process, which may reference the above

- litigation.

Complaints

If the purpose of a complaint is for inspection judgments to be reconsidered, the focus of correspondence should be on the evidence and how it has been evaluated against the standards or the grade descriptors. Judgments on educational quality are difficult to challenge as they are a corporate decision based on the professional experience of the inspection team which visited the school. In relation to compliance judgments, it may be worth considering questions such as:

- whether the standards have been correctly interpreted and applied – that is, whether issues reported as 'non-compliance' are indeed compliance requirements for independent schools

- whether any elements of the judgments are potentially *ultra vires* (not within the framework or standards) – for example, whether matters have been reported are properly within the remit of the inspectorate

- whether the evidence produced by the school was correctly evaluated, with an explanation of the school's perspective

- issues of multiple reporting

The latter point may be presentational but is often of great importance to a school. Some non-compliance issues have implications across a wide range of standards. It is a matter of judgment and protocol for inspectors whether to report a cross-cutting deficiency against every standard affected, with the effect that one issue leads to failure across many standards for the same reason, or whether to focus on the standards most pertinent.

Points which are unlikely to assist a school include complaints about the requirements themselves, because these are made by the DfE rather than the inspectorate, unprofessional comments about inspectors,[569] points about the potential impact on the school of negative judgments, comparisons with a neighbouring school, complaints that the bar has been raised since last time and – perhaps the ultimate own goal – comments that leaders did not understand the requirements, as this could itself be a regulatory failing (ISS paragraph 34). It is also not part of the role of inspectorates to explain the standards or how to run a school.[570] See Chapter Three on the role of inspection.[571]

---

[569] Inspector conduct is a legitimate ground for complaint but is unlikely to provide grounds to change inspection judgments as these are evidence based and arrived at corporately by the inspection team.

[570] Although this is not a requirement, some do it as part of their offer of added value. If so, care must be taken not to impact the independence of the schools or interfere with the proper exercise of inspection judgement.

[571] See also the judgment in Beis Aharon v Secretary of State [2016] UKFTT 270 (HESC)

Litigation

Attempts at restraining publication, overturning inspection reports and setting aside inspections are rarely successful. Inspection is a statutory process and it is well-established that there is a public interest in the publication of inspection reports. The following is a selection of reported cases where schools and others have litigated:

- R (City College Birmingham) v Ofsted [2009] EWHC 2373 – This case explains the principle that an injunction restraining publication pending a judicial review would only be granted for 'the most compelling reasons' and 'exceptionally strong grounds'.

- R (Interim board of X School) v Ofsted [2016] EWHC 2004 (Admin) – An injunction was granted to restrain publication but only for an interim period, pending determination of permission to bring a judicial review.

- The Old Co-operative Day Nursery Ltd v HMCI [2016] EWHC 1126 (Admin) – A report was ordered to be withdrawn and not re-published.

- HM Chief Inspector of Education of Children's Services and Skills v Interim Executive Board of Al Hijrah School [2017] EWCA Civ 1426 – The school could not rely on the lack of consistency with previous reports.

- R (Remus White Ltd (t/a) Heathside Preparatory School) v Ofsted [2018] EWHC 3324 (Admin) – The orthodox position, that reports should be published in the absence of exceptionally strong reasons, was restated.

- Ofsted v Secretary of State for Education and R(on the app of Durand Academy trust) [2018] EWCA Civ 2813 – The Ofsted inspection and complaints processes were found to be fair.

- R (governing body of X school) v Ofsted and DfE [2020] EWCA Civ 594 – A school was refused permission to apply for judicial review and refused interim relief.

- <u>Gallagher v Berwood School and Others</u> (Unreported) 7 October 1999, Court of Appeal – There was no proximity between a pupil in a boarding school and inspectors under section 77 of the Education Act 1944 for the purpose of an action in negligence.

Effective use of resources

Complaints and litigation do not usually stop the clock on the statutory processes set out above, which will in any event generally lead to reinspection and a new report. Constructive dialogue can be helpful for both schools and inspectors although when challenges become protracted they may lead to a school being involved in concurrent processes over many months. It is worth considering whether the most efficient path to compliance for a disappointed school is to focus efforts on understanding an adverse report and implementing the statutory action plan to put things right for the future. Although schools must publish inspection reports, it was confirmed in <u>R (governing body of X school) v Ofsted and DfE</u> [2020], at para.s 91 and 92, that they may provide parents with their perspective on the findings:

> *… public confidence in the statutory regime for school inspections is important in the public interest, and this requires Ofsted's concerns about a school's performance to be brought into the public domain promptly. But … the school is not powerless to minimize any potential reputational damage. There is nothing to stop it communicating to parents and pupils its criticisms of the Ofsted report, bringing to their notice other reports and surveys that – in its belief – cast doubt upon or disprove the conclusions of that report, and publicizing the measures it has taken to deal with the concerns expressed.*

CHAPTER TWENTY-FOUR

IN CONCLUSION – FUTURE DEVELOPMENTS

Education law continues to grow and change in response to events and emerging issues, and with it the standards for independent schools. As schools continue daily to deal with the consequences of the pandemic, there is no sign of the pace of regulatory change slowing. A number of developments are known to be imminent:

- The Independent Schools Inspectorate is consulting on a new inspection framework due to be introduced from September 2023. The proposal is to put the well-being of pupils at the centre of inspections, by structuring compliance expectations around ISS 34(1)(c).

- IICSA reported in March 2022 concerning safeguarding in day and boarding schools and is due to publish its final report and overarching recommendations in Autumn 2022. While the recommendations from March are still being processed, the final report is expected to cover further topics such as mandatory reporting and the effective leadership of child protection. Its findings are likely to influence future standards and guidance for schools.

- The NMS for boarding have changed from September 2022 in response to some IICSA recommendations. Even as the new NMS are being brought into force, some areas have already been flagged to be revisited such as provision for children experiencing gender-related distress. The DfE has committed to working with the EHRC to develop guidance to support schools.[572]

- The ISS are expected to be updated for implementation in September 2023, in response to recommendations from IICSA and to align with the 2022 iteration of the NMS.

- Provisions in the Schools Bill 2022 are expected to bring more settings within the regulated regime for independent schools and provide the Secretary of State a wider range of powers to respond to schools which do not meet the standards.

- The SEND review is underway and is expected to lead to legislative change, such as the creation of national SEND standards. These may directly affect specialist independent schools and be influential on the SEND provision of other independent schools.

- KCSIE is updated every year.

In addition, our understanding of the legal context around the standards continues to be developed through case law. As we go to press, judgments are awaited in a few cases concerning issues such as the protected characteristic of belief. These may have relevance to education.

In a context of change, this book can provide no more than an introduction and overview. It is hoped that this updated edition continues provide a useful starting point for those new to the independent sector; a sector which is far from the Wild West of its occasional reputation, but one which combines tradition with vision and creative energy and where there is a place for every child.

---

[572] See item 7 of the Summary of Main Findings, of *National minimum standards for boarding schools and national minimum standards for residential special schools: Government consultation response.*

MORE BOOKS BY
LAW BRIEF PUBLISHING

A selection of our other titles available now:-

'A Practical Guide to the EU Succession Regulation' by Richard Frimston

'A Practical Guide to Solicitor and Client Costs – 2nd Edition' by Robin Dunne

'Constructive Dismissal – Practice Pointers and Principles' by Benjimin Burgher

'A Practical Guide to Religion and Belief Discrimination Claims in the Workplace' by Kashif Ali

'A Practical Guide to the Law of Medical Treatment Decisions' by Ben Troke

'Fundamental Dishonesty and QOCS in Personal Injury Proceedings: Law and Practice' by Jake Rowley

'A Practical Guide to the Law in Relation to School Exclusions' by Charlotte Hadfield & Alice de Coverley

'A Practical Guide to Divorce for the Silver Separators' by Karin Walker

'The Right to be Forgotten – The Law and Practical Issues' by Melissa Stock

'A Practical Guide to Planning Law and Rights of Way in National Parks, the Broads and AONBs' by James Maurici QC, James Neill et al

'A Practical Guide to Election Law' by Tom Tabori

'A Practical Guide to the Law in Relation to Surrogacy' by Andrew Powell

'A Practical Guide to Claims Arising from Fatal Accidents – 2nd Edition' by James Patience

'A Practical Guide to the Ownership of Employee Inventions – From Entitlement to Compensation' by James Tumbridge & Ashley Roughton

'A Practical Guide to Asbestos Claims' by Jonathan Owen & Gareth McAloon

'A Practical Guide to Stamp Duty Land Tax in England and Northern Ireland' by Suzanne O'Hara

'A Practical Guide to the Law of Farming Partnerships' by Philip Whitcomb

'Covid-19, Homeworking and the Law – The Essential Guide to Employment and GDPR Issues' by Forbes Solicitors

'Covid-19 and Criminal Law – The Essential Guide' by Ramya Nagesh

'Covid-19 and Family Law in England and Wales – The Essential Guide' by Safda Mahmood

'A Practical Guide to the Law of Unlawful Eviction and Harassment – 2nd Edition' by Stephanie Lovegrove

'Covid-19, Brexit and the Law of Commercial Leases – The Essential Guide' by Mark Shelton

'A Practical Guide to Costs in Personal Injury Claims – 2nd Edition' by Matthew Hoe

'A Practical Guide to the General Data Protection Regulation (GDPR) – 2nd Edition' by Keith Markham

'Ellis on Credit Hire – Sixth Edition' by Aidan Ellis & Tim Kevan

'A Practical Guide to Working with Litigants in Person and McKenzie Friends in Family Cases' by Stuart Barlow

'Protecting Unregistered Brands: A Practical Guide to the Law of Passing Off' by Lorna Brazell

'A Practical Guide to Secondary Liability and Joint Enterprise Post-Jogee' by Joanne Cecil & James Mehigan

'A Practical Guide to the Pre-Action RTA Claims Protocol for Personal Injury Lawyers' by Antonia Ford

'A Practical Guide to Neighbour Disputes and the Law' by Alexander Walsh

'A Practical Guide to Forfeiture of Leases' by Mark Shelton

'A Practical Guide to Coercive Control for Legal Practitioners and Victims' by Rachel Horman

'A Practical Guide to Rights Over Airspace and Subsoil' by Daniel Gatty

'Tackling Disclosure in the Criminal Courts – A Practitioner's Guide' by Narita Bahra QC & Don Ramble

'A Practical Guide to the Law of Driverless Cars – Second Edition' by Alex Glassbrook, Emma Northey & Scarlett Milligan

'A Practical Guide to TOLATA Claims' by Greg Williams

'A Practical Guide to Elderly Law – 2nd Edition' by Justin Patten

'A Practical Guide to Responding to Housing Disrepair and Unfitness Claims' by Iain Wightwick

'A Practical Guide to the Construction and Rectification of Wills and Trust Instruments' by Edward Hewitt

'A Practical Guide to the Law of Bullying and Harassment in the Workplace' by Philip Hyland

'How to Be a Freelance Solicitor: A Practical Guide to the SRA-Regulated Freelance Solicitor Model' by Paul Bennett

'A Practical Guide to Prison Injury Claims' by Malcolm Johnson

'A Practical Guide to the Small Claims Track - 2nd Edition' by Dominic Bright

'A Practical Guide to Advising Clients at the Police Station' by Colin Stephen McKeown-Beaumont

'A Practical Guide to Antisocial Behaviour Injunctions' by Iain Wightwick

'A Practical Guide to Financial Ombudsman Service Claims' by Adam Temple & Robert Scrivenor
'A Practical Guide to Advising Schools on Employment Law' by Jonathan Holden
'A Practical Guide to Running Housing Disrepair and Cavity Wall Claims: 2nd Edition' by Andrew Mckie & Ian Skeate
'A Practical Guide to Holiday Sickness Claims – 2nd Edition' by Andrew Mckie & Ian Skeate
'Arguments and Tactics for Personal Injury and Clinical Negligence Claims' by Dorian Williams
'A Practical Guide to Drone Law' by Rufus Ballaster, Andrew Firman, Eleanor Clot
'A Practical Guide to Compliance for Personal Injury Firms Working With Claims Management Companies' by Paul Bennett
'RTA Allegations of Fraud in a Post-Jackson Era: The Handbook – 2nd Edition' by Andrew Mckie
'RTA Personal Injury Claims: A Practical Guide Post-Jackson' by Andrew Mckie
'On Experts: CPR35 for Lawyers and Experts' by David Boyle
'An Introduction to Personal Injury Law' by David Boyle

These books and more are available to order online direct from the publisher at www.lawbriefpublishing.com, where you can also read free sample chapters. For any queries, contact us on 0844 587 2383 or mail@lawbriefpublishing.com.

Our books are also usually in stock at www.amazon.co.uk with free next day delivery for Prime members, and at good legal bookshops such as Wildy & Sons.

We are regularly launching new books in our series of practical day-to-day practitioners' guides. Visit our website and join our free newsletter to be kept informed and to receive special offers, free chapters, etc.

You can also follow us on Twitter at www.twitter.com/lawbriefpub.